ROBERT BURNS

This book is both a biography of Burns and a study of his work. It was translated into English by Jane Lymburn, from the German of Hans Hecht who was Professor of English first at Basle and later at Gottingen Universities.

It is a thorough, fair and balanced study and sets out to debunk some of "the idolatrous and cynical nonsense" written about Burns by his Scottish admirers. And he has indeed been so regularly over-praised and over-criticised by Scottish writers that one is tempted to wonder if they lose all sense of proportion when they are dealing with their compatriot.

Hans Hecht, on the contrary, has tried to put Burns' life and work into proper perspective, and deals more with his unique commonsense genius than his so called failings.

ROBERT BURNS
the man and his work

hans hecht

TRANSLATED BY JANE LYMBURN

ALLOWAY PUBLISHING
AYR.

First published 1936
by
William Hodge & Co. Ltd.
Reprinted 1971
by
Cedric Chivers Ltd.,

This edition published
by
Alloway Publishing Ltd.
1981

ISBN 0 907526 04 7

The Publisher acknowledges the financial
assistance of the Scottish Arts Council in
the publication of this volume.

Reproduced from copy supplied
printed and bound in Great Britain
by Billing and Sons Limited
Guildford, London, Oxford, Worcester

PREFACE TO FIRST EDITION

THE German edition of this book was published in 1919 by the firm of Carl Winter at Heidelberg. The Great War had intervened between the preparation of the material and its publication, and the stress of the time is evident in many details of the general get-up of the volume, although the sympathetic interest shown in the work by my old friend Otto Winter must be gratefully remembered. Since then an English translation of the book has been repeatedly suggested, not only in conversations and letters, but also in the publicity of the press. The subject-matter recommended compliance with this wish, and the author was ready enough to satisfy it, but obstacles of a practical nature stood in the way of its fulfilment, so that several attempts proved abortive, until the efforts of the translator, Jane Lymburn, the generous support of Harry Hodge, the Edinburgh publisher, and the courtesy of Messrs. Winter finally succeeded in overcoming the difficulties. It now remains for the critics of the English-speaking countries to judge whether the result is equal to the expectations and justifies the labour expended upon it.

It seemed essential that the structure and the fundamental conception of the book should remain unchanged in its English dress. This fortunately proved to be possible, though, of course, the Burns literature published since 1919 had to be taken into account, with the result that almost every page has undergone changes, amplifications, and omissions. Quotations from Burns's letters are no longer taken from Chambers-Wallace, but from the edition of the Letters by De Lancey Ferguson, Oxford 1931. This applies also to the spelling, punctuation, &c. As a matter of fact, every new Burns MS. that turns up shows the unreliability of any text that is not based on the original. F. B. Snyder's "Life of Burns," New York 1932, a work whose merits are not impaired by an occasional outburst of unfounded scepticism, has been utilized with advantage throughout the whole course of the preparation of this new edition. The volumes of both series of the *Burns Chronicle,* which are not yet sufficiently known or appreciated, have in a considerable number

of cases contributed valuable and otherwise unattainable material.
This organ of the Burns Federation, the honorary editor of which
is Mr. J. C. Ewing, is yearly growing in importance.* In addition
to fulfilling its other obligations, it is increasingly successful in its
service to the scientific study of Burns in the strict sense of the
word: it consolidates the foundations upon which later particular
and general representations of the poet will have to be built.

The Bibliography had to be rewritten and rearranged. Without
aiming in any way at completeness, it contains what I believe to
be the most essential in Burns literature, books and essays which
the author himself has found to be of intrinsic value, and may
serve as a signpost to those who desire to penetrate deeper into
the vast field of Burns criticism. The backwaters of antiquated
and merely dilettantish stuff have been skipped without reference;
on the other hand the author has refrained, as far as possible, from
critical or descriptive remarks on the items mentioned in the
selection. The list of the extant Burns MSS. (Section II in the
German edition) has been omitted. The reprint of the *Memoir* by
Heron in an Appendix is intended to fill an oft-felt gap (*Cf.* Introduction to our reprint.)

Wherein, then, does the fundamental conception of which we
have spoken consist? Burns is so deeply rooted in the soil of his
native land; he is so typically the expression of his environment and
his time that it may seem presumptuous for a foreigner to attempt
to do justice to his achievement. The last idiomatic subtleties, for
instance, will by necessity escape him. Furthermore, a vast number
of books and treatises have been devoted to the subject in general
and in detail, dealing with the poet as an entity as well as with
every individual aspect of his life and work. Local research has
spared no pains in collecting documents and anecdotes, accounts and
appreciations from every class and stratum of the Scottish people,
and will doubtless continue in the future to carry on this praiseworthy task with undefatigable zeal. In spite of this, or, perhaps,
because of it, it proved impossible to arrive at a clear-cut and final
verdict, even in questions of outstanding importance. We all know
that too close proximity obscures the vision, and that too great
love blinds the judgment as much as too violent antipathy. In the

---

* Now under the Editorship of Mr. Wm. Montgomerie.

case of Burns there is the further difficulty that the controversial points move along the dangerous lines of sexuality, alcoholism, religion, politics, and class prejudices or preferences. The result of this is a confusing wealth of individual differences of opinion, which become all the more heated the more conscious their holders are of their responsibility for the inviolability of the great national character. But no man is inviolable viewed from the purely human standpoint, and what would Burns be without the often unguarded vitality of his human qualities?

The foreigner's privilege, then, consists in his greater distance from the subject. Between him and it there lies a broad open space. His vision is perhaps less acute, but it is also less biassed. I have, of course, endeavoured to do justice to the results of the topological, biographical, and ethical Burns literature. The expert reader will find my attitude to the individual problems indicated at least. But this book is not intended to be a study of details. Rather does it strive, while fully appreciating the definite local data, to show the universal aspect of Burns by presenting him against the broad backgrounds of British civilisation, of the eighteenth century, and of European culture in general. Whether such a high standard can be applied may be questioned. The present writer would answer the question most emphatically in the affirmative. If certain Hotspurs of our days believe that they can dismiss Burns as a poet of purely local importance, they are in my opinion making a fatal blunder, not for him, but for themselves. Burns belongs to the very few poets who were capable of symbolism; who had the gift of being able to grasp and to form the fleeting incident *sub specie æternitatis.* Therein lies the guarantee for the lasting value of his work; and it is also this fact which forces us to give serious attention to this conception of the poet, even at the risk of leaving out of account—in this book at least—much that is merely ephemeral, however characteristic it may be.

There remains the pleasant task of thanking the numerous friends on both sides of the Border who have again shown an indefatigable interest in my work, making it possible for me, for instance, to have access to the collections in their charge: to Dr. H. W. Meikle of the National Library of Scotland; Dr. C. A. Malcolm, Librarian of the Signet Library, Edinburgh; Mr. S. A. Pitt, City Librarian of Glasgow, who kindly gave me access to the important Burns Collection in the Mitchell Library; Mr. J. C. Ewing, and to the authorities of the British Museum. The valuable information which I received through my daily intercourse with that conscientious and circumspect scholar, Mr. Ewing, has been of more frequent service to the book than I can express here. John McVie, the Secretary of the Burns Federation, was my friendly guide to the most remote spots connected with the poet's life in Edinburgh, and his profound knowledge never failed me when it was a question of clearing up one of the many knotty points that arose in the course of our discussions. In addition to them my thanks are due to the devoted and disinterested translator of the book, Jane Lymburn, and to the encouragement which I received from the publisher, Harry Hodge, without whose help the book could not have been published. In matters of style Dr. J. W. Oliver, Edinburgh, was always ready to give his advice. I had the privilege of spending unforgettable weeks with all of them in the service of a great cause. The nature of their co-operation made me clearly feel the position which Burns holds in the history of Scottish Literature: as he is the finisher of a long tradition, so the occupation with his work is not the privilege of an individual, but the heritage of a community, of a people in being, and of those who from far and near have found their way to it.

HANS HECHT.

LONDON, *December*, 1935.

CONTENTS

ABBREVIATIONS

Archiv   = *Archiv für das Studium der neueren Sprachen,*
                      edd. A. Brandl and G. Rohlfs.

B. Chr.   = *Burns Chronicle and Club Directory.* Two
                      Series. Kilmarnock 1892 ff.

Ch. W.   = *The Life and Works of Robert Burns,* ed. R.
                      Chambers, revised by William Wallace,
                      4 vols., 1896. Bibliography, II, a, 5.

Dunlop Corr.   = *R. B. and Mrs. Dunlop. Correspondence,* with
                      elucidations by W. Wallace, 1898. Biblio-
                      graphy, II, e, 4.

H. H.   = *The Poetry of R. B.,* edd. W. E. Henley and
                      T. F. Henderson, 4 vols., 1896-97 (1901).
                      Bibliography, II, b, 3.

Letters   = *The Letters of R. B.,* ed. De Lancey
                      Ferguson, 2 vols., 1931, quoted by number.
                      Bibliography, II, e, 1.

Mus.   = Janes Johnson, *The Scots Musical Museum,*
                      6 vols., 1787-1806.

Sinton   = J. Sinton, *Burns, Excise Officer and Poet,* 1897.
                      Bibliography, IV, c, 7.

Snyder   = F. B. Snyder, *The Life of R. B.,* New York
                      1932. Bibliography, IV, b, 10.

Earth, and the snow-dimmed heights of air,
And water winding soft and fair
Through still sweet places, bright and bare,
By bent and byre,
Taught him what hearts within them were:
But his was fire.

SWINBURNE, *Burns: An Ode.*

PART ONE: AYRSHIRE
1759-1786

CHAPTER I

ALLOWAY

1759-1766

LATE in the autumn of the year 1757 the gardener William Burns[1] put the finishing touches to a modest but not uncomfortable clay cottage which he had planned and built with his own hands on a small plot of ground in the parish of Alloway, some two miles south of the busy little seaport town of Ayr on the Firth of Clyde. In December of the same year he brought his wife, Agnes Brown, who like himself came of old peasant stock, to this white-washed, thatch-roofed home; and there, in the little alcove, on 25th January 1759, was born the first of their seven children: a son, Robert Burns.

A typical Scottish storm—so the story has it—a few days later did such damage to the somewhat unstable gable-end of the house that mother and child had to be given shelter by friendly neighbours:

> " 'Twas then a blast o' Janwar win'
> Blew hansel in on Robin."[2]

We may regard this stormy greeting as symbolic not only of the turbulent life which had just begun, but also of the intense activity which at that time possessed the minds of men both at home and abroad. The year 1759 proved to be strikingly eventful for literature in general. In England, Edward Young, the renowned poet of "Night Thoughts," set forth in an enthusiastic epistle to Richardson the doctrine of Original Composition; in France, Jean-Jacques Rousseau, in the passionately welcomed seclusion of the woods at Montmorency, was composing "La Nouvelle Héloïse," "Le Contrat Social" and "Emile"; in January of the same year

---

[1] Also spelt Burnes or Burness, the two-syllabled form corresponding to the pronunciation of his native dialect (Kincardineshire). The one-syllabled form is that used in the South of Scotland.

[2] H. H., iv, 13. (For abbreviations see above, p. xiii.)

(the year in which Schiller was born!) Lessing gave to Germany
the first of his illuminating Letters on Contemporary Literature.
And now, in Scotland, there appeared the poet of whom Carlyle
wrote to Goethe:

> "Perhaps you have never heard of this Burns, and yet he was a man
> of the most decisive genius; but born in the rank of a Peasant, and
> miserably wasted away by the complexities of his strange situation; so
> that all he effected was comparatively a trifle.—We English, especially
> we Scotch, love Burns more than any other Poet we have had for
> centuries."

(Letter of 25th September 1828.)

In the same essay,[3] which includes his translation of this part
of the letter, Goethe, after briefly comparing Schiller and Burns,
sums up his own opinion of the latter in these words:

> "We [too] esteem this highly-praised Robert Burns amongst the
> first poetical spirits which the past century has produced."

The present volume is an attempt to explain the personality and
the writings of the Scottish national poet by placing them against
the background of his time, his environment, and the tendencies
of the literary life of which his work forms a part.

There is ample material to draw upon in reconstructing the
poet's early life. Burns himself must be named first among his
own biographers. In his elaborate letter of 2nd August 1787 to Dr.
John Moore, who then resided in London, he takes us back in
reminiscence to the threshold of his Edinburgh triumphs, to the
moment when "the baneful Star that had so long shed its blasting
influence in my Zenith, for once made a revolution to the Nadir."[4]
In addition to this, several letters from his intelligent younger
brother, Gilbert (b. 1760), to Mrs. Dunlop, the poet's noble friend,
and to James Currie, the first editor of his works, fill in the gaps
and clear up many doubtful points. We owe further details to
John Murdoch, the teacher of Robert and Gilbert, who, in February
1799, noted down his recollections of the household in which he
had worked, for J. C. Walker of Dublin. Lastly, Robert's youngest
sister, Isobel Burns (b. 1771), who later became Mrs. Begg, has,
at Chambers's request, added valuable details to the picture which

---

[3] Thomas Carlyle, Leben Schillers. Translated from the English. Introduction
by Goethe. Frankfurt a. Main, 1830. Jubilee Edition, vol. 38, 211-226.
[4] Letters, 125.

we are justified in forming of the poet's childhood and of the influences at work upon him at that time, so that, on the whole, we have at our disposal a wealth of first-hand evidence which in spirit at least is true to life.[5]

When we examine the poet's early days, we find that conditions, though simple, were neither unpleasant nor unfavourable. Poverty weighed heavily upon the family, but at the same time there was no lack of promising and encouraging factors. When telling the story of the development of a genius, one's glance involuntarily falls first upon the woman who watched over the dawn of his life. In Burns's case, however, we know so little of his mother that it is not easy for us to form a clear impression of her. Murdoch mentions her in passing as a woman who was always busy, and who had difficulty in wresting from her never-ending domestic duties the moments in which she listened admiringly to her husband's discourses. A somewhat commonplace delineation shows us Agnes Brown as an old woman with horn-rimmed spectacles and little lace mutch, sitting in an arm-chair: grandmother telling fairy tales to the children. Isobel Begg, however, could remember her before the buffetings of Fate had bent that valiant little woman's back, in the days when her eye was dark and glowing, and the dark red of her hair gleamed above the most delicate and transparent of complexions. Her active, supple body knew no rest, and her sweet singing was heard as she went about the heavy work of the day, for she had a good voice and a wonderful stock of old and new ballads and songs, such as were current among the people. These she passed on to her children in hours that were destined to prove fateful to at least one of them. In the art of story-telling she had a rival in an old kinswoman, Betty Davidson, who was frequently a guest in the little household at Alloway.

> "She had, I suppose, the largest collection in the county of tales and songs concerning devils, ghosts, fairies, brownies, witches, warlocks, spunkies, kelpies, elf-candles, dead-lights, wraiths, apparitions, cantraips, giants, inchanted towers, dragons and other trumpery,"

wrote Burns to Dr. Moore, adding the significant words:

> "This cultivated the latest seeds of Poesy."

---

[5] The reader will find the documents mentioned here more or less fully quoted in almost any biography of Burns. Currie first used them in his four-volume edition of the "Works of Robert Burns," 1800.

Much stronger was the influence which two men, each excellent in his own way, exercised upon the boy: his father and his teacher, John Murdoch.

There is no doubt that William Burns was a man, the peculiar qualities of whose character and whose craving for knowledge were above the average of the Scottish peasantry, high though the standard of intelligence in that peasantry was. He had been trained in a hard school of life. Born in Kincardineshire in 1721, within the magic circle of the North Sea, he had migrated, poverty-stricken, to the South,[6] managing with difficulty to keep himself going with gardening work. He reached Edinburgh and then went to Ayrshire, where he settled down and founded his family, hoping to labour under more propitious stars. In Alloway he worked as gardener and overseer to Dr. William Fergusson, then Provost of Ayr, a man who was kindly disposed to him. Soon he leased seven acres of ground, intending to carry on business as a market-gardener. This comparatively carefree spell of young married bliss and manly striving for the necessities of life lasted eight years. At the end of that period William Burns, for his children's sake, took a bold, and, as it turned out, a fateful step: he leased a farm. The tribulations which then began for the father of the family were infinitely harder and sadder than the roving life of his bachelor days, but these very days had been the means of turning the bright-faced, hot-blooded youth into a strong, upright and self-reliant man: a man, moreover, who knew men, who weighed consequences before he committed himself to a decision, and who always kept his head high. His son, in whom we plainly recognize the father's nature in a more strongly developed form, says of him in the somewhat high-flown, affected phraseology of his epistolary style:

"I have met with few who understood 'Men, their manners, and their ways' equal to him; but stubborn, ungainly Integrity, and head-long, ungovernable Irrascibillity are disqualifying circumstances: consequently I was born a very poor man's son."

In the tall, gaunt, somewhat bent figure with the grave, expressive face framed in scanty grey locks, there lived an active, receptive spirit, a strong faith and an invincible pride. This stern

---

[6] See B. Chr., 1935, pp. 94-97.

exterior hid great inward kindness. He was above all an excellent teacher of his children, a real educator of young human souls. Gilbert tells how his father used to talk to him and his brother as though they were grown men, allowing them to discuss any subject they liked. We could scarcely quote a better proof of his remarkable insight, even if we mention a little tract in the form of a dialogue between father and son, a copy of which has been preserved, and of which William Burns is supposed to have been the author. This "Manual of Religious Belief" is in the handwriting of Murdoch, who probably touched it up both in language and in form. It consists of a few easily grasped biblical precepts, free alike from doubts and from the harsh dogma of Calvinism; precepts which put forth as an ideal for life contemplative contentment and the pursuit of a calling upon which one can depend to supply one's daily wants; precepts which laud as happy the man who has learned to control his senses by his reason.[7] Of greater importance, however, was the exemplary life of the intelligent, high-principled man himself, who left a strong impression upon all who came into contact with him: the impression of one who strove untiringly to obtain the blessings of peace. "O for a world of men of such disposition!" exclaims Murdoch enthusiastically in the letter in which he has set down his memories of the unforgettable father of his great pupil.

It was natural that a man of the high ideals and strong sense of responsibility of the cotter Burns should do his utmost to let his sons have good schooling as soon as possible. Anyone who has studied the wretched conditions of primary and secondary education then prevalent in the rural districts of Scotland can appreciate the difficulties of this undertaking. Money was scarce, consequently there was a dearth of teachers and of school-buildings. The teacher could safeguard himself from starvation only by taking on all sorts of subsidiary jobs. He might (at the risk, it must be admitted, of being dismissed from his post) keep a small shop, or serve the community and its governing body as clerk, precentor, beadle, or even grave-digger. It is not to be wondered at that under such conditions people of adequate culture were scarcely to be got and that the school holidays sometimes lasted for years.

---

[7] Printed by Ch. W., i, 455-459. Separate edition with a specimen of handwriting, Kilmarnock, 1875. See B. Chr., 1933, pp. 78-83 (J. Muir).

Misfits of every kind, discharged soldiers, cripples unable to work,
the village cobbler or the village blacksmith set the not over-zealous
children to study in some ill-lighted, chilly barn; and with all the
urge for education, which in spite of everything was awake in the
minds of the Scottish people, the results were, until the nineteenth
century, what might have been expected from such an unsatisfactory
system.[8]

How far conditions in the district of Alloway conformed to these
generally prevailing at the period with which we are dealing, we
do not know. The rudiments of a village school seem to have been
in existence. Moreover, William Burns strove to speak as pure
English as possible, with the result that a modest foundation of
culture had already been laid by the time he, supported by a few
neighbouring families, resolved to establish a small private school.
The vicinity of the town of Ayr made his choice of a teacher
easier. His choice was a happy one. It fell upon a young student
of languages, who, at the time of his appointment by Mr. Burns,
was only in his nineteenth year himself—John Murdoch (b. 1747),[9] a
man who had so profound an influence upon the poet's early mental
development that we dare not entirely disregard his life and work.
Murdoch describes how William Burns, to whom he had been
highly recommended, came to Ayr one March day in the year
1765 and summoned him to an interview at a certain inn, telling
him to bring his writing-book with him. Burns must have been
favourably impressed by the young man himself and by his skill
in writing, for a few weeks later, in May, the school opened in
Alloway. Murdoch lived with the parents of his pupils in turn,
an arrangement which relieved him of immediate worries; and he
was assured of a fixed yearly salary besides. His method, which
was approved by William Burns, aimed principally at teaching his
pupils, once they had mastered the elements of education, the
accurate use of literary English, this being accompanied, of course,
by constant study of the Old and New Testaments. The learning
of poems by heart was considered to be a particularly helpful
means of achieving this end, and was rendered easier by the care-

---

[8] H. G. Graham describes these conditions in the 11th and 12th chapters of
his book "The Social Life of Scotland in the Eighteenh Century." London, 1906.
[9] For Murdoch, see W. Will, *B. Chr.*, 1929, 60-69. This essay, also published
separately, contains all the available data concerning Murdoch's career.

ful explanation of every clause in the passages to be memorized. Added to this there were exercises in style: poetry was translated into prose, synonyms being substituted and ellipses filled in, which not only ensured an understanding of the text, but also generally developed and improved the pupils' feeling for language. Besides the primer and the Holy Scriptures, the schoolbooks consisted of an English grammar by A. Fisher and a well-stocked reader by Arthur Masson, "A Collection of Prose and Verse, from the best English Authors," in which young Burns came face to face for the first time with an abundance of English masterpieces in prose and poetry. Amongst these were his two earliest favourite pieces, Addison's hymn, "How are Thy servants blest, O Lord" and "The Visions of Mirza" from the *Spectator*. Murdoch found Robert and Gilbert apt pupils, though the two boys, especially Robert, seemed lacking in musical talent, both having considerable difficulty in distinguishing between the tunes in the song-book. Robert's face generally wore a serious expression and reflected a thoughtful mind.

The little school at Alloway carried on work for nearly two and a half years, when changes within the families upon whose support it depended made its further existence impossible. The Burns household had already, in 1766, been transferred to the farm of Mount Oliphant, and though Robert and Gilbert made their way across the fields to Alloway as often as they could, the regular hours of tuition had suffered considerable curtailment through the more difficult external conditions. Once more the duty of advancing his children's education rested solely upon William Burns, although Murdoch, who was devoted to him, never wholly withdrew his support. Murdoch had been working in Ayr since 1772 as a teacher of English and was there able in the following year to take Robert as a pupil again. Burns came to him to brush up and to amplify what he had already learned, so that he "might be better able to teach his brothers and sisters at home." Every step taken by this remarkable family seems to have been influenced by the conviction that, wherever one's lot may be cast, one should face life armed with knowledge. At that time Burns had at his disposal three weeks before the harvest. The first week he devoted chiefly to the study of English grammar, while Murdoch made use of the last two to introduce his enthusiastic pupil to the elements of French. Burns brought to his teacher's progressive, intuitive method the whole vigour of his strong power of assimilation, which was already exciting admiring comment. When he returned home, he could produce, with justifiable pride, a French grammar, a dictionary, and Fénélon's "Télémaque," with the reading of which he had already made a start. With the aid of these books and some practice in the conversational idiom of the language whenever he could manage it, Burns was soon able to understand French prose authors without difficulty. On the advice of a pedagogue, a friend of Murdoch's, he at the same time ventured upon Latin, but he never succeeded in getting beyond the rudiments of this language. According to Gilbert, he used often to take it up, but always in a half-penitential mood, when he wished to overcome some mortification or disappointment, particularly after amorous adventures. His Latin studies were confined to these fleeting attempts. If, while we are still on this subject, we mention a few weeks of intermittent instruction in the neighbouring village of Dalrymple (1772) for the improvement of his handwriting, and in the more distant village of Kirkoswald (1775), where he studied land-surveying and the elements of mathematics pertaining to it, we have given the full extent of Burns's education in the strict sense of the word. In discussing the boy's teachers, amongst whom Murdoch was by far the most outstanding, we must not, however, forget the continually stimulating influence of the father, who till his death dominated the spiritual and mental life of his family, nor must we lose sight of the constant, almost passionate yearning for knowledge of the boy and youth himself. Assimilation of knowledge is the first instinctive expression of creative power : it is like the forging of the weapon which is later to be brandished in battle.

Carlyle says in one passage of his famous essay on Burns :

> "Mighty events hang upon a straw; the crossing of a brook decides the conquest of the world. Had this William Burns's small seven acres of nursery ground anywise prospered, the boy Robert had been sent to school; had struggled forward, as so many weaker men do, to some university; come forth not as a rustic wonder, but as a regular, well-trained intellectual workman, and changed the whole course of British literature, for it lay in him to have done this."[10]

This pronouncement gives us food for thought, though we are

---

[10] Standard Edition, vol. v, 262.

far from agreeing unreservedly with so exaggerated an estimate of
the influence of education on the development of native genius.
From the point of view of the time spent on it the education
which Burns enjoyed was narrowly limited. From the point of view
of quality it could scarcely have been bettered under the given conditions. It yielded its full value, however, only through the personal
worth of the two men who, as faithful guardians, carefully watched
over the awakening of this young mind.

CHAPTER II

MOUNT OLIPHANT

1766-1777

ONLY too soon in this tragic story we notice the appearance of antagonistic influences against which battle had to be joined with ill-equipped forces and under conditions which from the first gave little hope of final victory.

William Burns's chief reason for taking on the lease of Mount Oliphant Farm,[1] a few miles to the south-east of Alloway, was completely in keeping with that remarkable man's lofty conception of life. Had he remained a gardener, he would have had to put his children out to service with strangers, thus exposing them to incalculable influences. As a farmer, he could keep them under his own eyes, and continue to exert decisive personal control over their development. His friendly employer, William Fergusson, having advanced him the necessary means, he removed to Mount Oliphant at Easter 1766, and in so doing embarked upon an enterprise which only a peculiarly favourable combination of circumstances could have brought to a happy issue. As is was, what happened was a series of catastrophes, intolerable physical strain being added to spiritual humiliations of so depressing a nature that Burns, looking back on this part of his youth, afterwards wrote bitterly that this period combined "the cheerless gloom of the hermit with the unceasing moil of a galley slave."

It has been rightly pointed out[2] that from the farmer's standpoint the choice of Mount Oliphant proved to be just as unfortunate as that of all the other farms with which the fate of the Burns family was bound up. It is true that the property was beautifully situated high above the well-wooded banks of the Doon, and that it commanded an uninterrupted view far over hill and dale. It was indeed a peaceful spot, yet not too far removed from the busy scenes

---

[1] A picture of Mount Oliphant (from a drawing, probably by W. L. Leitch) is in *B. Chr.*, 1932, facing p. 79.

[2] C. S. Dougall, "The Burns Country." London, 1925, p. 46.

of town life—but the land was poor and barren. How far William
Burns thought of rational improvements, such as were recommended
by various books at his disposal, we have no means of ascertaining.
In any case, it is more than doubtful whether he could have afforded
to carry them out. Thus, ere long, hard times came upon this
household, and the efforts of the hard-working little community
to ward them off were of slight avail. Though all did their utmost,
the feeling that the struggle was hopeless must have been repeatedly
borne in upon them with paralysing effect. Gilbert conjures up
the situation and its consequences in a few vivid sentences.

"To the buffetings of misfortune," he wrote in 1797 to Mrs.
Dunlop, "we could only oppose hard labour, and the most rigid
economy. We lived very sparingly. For several years butcher's meat
was a stranger in the house, while all the members of the family exerted
themselves to the utmost of their strength, and rather beyond it, in
the labours of the farm. My brother, at the age of thirteen, assisted in
thrashing the crop of corn, and at fifteen was the principal labourer on
the farm, for we had no hired servant, male or female. The anguish
of mind we felt at our tender years under these straits and difficulties
was very great. To think of our father growing old (for he was now
above fifty), broken down with the long-continued fatigues of his
life, with a wife and five other children, and in a declining state of
circumstances; these reflections produced in my brother's mind and
mine sensations of the deepest distress. I doubt not but the hard
labour and sorrow of this period of his life was in a great measure
the cause of that depression of spirits with which Robert was so often
afflicted through his whole life afterwards. At this time he was
almost constantly afflicted in the evenings with a dull headache,
which, at a future period of his life, was exchanged for a palpitation
of the heart, and a threatening of fainting and suffocation in his bed
at night-time."[3]

These hardships reached their climax when William Fergusson
died, and his tenants had to deal not with their kindly landlord,
but with a relentless factor. This man took care that they should
not only realize that they were faced with ruin, after having
expended their health and strength for years, but that they should
also taste the bitter draughts of repeated humiliation: he sent them
threatening letters which brought the tears to the eyes of all of them.
They felt his insults all the more deeply because of the high mental
standard they had reached under the guidance of their patriarchal
father. A novel-writer, as Burns remarks, might have lingered

---

[3] Ch. W., i, 35.

over these scenes with some satisfaction, but his indignation always boiled at the recollection of them.

For all that, Mount Oliphant had its happier·hours, and Murdoch, whose unfailing devotion to the Burns family has been mentioned, was frequently and willingly the cause of them. On a free afternoon he would make a pilgrimage from Ayr to Mount Oliphant with one or other of his town-acquaintances—persons more intelligent than himself, he modestly calls them—in order to give his old friend the pleasure of a "mental feast." At such times the work would be laid aside, father and son would sit down beside their welcome guests, and there would ensue for all of them a delightful, instructive conversation, flavoured with a moderate—probably very moderate!—seasoning of jocularity. Robert, Murdoch tells us, would be brimming over with questions about French, while his father's enquiries dealt with more lofty topics such as ethics or natural philosophy, and needed the greater erudition of Murdoch's companions to answer them. We notice how William Burns worked constantly not only at the advancement of his children's education, but also at the widening and deepening of his own intellectual horizon. The only effective teacher is he who, conscious of the gaps in his own knowledge, never ceases to learn himself. At the same time, we clearly recognise the channels through which a certain by no means contemptible measure of contemporary learning reached the receptive tenants at Mount Oliphant, who probably valued knowledge all the more highly because it was hard to obtain. When the school came to an end, the schoolmaster continued to help, and when the pupil was caught fast in the clods, the teacher found his way from the town to the country.

It is in this atmosphere, so strangely compounded of worry and strength of mind, physical toil and mental endeavour, that we get our first personal glimpse of Robert Burns, in a significant scene where he gives vent to a characteristic outburst of emotion. Gilbert is our authority for the incident, the time of which is rather vague. Again the stimulus came from Murdoch, who turned up at Mount Oliphant one evening, in order to spend a little time with his friends, before taking up a new appointment. As a parting-gift he had brought with him some books, among them Shakespeare's gruesome youthful drama, "Titus Andronicus." Murdoch began to

read the play aloud, his audience listening eagerly, until he reached
the fourth scene of the second act, where the ravished and mutilated
Lavinia, whose hands have been cut off and whose tongue has been
torn out, is bidden by Queen Tamora's sons to call for water
to wash her hands:

Chir.: Go home, call for sweet water, wash thy hands.
Dem.: She hath no tongue to call, nor hands to wash;
And so let's leave her to her silent walks.

At this point Murdoch's friends interrupted him, begging him to
read no further: they even went the length of saying that it would
be better if the appalling play did not remain in the house. Robert's
wrath transcended that of the others. He embraced the cause of
the suffering Lavinia, and, transferring his righteous indignation
from the text to the book, threatened to throw it into the fire unless
Murdoch took it away with him. The father wished to rebuke the
ill-mannered, ungrateful lad sharply, but Murdoch, who knew his
pupil's high-strung nature, intervened, saying that he thought such
sensibility most estimable. In place of the Shakespearean play he
left behind him a comedy, "The School for Love,"[4] translated from
the French, and went his way in peace.

The bond between Burns and his teacher lasted, despite absence
and the passing of time, for many a long day. It was based, we are
sure, on a certain similarity of temperament in the two men,
although we have, unfortunately, not enough data to enable us to
go into this question more thoroughly. In 1776 Murdoch lost his
postion in Ayr, because in a moment of anger he had expressed an
opinion to the effect that Dr. William Dalrymple, minister of the
First Charge in Ayr (the same man, by the way, who had baptized
Burns, and who plays a sympathetic rôle in his later poems), was
as revengeful as Hell and as false as the Devil, and a liar and
hypocrite to boot—certainly an example of frankness towards an
influential Church dignitary which must have left its mark upon
Burns! He passed the rest of his life in London teaching languages
and selling stationery, at the same time publishing a few by no
means uninteresting manuals of French. He died in that city in
extreme poverty in the year 1824.

---

4 Gilbert writes: "The School for Love." We are unable to trace a comedy
with this title. Probably it was William Whitehead's "School for Lovers" (London,
R. & J. Dodsley, 1762), which was, according to the preface, "formed on a plan
of Monsieur de Fontenelle's." See also Henley's Essay, Cent. Ed., iv, 239, note.

To these refreshing interruptions in the life of Mount Oliphant
we must add a few summer months in the year 1775 which the
seventeen-year-old Burns spent in the little village of Kirkoswald.
He went there to study land-surveying, geometry and trigonometry,
with a teacher of some repute, Hugh Rodger by name; and he combined with this object a visit to a maternal uncle, Samuel Brown, at
whose farm of Ballochniel he was hospitably received. Various tales
of friendships which he is said to have made at this time, of his
successes in debates and of first drafts of what were later very famous
poems, have too little authority behind them to justify their being
discussed or even quoted here.[5] The poet's autobiographical letter
brings out the essential facts clearly, and shows how, just as had
been the case in previous excursions to Ayr, Kirkoswald revealed to
his acutely observant mind a glimpse of busy life: the life, moreover, of a rather disreputable smugglers' nest, with adventures,
carousals and brawls. Amid all these distractions Burns worked,
read and corresponded diligently—unfortunately, only a few of the
numerous letters which he mentions have been preserved—until
the appearance of a maiden, Peggy Thomson, set aflame the
slumbering passions of this remarkable peasant lad, and made any
further attempt at serious study futile. Thus he returned home
richer, not so much in technical knowledge as in knowledge of
men and books.

Previous to the Kirkoswald episode Burns had already been in
love. Special interest attaches to this love-affair, in that it was
the first event to give direction and form to his still vague urge
towards poetry. His sweetheart's name was Nelly Kilpatrick, and
Burns himself places the great hour of his artistic awakening in his
fifteenth year (1773). The memory of that rapturous state in which
first love and first poetic achievement coincided, continued to
stimulate him with unabated intensity for many a day. An entry
in his commonplace-book dated April 1783[6] refers to the episode,
the autobiographical letter makes us familiar with every detail of
it, and the Epistle to Mrs. Scott of Wauchope House (March 1787)[7]
commemorates it in enthusiastic verse. In this last-named rhyming

---

    [5] J. Muir, R. B. till his Seventeenth Year. Kilmarnock, 1932. (See B. Chr.,
1932, p. 114.)
    [6] Ch. W., i, 103.
    [7] H. H., ii, 104-106.

letter we see the poet as a shy, young, beardless lad, who has just crossed the boundary between boyhood and manhood, and, filled with heart-felt pride at being put on the same level as the other men, is toiling indefatigably in the fields. One thing alone distinguishes him from his companions: the desire to do something for his native Scotland, be it only to write a song in its praise; and he "turns the weeding-clips aside" from the prickly thistle and the bearded barley, out of respect for the symbols of his country. And all the while the elements of song are surging wildly but inarticulately through his soul, until his partner in the merry throng helps them to take form, for the first time:

"She rous'd the forming strain."

He can still see her, each glance from her roguish eyes setting him on fire and inspiring him, but at the same time making him so confused that he is tongue-tied and forced to call poetry to his aid. He was far from being so presumptuous, he said later, as to hope to succeed in making poetry like that printed by those conversant with Latin and Greek, but his girl had a sweet voice and used to sing a song made by the son of a neighbouring "small country laird on one of his father's maids." Burns thought he could at least equal this performance, and so, to Nelly's favourite reel-tune, he wrote verses such as had been familiar to him since early childhood in well-thumbed contemporary collections of songs and in various broad-sheets. Thus his first song, "O, once I lov'd a bonie lass,"[8] was written: the direct result of a personal experience, it was based on a now forgotten melody and was manifoldly influenced by printed models. It praises the external charms of the beloved in conjunction with her moral virtues, and assures us that she is the unqualified mistress of the poet's heart:

"For absolutely in my breast
She reigns without controul."

In the entry in the diary already mentioned, Burns has subjected this first effort of his muse to a thorough, penetrating and not unjust criticism, describing it as "silly and puerile," but for all that the outcome of a mood of honest emotion. The song, "O Tibbie, I hae seen the day,"[9] written a few years later, and, like its pre-

---

[8] H. H., iii, 197-198.
[9] H. H., iii, 37-38.

decessor, to a reel-tune (Invercald's Reel, first printed in 1762), shows greater sureness, and is more successful, both as regards form and content, in catching the real spirit of the folk-song. The chorus will give the reader a good idea of its character and theme:

> "O Tibbie, I hae seen the day
> Ye wadna' been sae shy!
> For laik o' gear ye lightly me,
> But, trowth, I care na by."

A well-known and very widespread motif this: the rich maiden sweeping past the poor working lad, without deigning to cast him a glance, while he, making a virtue of necessity, exclaims: "I'd rather have the other—you know which!—in her sark, than you, with all your money." The vocabulary is strongly flavoured with the vernacular, the treatment is fresh, and the words are most happily wedded to the air.

Two other poems of this early period clearly show the influence, in form at least, of a well-known lament by Mrs. Alison Cockburn (1712-94): "I've seen the smiling of Fortune beguiling," a poem which is itself based on an old fragment of verse dealing with the transitory nature of human happiness: "The flowers of the forest are a' wede awa."[10] In his poem "I dream'd I lay"[11] it is more the sententious tone of his model that Burns has elaborated, while in "A Ruined Farmer" with its wailing refrain, "And it's O fickle fortune, O!"[12] he has described, from personal observation, the misfortunes and the sorrows of an honest farmer, who one stormy night, wellnigh despairing as he remembers happier days, passes apprehensive, care-laden hours beside his sleeping dear ones. It is the portrait of his own father that Burns has drawn for us here. The artistic value of both poems is slight.

Such are the gloomy strains with which the years at Mount Oliphant reach their end. The child has become a youth. Worry and struggle, poetry and love, have begun. Burns has felt the heavy hand of oppression and has learned the meaning of social misery at his own fire-side. At the same time there have been vouchsafed to him glimpses of broader horizons of human life and

---

10 A. Whitelaw, "The Book of Scottish Song," 368-369.

11 H. H., iii, 18-19.

12 H. H., iv, 1-2.

a certain insight into the literature of his country, all of which
has enriched his mental and emotional experience. Ardent, tender-
hearted, sensitive, an eager and receptive listener, whose first steps,
moreover, into the creative world have been attended with some
success; with the faith of childhood still strong in his heart; burning with passionate love for his native land; highly strung, intense,
and filled with the joy of life, despite his poverty; his mind open
to every great thought and seeking a suitable vehicle for its
expression: that is how the poet of these years appears before us—
full of promise, but also set about with many dangers.

The year 1777 at last brought deliverance from the depressing
conditions at Mount Oliphant. The first period of the lease had
run out, and the family resolved to try their luck on a larger
farm farther inland, in the parish of Tarbolton, only to be more
bitterly disappointed than before.

CHAPTER III

LOCHLIE AND TARBOLTON

1777-1784

OUTWARDLY, life at Lochlie, as the new farm was called, ran strikingly parallel to that at Mount Oliphant, except that everything now appears in a more significant and more portentous light.

From the road which runs from Tarbolton to Mauchline, a road situated about midway between these two places leads through the fields in a northerly direction to Lochlie. To-day the farm is in a flourishing condition. In Burns's time, however, the small loch which gave it its name was still undrained and made the otherwise hard and barren land marshy. Besides this, we gather from a letter written by Robert on 21st June 1783,[1] to a relative, that the methods of cultivation were unsuitable, the rent too high, and the whole country suffering heavy loss because of the wretched political and economic conditions due to the American War and the failure of a provincial bank. The picture of the times which he outlines in this letter is as interesting as it is sad : industry, which up till a short time before had been flourishing, now appears to be in desperate straits, agriculture has reached a very low ebb, the aristocracy and the middle-classes are financially reduced or ruined, smuggling is in full swing on the adjacent coasts, and the misery and decay which everywhere abound are as apparent in the farmers' steadings as in the low, white, thatched houses in Tarbolton, where the rattle of the looms is being less and less heard from year to year.

Lochlie[2] is so near Tarbolton that its inhabitants could reach the village in less than an hour, and yet it was far enough away from that small social centre to have guaranteed complete seclusion to those who sought it. The farm buildings lay hidden behind a rise in the ground; but when Burns, who in contrast to his father

---

[1] Letters, 14.
[2] See plate in *B. Chr.*, 1933, facing p. 3.

was drawn towards the society of his fellows, walked along the road to Tarbolton or to Mauchline, though the scene which he beheld might not be distinguished by any overwhelming natural beauties, his gaze could roam unimpeded over undulating ranges of hills to far, free horizons. Invisible, but easily traced by means of the vegetation fringing their banks, the Ayr and the Irvine flow down to the sea. Here and there rise groups of old trees or small patches of denser wood, to South and West hills of a considerable height shut in the horizon, and everywhere, nestling in the countless folds and hollows of the landscape, lie villages and farms. The air, sweeping over moor, meadow, and ploughed land from the North Sea or the Atlantic Ocean, is spicy, stimulating, and so pure that one can hear the sound of the bells and the striking of the steeple-clocks a long way off. Serene and lofty Heaven's great vault extends, impressive alike in the glare of undimmed sunshine or when the winds rise and drive the clouds before them in ever-changing masses, sending cold showers of rain scudding across the open country. The idyllic quality in this landscape never becomes insipid, as occasionally happens in the more southern districts of Britain, and, especially in the times with which we are dealing, poverty and the constant struggle to win a living from the soil caused a certain harshness and severity to mingle with the peace that lay over the many scattered homesteads. It was here that Burns had his roots, this was the ground from which his nature drew its nourishment; from this soil came his happiness and his sorrow, his stubbornness and his all-embracing love; from this environment his spirit, permeated with the forces of his native earth, soared out into the world, returning again and again, as long as Fate allowed it, to the place of its birth. A traveller, passing through this country-side, ignorant of Burns, would scarcely feel tempted to linger there, but would rather try to reach the more imposing North or the more friendly South. Anyone, however, who visits it for the sake of Burns, finds a thousand things that hold him fast in these wide solitudes; he looks with new eyes upon the harsh thistle and bearded barley, and upon the daisies which in spring cover the ground in thousands; and if he is passing Mossgiel or Lochlie in the fragrance of the early morning, he probably glances back involuntarily to see if he may not catch a glimpse of the Bard walking to and fro behind his team of four horses, his hand on his plough and a

well-thumbed book in his pocket, humming an old tune to himself as he goes.

There can be no doubt that the family at Lochlie soon attracted
attention to itself. The austere, self-absorbed character of the father
was not calculated to win him many friends. He continued to
lead a severe, patriarchal existence in deliberate, self-imposed retire-
ment, keeping his family not only hard at manual labour but busily
employed with subjects likely to benefit their minds. In this he
anticipated the intellectual needs of his eldest son, whose habits may
have caused him worry, if not disgust, with regard to other matters.
Neighbours could tell how the members of the Lochlie household
might be seen gathered round the dinner-table, each with a spoon
in one hand and a book in the other. As for Robert, he evoked
grave head-shaking in one person and loud approbation in another.
He was respected, but was also looked upon with suspicion, if not
dislike, because at one time, in the bitter agony of developing
genius, he would shun the society of his equals, and at another—
and this was far oftener the case—would seek out their company
and gather them round him, fascinating them with the flow of his
eloquence, which was able and willing to cope with any subject,
however difficult. He was, moreover, a keen observer and satirist,
in religious matters suspiciously free in his opinions, so that the
honest Tarbolton "bodies" hardly knew what to think of the restless hot-head from Lochlie who was so fond of visiting their village.
Was he not the only man in the parish who wore his hair carefully
tied and his filemot plaid in a fashion which he had made his own?
"They couldna' tell what to mak' o' young Burns o' Lochlea."[3]

We may conclude from various indications that Tarbolton, a
little village of some five hundred inhabitants, did not lack a
certain intellectual activity. Religious squabbles between the strictly
orthodox Calvinists and the more liberal, modern-minded members
of the community were at that time, to use Burns's own expression,
putting the country half-mad. The Scot has always taken a
passionately active interest in ecclesiastical questions, and controversies of that and a similar kind have recurred with remarkable
violence to the present day. However much these may have
harassed the life of the individual and occasionally interfered with

---

[3] Account by the Rev. J. C. Higgins. See Ch. W., i, 69 (note).

the peaceful earning of a living, they kept up the intellectual vigour of the people and gave them a deeper insight into problems which at least possessed the merit of lifting their minds out of the rut of everyday routine. Apart from these religious factions, there were various friendships and enmities of another kind. Among Burns's personal friends we must here mention David Sillar (1760-1830), the son of the farmer on the small neighbouring farm of Spittalside. Gilbert Burns brought the two together, and Sillar was soon Burns's companion on many a ramble between the Sunday sermons, and his confidant in the almost unbroken series of his love-affairs, as well as his comrade in debating and rhyming; for Sillar made poetry too, though certainly as yet just as Burns used to do, without any thought of publishing his verses. In 1789, following in the footsteps of his celebrated friend and encouraged by him, he had his Poems printed by Wilson of Kilmarnock. They are unimportant productions, whose only interest for us lies in their association with Burns. We must not forget to mention that Sillar was musical and a good fiddler. His recollections of the Tarbolton days show us Burns as the eager reader and dreamer, passionately fond of female society; as the theological sophist, whose opinions were not above suspicion; as a man whose social gifts always won him a willing audience, but whose satire at the same time roused antagonism and distrust in many of his listeners. This is the picture we get of him from other sources belonging to this period.[4]

Sillar had also to share certain enmities with Burns, among them that of the local poet and tailor Alexander Tait, an "original" of adventurous habits, who used to place his very limited poetic gifts at the service of Tarbolton, where he acted as chronicler of local events, to his own great satisfaction. His Poems, published at Paisley in 1790,[5] contain scathing descriptions of the ongoings of Burns and Sillar, and are full of venomous accusations, coupling their names with those of various girls in a very scandalous manner. These effusions, however, must not be taken too seriously. The

---

[4] See J. M'Vie, "Burns and Stair." Kilmarnock, 1927, chaps. 5-7, pp. 31-53.

[5] At present one of the three known copies of the book is in the Mitchell Library, Glasgow. For Tait see Paterson's "Contemporaries of Burns," Edinburgh, 1840, 142-157; Kay's "Edinburgh Portraits," ii, 119-120; H. H., iv, 248-250 and 254-255; Lowe, "Burns's Passionate Pilgrimage," Glasgow, 1904, 117-133 (Saunders Tait: The Tarbolton Poet Laureate). Border Magazine, May 1924, 68-71 (T. A. A.). For some specimens see Snyder, pp. 498-503.

whole family at Lochlie, with their pride of spirit and their ill-concealed poverty, seem to have been repugnant to Tait's spiteful nature. Even their unfortunate financial position finally served him as the theme of a malicious poem, "Burns at Lochly," written in Burns's favourite stanza. How Burns and Sillar first roused his anger we know not.

That intellectual interests and the joys of social intercourse were not confined to individuals among friends or foes, is shown by the founding in Tarbolton of a Bachelors' Club, of which Burns was obviously the life and soul. From the seventeenth century onward, such social clubs had abounded in the principal cities of the country, and whether serious or convivial in their purpose, had served to promote mutual understanding, an uninterrupted exchange of thought, and the strengthening and expansion of the common intellectual interests of their members. We need not mention that the interests of these clubs were not confined to these and similar lofty matters. Eating and drinking filled a large place in their activities, but at the same time room was also found for the delights of music and poetry; and although all kinds of absurdities—perhaps even an occasional bout of dissipation—caused them to be a target for criticism, the spirit of brotherly love which permeated them kept them in a happy and flourishing condition. In the ninth number of the *Spectator* (dated 10th March 1711) Addison writes with benevolent humour of these "little nocturnal assemblies, which are commonly known by the name of clubs," and finds much that is praiseworthy in them. "When men," he says, "are thus combined for their own improvement, or for the good of others, or at least to relax themselves from the business of the day, by an innocent and cheerful conversation, there may be something very useful in these little institutions and establishments." The example of the big towns was imitated throughout the country, as witness the club in Tarbolton under Burns's leadership. From the documents of the Tarbolton Bachelors' Club, first quoted by Currie in his biography of Burns,[6] we plainly recognize the spirit which prevailed at its meetings. The members were enjoined to hold fast to what were accepted as the highest ideals of club life, which aimed at improving humanity; and to avoid "all excesses,

Works, vol. i, 104-107, 363-367.

extravagances and follies, the end of which is guilt and misery."
According to the short annals of the club, of which Burns was
probably the author, the first meeting was held on the evening of
11th November 1780. Burns presided, and the following subject
was down for debate: "Suppose a young man, bred a farmer, but
without any fortune, has it in his power to marry either of two
women, the one a girl of large fortune, but neither handsome in
person nor agreeable in conversation, but who can manage the
household affairs of a farm well enough; the other of them a girl
every way agreeable in person, conversation and behaviour, but
without any fortune: which of them shall he choose?" It transpires
from notes, the publishing of which we owe to Currie, that in this
debate Burns fought on the side of the imprudent. Currie also
gives us, in the same passage, a short list of other subjects which
were dealt with from time to time in the Bachelors' Club. They
all testify to the ambitious spirit which dominated the little club, and
are by no means uninteresting as regards the questions they raise.
Thus on one occasion we clearly recognize the influence of
Rousseau: "Whether is the savage man or the peasant of a civilized
country in the most happy condition?" or "Whether is a young
man of the lower ranks of life likeliest to be happy, who has got a
good education and his mind well-informed, or he who has just
the education and information of those around him?"[7]

The rules of the club have likewise been preserved,[8] and afford
us a glimpse into the customs which prevailed on debating evenings, the meetings being held every fourth Monday: they regulated
the choice of members and the initiation ceremony, imposed fines
upon recalcitrant and dilatory members, decreed secrecy, and were
directed with particular severity against such as in any way made
merry in public over what took place in the privacy of the club.
Obscene and blasphemous talk was forbidden. When the business
of the evening had been exhausted, the members parted after drinking "a common toast to the mistresses of the club." The tenth and
last paragraph sums up the regulations thus:

> "Every man proper for a member of this society must have a
> frank, honest open heart; above everything dirty or mean; and must .
> be a professed lover of one or more of the female sex. No haughty,

[7] *Ibid.*, 118 (note).

[8] *Ibid.*, 363-367.

self-conceited person, who looks upon himself as superior to the rest of
the club; especially no mean-spirited, worldly mortal, whose only will
is to heap up money, shall upon any pretext whatever be admitted. In
short, the proper person for this society is a cheerful, honest-hearted
lad, who, if he has a friend that is true and a mistress that is kind,
and as much wealth as genteelly to make both ends meet, is just as
happy as this world can make him."

Even to-day those sentences conjure up, without much imagination on our part, the voice of young Burns, as he presides with
joyous pride at the Round Table of the Tarbolton Club, his eye
sparkling, his whole being alive with the inexhaustible vitality of
his developing talents, while the company listens entranced to his
words, carried away by the rushing torrent of his eloquence, or
borne aloft on the pinions of his genius, which despite all obstacles
soars ever upwards. As time went on, it turned out that the Tarbolton Club, whose twelve members, some of whom are completely
unknown, included Gilbert Burns and David Sillar, could not carry
on its existence without the magnetic centre of Burns's infinitely
stimulating personality. When he left Ayrshire, the club, in spite
of the tenth paragraph of its rules, fell a prey to mediocrity and
ended its sessions in inglorious discord.

Burns's social urge found wider and more adequate satisfaction in his admission into the Freemasons' Lodge on 4th July
1781. Tarbolton was at that time very strongly under the influence
of freemasonry. Before Burns became a mason, it had two lodges:
St. James Tarbolton Kilwinning and St. David Tarbolton, St.
David having seceded from St. James in consequence of some
internal friction. In 1781 the two lodges reunited under the name
of St. David Lodge, which was established by the Scottish Grand
Lodge. Before a year had elapsed, however, St. James Kilwinning
was resuscitated through a seccession in which Burns took part,
and from that time onward exercised considerable influence on the
intellectual life of Tarbolton and its immediate vicinity.[9] Burns's
masonic activity is intimately associated with this lodge, and its
archives contain to this day notable original memoranda on his
doings in it. He quickly mounted the ladder of honours, becoming a member in October 1781, and being appointed deputy master
in July 1784, when he was already settled at Mossgiel. In this

---

[9] D. M. Lyon, "History of the Lodge of Edinburgh (Mary's Chapel)," 1900,
367-369.

capacity he presided over numerous meetings of the "brothers of
the mystic tie," never finding the road from Mossgiel and back
irksome, rejoicing in the thought of the festive hour and the
inward exaltation which was granted to "the sons of light."
Masonic thoughts are frequent and always easily detectable in
Burns's writings.[10] They reach their climax in the hymn in praise
of honest manly worth: "Is there for honest poverty" written in
January 1795. The reader must not, however, get the impression
that it was freemasonry that first roused the sentiments underlying
these poems: Burns is inconceivable without them. He was a
freemason, in Lessing's sense of the word, before he ever bore the
name.

While Burns was in deep sympathy with the spiritual element
in the movement, he admittedly found in freemasonry certain
material advantages, the chief of which was that his circle of
acquaintances grew in extent and in importance. In the Tarbolton
Lodge he probably came into contact for the first time with respected
citizens of Mauchline who were later to be more closely associated
with him, and to spur him on with friendly patronage. He met,
for example, the lawyer Gavin Hamilton, who a few years later
became his landlord; Dr. John Mackenzie, who in turn introduced him to Dugald Stewart, the philosopher; James Dalrymple
of Orangefield, to whose recommendation he owed the interest
taken in him by the noble Earl of Glencairn when he went to
Edinburgh; and many others, of higher or lower rank. In Kilmarnock, Edinburgh, and Dumfries he benefited by masonic connections. They were responsible for many an honour conferred
upon him; but they were also the cause of many of the bouts of
dissipation indulged in by him, for he was easily led. We shall
have occasion to touch upon these matters later on.

Life for Burns had hitherto flowed tolerably smoothly at
Lochlie, but almost simultaneously with his admission to the lodge
its even tenor was disturbed by an episode which took place in
the little seaport and smuggling town of Irvine, and which did
not reach its conclusion till March 1782. It is one of the least

---

10 See the following poems: "The Farewell," i, 184-185; "Tam Tamson's
Elegy," i, 221; "No Churchman am I," i, 256-257; "To Dr. Mackenzie," ii, 89;
Masonic Song ("Ye sons of old Killie, assembled by Willie"), iv, 19; "Libel
Summons," l. 93-125) *Archiv*, vol. 130, 69-70).

edifying chapters of his early history, for it found him weak, moody, and depressed, owing to the fact that his resistance was temporarily lowered by illness; and he allowed himself to break out into sentimental lamentations about his lot, which he soon afterwards faced once more with courageous resolution.

Burns gives as the motive for his excursion to Irvine partly a fit of caprice, partly the intention of taking up a new profession. The new profession was to be that of flax-dressing, from which he thought he might more quickly expect independence than from agriculture. Gilbert Burns supplements the story with a few interesting details, telling us that he and his brother had leased a piece of land from their father some years previously and had cultivated flax upon it. Robert now evidently wished to complete his training by learning how to dress this material properly. Gilbert adds that his brother had also been preoccupied with thoughts of matrimony, and had in consequence been looking round for means to set up a household of his own, realizing that these dreams must be relegated to the dim and distant future as long as he was condemned as a penniless farmer to carry on the galling battle with the soil.[11] Seldom has the truth of his own words

> "The best-laid schemes o' mice an' men
> Gang aft agley"

been more strikingly illustrated than in the development and carrying through of this well-thought-out and rational plan. In the first place, he was disappointed in the hopes which he had set upon his sweetheart, Alison Begbie, who was serving as a maid on a neighbouring farm, and who, for some unknown reason, rejected the hand he offered her, in spite of his letters, which were filled with the highest moral precepts and sentiments of universal benevolence.[12] Nevertheless, Burns went to the place of instruction in Irvine, only to find that he had been mistaken in his partner, who was "a scoundrel of the first water" and "made money by the mystery of Thieving," that is, if we interpret the words of the autobiographical letter rightly, he was either a smuggler or a receiver of stolen goods. The unfortunate venture ended in catastrophe on New Year's Eve, 1781-82: Burns, his partner and

---

[11] Currie, i, 72-73.

[12] Letters, 5-9. The poem "The Lass or Cessnock Banks" is also said to have been written in her praise. H. H., iv, 3-6.

the latter's wife were bringing in the New Year with much carousing, when, owing to some drunken carelessness on the part of the wife, the workshop went on fire and was burned to the ground—leaving Burns, as he expressed it himself, "like a true poet, not worth a sixpence." Previous to this decisive event, however, on 27th December 1781, he had sent his father a disillusioned letter,[13] revealing a state of self-torturing melancholy and hopeless despondency, which was assuredly due in part to nervous disorders brought on by excessive bodily strain, and was probably also caused by the conflict between his creative will and the necessity of eking out a miserable existence: by the consciousness of strong mental powers hampered by the most primitive demands of his daily duties. This depression returned periodically during his life-time. A constitution not of the strongest to begin with, unsettled by the painful development of the artistic, creative urge, and at the same time lowered in resistance by the season of the year, which was unfavourable for him, combined with the uncongenial environment, completely explain the gloomy mood of those months in which he yearned to be set free from this earthly life. In later years he could not remember this period without a shudder.

The one bright spot in his sojourn in Irvine was the friendship he made with a sailor named Richard Brown, in whose life and nature he saw himself reflected in many respects. Brown (who shortly afterwards became a captain) was poor, dogged by misfortune, and full of the joy of life. Burns in his autobiographical letter has endowed him with all the virtues of the hero of a novel. Possessed of what the poet then called "knowledge of the world," he was, in the way of sailors, even more of a worshipper of the female sex than Burns himself, and spoke with levity of a "certain fashionable failing" on which the latter had hitherto looked with horror. "Here his friendship," writes Burns, "did me a mischief." Brown was evidently a full-blooded person in whose nature Burns found support, and he was at the same time well enough educated to view his friend's intellectual efforts with understanding. Letters written to him by the poet right up to November 1789 show that Burns faithfully remembered the hours they had spent together.

"Do you recollect a sunday we spent in Eglinton woods?" he

---

[13] Letters, 4.

writes. "You told me, on my repeating some verses to you, that you
wondered I could resist the temptation of sending verses of such merit
to a magazine: 'twas actually this that gave me an idea of my own
pieces which encouraged me to endeavour at the character of a
Poet."[14]

It is doubtful to which poems he refers here, especially as the period
in question is characterised in both the autobiographical letter and
an entry in his diary as being barren of poetic achievement. It
was only later, and so probably after his return to Lochlie, that,
meeting with Fergusson's poems, he—to use his own words—
"strung anew his wildly-sounding lyre with emulating vigour."

The next letter of importance written by Burns which we
possess was sent on 15th January 1783 from Lochlie to his old
teacher, Murdoch, who was then busy in London as a teacher of
languages.[15] It is an unusually interesting and self-revealing letter,
which gives us a clear picture of Burns's life during the last year
of his residence at Lochlie. It speaks of his extremely delicate constitution, which makes it easy for him to resist the temptations
which come his way: as far as these are concerned, he has little
to reproach himself with; but somehow he cannot fall into line
with the practical demands of life. Money-grubbing and market-
prices are matters of indifference to him: "I seem," he says, "to be
one sent into the world, to see, and observe." His attention is
concentrated on men and their ways. He can forgive the knave
who has tricked him of his money, provided he is different from
other men in that he has something original about him. He lives
for the hour and its countless distractions, and beyond that he has
no cares. Even the prospect of one day having to wander about
the country as a beggar has no terrors for him, for he feels that
his talent for conversing with men will save him from utter want,
and the pride which is his inseparable companion will not let him
lose faith in himself. Of the satisfaction which the writing of
poetry can give him, or of any artistic plans whatever, there is still
no word here: rather does he refer in characteristic fashion to the
dynamic and soul-stirring impression which a wide study of literature, especially of authors with a sentimental bias, has made upon

---

[14] Dated 30th Dec. 1787. Letters, 168.
[15] Letters, 13.

him. He mentions a number of his favourite poets by name, and then, becoming very sentimental himself, exclaims:

> "These are the glorious models after which I endeavour to form my conduct"—notice that he speaks of *conduct* and not of poetry!— "and 'tis incongruous,—'tis absurd to suppose that the man whose mind glows with the sentiments lighted up at their sacred flame—the man whose heart distends with benevolence to all the human race— he who can 'soar above this little scene of things'[16]—can he descend to mind the paltry concerns about which the terraefilial race fret, fume and vex themselves! O, how the glorious triumph swells my heart!"

The important part which the zealous study of books played in developing and shaping Burns's poetic faculties has long been known, and has been carefully and thoroughly analysed by a number of authorities. Instead of being the prodigy, the poet of nature, "without help, without model, or with models only of the meanest sort," the man of pure, unadulterated inspiration so rhetorically described by Carlyle in his famous essay, Burns, according to them, was a poet who let himself be influenced by contemporary and past literature to the point of endangering his own originality; who did not create one single new form; who in those of his poems which are free from dialect often sinks to mediocrity, and who even in the domain of his most inspired work—that of description, satire and the folk-song—is not the original creator or founder, but the great finisher of a tradition already far advanced through the efforts of notable forerunners. This calmer view is quite clearly expressed as early as 1797 by Robert Heron, who rightly draws attention to the Bible, the ballads which were still popularly sung in the South of Scotland, Ramsay, and the stimulating magazines, as Burns's models. Those who have taken this point of view have been led, with ever-increasing conviction, to conclusions which can no longer be overlooked. Angellier in France, the editors of the Centenary Edition in Scotland, and various investigators in Germany have accepted and developed these conclusions, and in so doing have sometimes swung to the other extreme, laying undue emphasis on what he borrowed, at the expense of the greatness of what he created.

It is easy, from Burns's letters and "commonplace books" and his brother Gilbert's supplementary contributions, to draw up the

---

16 From Thomson's "Autumn," l. 966.

catalogue of a little library with whose contents he made himself
intimately acquainted during his more reproductive period which
came to an end at Lochlie. The importance of his later reading,
which grew more and more comprehensive, is to be otherwise
assessed. If we leave out of account the Bible, the catechism, the
schoolbooks in the narrower sense of the term, Tooke's "Pantheon,"
a number of treatises on agriculture, and a collection of model
letters (as yet unidentified) of the time of Queen Anne, we come
first of all to a Life of Hannibal[17] and William Hamilton's "Life
and Heroick Actions of the Renoun'd Sir William Wallace"
(1722), a popular modernized version of the epic of the same title
written by Blind Harry in the second half of the fifteenth century.
One of these two books brought him for the first time into close
touch with a heroic figure from classical antiquity, the other made
him familiar with the foremost champion of Scotland's national
freedom, whose history was very closely associated with Ayrshire
and, in particular, with the districts Burns knew best. He early
got to know Pope's translation of Homer, and the works of the
leading rationalists were soon added to his list. The pungency of
Pope's satire always attracted him, and he repeatedly, if vainly,
attempted to follow in his footsteps, but the difference in temperament of the two poets was unbridgeable, and what passed from
Pope into Burns's intellectual possession was confined to formal
imitations and the borrowing of some half-philosophical thoughts
and a few sharply moulded epigrams. Nor can one speak of
Shakespeare's influence as being deep. Milton, on the other hand,
left a deeper impression on the poet: we see the defiant figure of
Satan clearly reflected in Burns's poems as his heroic type. Apart from
this, his sympathy turned to the sentimental poets, as he was fully
justified in calling them: Thomson, Young, Blair, Shenstone,
Beattie, Goldsmith, and Gray. Macpherson's prose rhapsodies,
which went under the name of Ossian, take pride of place. Burns
was already familiar with less famous but not less influential
names through his school reader, the well-stocked "Collection of
Prose and Verse from the best English Authors," compiled by
Arthur Masson. Periodicals like Addison's and Steele's *Spectator*

---

[17] This book has not yet been identified. Perhaps it was "The Life of Hannibal
translated from the French of Mr. Dacier"; London, 1737. The heroic tone of the
preface, signed by Sam. Chandler, has much that would appeal to Burns.

and the *Weekly Magazine or Edinburgh Amusement,* published in
Edinburgh since 1768 by Walter Ruddiman and his brother Thomas,
elated and instructed him, and kept him in touch with the intellectual and political life of the great world. Of the eighteenth
century novelists, selections of whose work were known to him
through isolated volumes, sometimes picked up at random, we
may name Richardson, Fielding, Smollett, Sterne and Mackenzie:
here again it was the sentimental note which moved him to tears
and drove him to the wildest, though of course sincere, exaggera-
tions, so that he once said that Mackenzie's novel, "The Man of
Feeling," which is brimful of sentimentality, was the book which
he prized next to the Bible; and, in truth, it made a very lasting
impression upon him. To his serious-minded father's choice of
books he probably owed his knowledge of popular, and at that
time widely read, works such as Thomas Salmon's "New Geographical and Historical Grammar" (first published 1749) and William
Guthrie's "New Geographical, Historical and Commercial
Grammar" (first published 1771, then running into frequent new
editions), theological books such as Thomas Stackhouse's "New
History of the Holy Bible" (four volumes, Edinburgh and Kilmarnock, 1767), John Ray's "Wisdom of God Manifested in the
Works of the Creation" (first published 1691, followed by numerous
editions), William Derham's "Physico-Theology" (1713) and
"Astro-Theology"[18] (1715), and, finally, John Taylor's "Scripture
Doctrine of Original Sin"[19] (1740). Of philosophical works, he
already knew at the time in question John Locke's "Essay concerning Human Understanding" (1690), Adam Smith's "Theory of
Moral Sentiments" (1759), and the pious James Hervey's "Medita-
tions and Contemplations" (first edition 1745-47, followed by several
new impressions). We need only mention here the deep and lasting impression made upon him by the poets of his native country,
especially Ramsay and Fergusson, as well as by the collections of
song, folk-ballads and street ballads, which from his childhood he
studied with love and respect, and in later years with considerable
critical acumen.

---

[18] The two last named are the "Boyle's Lectures" mentioned in the autobiographical letter. Robert Boyle (1627-91) in his will left an endowment of £50 to
found lectureships in these subjects.

[19] See Ch. W., i, 461-462.

The question whether the influence of this reading, which was extremely comprehensive for a man in his station, was advantageous or the reverse, is a most difficult one to answer. The fact is that this element is inseparably bound up with his intellectual life, and that much of his poetry, including the poems which are written in the vernacular and deal with scenes from the life of the people, is very deeply permeated with it. He had no intention whatever of setting himself up in opposition to the classicists or the sentimentalists, as the representative, let us say, of popular poetry. He looked up to poets such as Thomson, Blair, Shenstone, and Beattie as to inaccessible masters, and, indeed, whenever he tried to imitate them in form and speech, he failed to reach their standard. But they helped him inwardly. They made it easier for him to find adequate expression for the rich store of emotion that was striving to find an outlet, and thus through them his originality came into its own. It is from this need of support that his love of quotations springs. As he says in a letter to Mrs. Dunlop, he "stores them in his mind as ready armour, offensive or defensive, amid the struggle of this turbulent existence."[20] There is no mistaking the fact that in certain groups of poems it is very easy to detect the particular stimuli: Pope influences the satire, Ossian and Thomson the description of scenery, Young, Hervey and Blair contribute grave reflections, often of pessimistic tendency, on the aspect of the tomb and the transitoriness of human life; while love of nature is common to the group of sentimental poets whose not very strongly differentiated style is reflected in numerous stanzas and lines written by Burns. Research into the sources, however, has reached absurd conclusions when it has tried from time to time, by pointing out parallel passages, to isolate these influences line by line. That they exist is certain. They are even so pronounced that quite a number of his poems may be excluded from the survey of his collected works without harm, as being totally lacking in the personal note. As a rule, however, their effect is general, and is not confined to single passages. Although he studied the poets, Burns even in his earliest days never modelled himself on any particular one of them, unless, perhaps, where some external or internal experience reminded him of the exemplary treatment of similar ideas by the

[20] Letters, 524.

older masters. Investigators must guard against seeing separate factors where there is in fact only an indivisible product. It is noticeable that the intensive study of literature during the Lochlie period was not accompanied by anything like a correspondingly vigorous output.

Burns now began for the first time to keep a diary or "Commonplace Book,"[21] though only a few pages of it were written at Lochlie. It was intended to contain "observations, hints, songs, scraps of poetry, &c.," to show the observer of human nature how a ploughman managed his cares and passions, and, in particular, to give a picture of the diarist himself, "a man who had little art in making money, and still less in keeping it; but was, however, a man of some sense, a great deal of honesty, and unbounded good-will to every creature rational and irrational." These words are followed by two mottoes from his favourite poet, Shenstone, one in prose, the other in verse; thoughts on the delights of love; the first song, with the discerning criticism of it already mentioned in a previous chapter; and arguments on the torments of remorse, with reference to a quotation from Smith's "Moral Sentiments," followed by a note on the spiritual greatness of the man who knows how to bear his self-incurred mental torture with manly resolution. These last thoughts are then expressed in rather pathetic blank verse.[22] The next entries were probably not made until the Mossgiel period. As before, poems, personal reminiscences and reflections are all set down together. One entry refers to the noble features discernible even in the meanest person; another speaks of the sublime beauty of the winter landscape (Thomson's influence is obvious here!); another affirms that "the whole species of young men" may be divided into two groups, the "grave" and the "merry," and this remark leads to the insertion of the song, "Green grow the rashes, O," (August 1784). Gradually philosophy is driven into the background by poetry, until in the summer and autumn of 1785 there reappear extremely interesting notes, chiefly about folk-songs, which bear witness to an astonishingly rapid maturing of Burns's mind. These will be fittingly dealt with in

---

21 Ch. W., i, 102 ff. Printed separately from the original MS., then in the possession of John Adam, Esq., Greenock, Edinburgh, 1872 and more accurately by W. Scott Douglas, iv, 51-98.

22 H. H., ii, 234.

the proper place. The first entries in the diary are still marked by
a certain awkwardness in self-expression on the poet's part; they
are very conscious, and so far show no trace of the desire, to which
Burns soon afterwards gave passionate utterance, to bring fame to
himself and to his country by his poetry.

The few poems and songs belonging to this period are of no
great value. The gloomy months in Irvine, with their physical
and spiritual despondency, are reflected in rhymed prayers and
paraphrases of psalms, and in the imitative melancholy poem of
resignation, "Winter, a Dirge";[23] autobiographically, we have "My
Father was a Farmer," in the style of the street-singers' ballads;[24]
amongst a number of songs "Mary Morison"[25] is so outstanding
that one is inclined to assign it to a later period in Burns's literary
life; and the cheerful ballad of "John Barleycorn" has been reconstructed on the basis of older versions.[26] The little poem on the
death and dying words of the poor sheep Mailie, written in the
stanzas of Allan Ramsay's fables, is particularly praiseworthy. Concerning the origin of this humorous masterpiece of animal charac-
terisation Gilbert Burns gave Currie the following details: Burns
had bought a ewe and two lambs from a neighbour and had
tethered them in a field near the dwelling-house at Lochlie. While
the brothers were busy ploughing, a herd-laddie of extraordinary
appearance, named Hugh Wilson, suddenly came on the scene
almost distracted with horror, and reported that the sheep had
strangled itself and was lying in the ditch. Burns, who was highly
amused by the grotesque spectacle presented by the boy, rescued
the animal, and when he was returning home with his brother from
the ploughing in the evening, is said to have produced the poem
almost in the form in which it appears to-day in the Kilmarnock
Edition under the title "The Death and Dying Words of Poor
Mailie."[27] In the poem, which is in dialect, the sheep is represented as speaking: turning to the herd-lad, Hughoc, who stands
gaping as helpless as a statue on the scene of the tragedy, she gives

---

[23] H. H., i, 134-135.

[24] H. H., iv, 8-10.

[25] H. H., iii, 286-289, sent to Thomson on 20th Mar., 1793. See Letters, 540.
Burns there calls it "one of my juvenile works."

[26] H. H., i, 234-246. See also Ritter, "Anglia," xxvii, 450-452.

[27] H. H., i, 53-56. Kil. Ed., 62-65.

him her last messages, warnings and wishes, recommending her two lambs to her ever-kind master, and expressing the hope that her son, the "toop-lamb," will always conduct himself in a seemly fashion and not stray far a-field at mating-time; that her daughter, the "yowie," will not throw herself away on any nasty moorland tup, but will consort only with respectable rams; and that her master will, for pity's sake, burn the cursed rope! The portrayal of the dying animal's thoughts, which is not without a precedent in Scottish literature, is quite free from sentimentality, and is far removed from the manner of the pastoral poetry in which city poets used to represent the little lamb on the meadow. It is the first of a series of delightful poems, in which the peasant-poet describes his faithful companions of the lower kingdom with the understanding which comes from constant association with them. Somewhat later Burns seems to have added a sequel to it, entitled "Poor Mailie's Elegy,"[28] in which the half-melancholy, half-humorous flashes of happy inspiration are most successfully intermingled, the poet being the speaker on this occasion.

"The Death and Dying Words of Poor Mailie," which, as we have seen, seems to have been the result of one happy effort, remained for a time an isolated production, for there dawned at Lochlie days which brought the poet's growing joy in song face to face with the deep melancholy of a tragic death-bed. It was obvious to wife and children that William Burns was in the last stages of consumption. As early as the summer of 1783 it was apparent to everybody that he had only a few months to live. What made this fact doubly bitter, however, was the realization that his death would be accompanied by the bankruptcy with which his family had already several times been threatened, and which was now at their very door.

After the first four years at Lochlie had passed without any great friction on the whole, William Burns found himself involved in an unedifying lawsuit with his landlord, a certain David M'Clure, a merchant in Ayr. Previous accounts of the case have shown William Burns in no favourable light, but these have been one-sided and have been based on the statements made by the plaintiffs only, whom the malicious rhymes of that scandal-monger

---

[28] H. H., i, 56-58, also four stanzas of an earlier draft, 345-346. *B. Chr.* 1932, 25-27, with fascimile.

Tait seemed to justify.[29]   The official documents pertaining to the
lawsuit have now come to light and have been published,[30] and
while they are not complete, they are sufficient to absolve the upright
man from the reproaches of illegal practices which have hitherto
been levelled against him.   The financial difficulties of the whole
county were in the background: not only Burns, but also M'Clure,
his opponent in the lawsuit, fell a victim to them, and, indeed,
there is scarcely a doubt that it was his own pecuniary embarrassment that drove the latter to institute proceedings against his tenant
at Lochlie.   Curiously there was no written agreement between the
parties.   There was a vagueness about the whole matter.   What
was certain, however, was that William Burns had for several
years fallen behind in his payments of the stipulated rent of £130.
When the case came up before the arbiters, the sum claimed by
M'Clure amounted to £775.   On the other hand, the "oversman,"
John Hamilton of Sundrum, allowed William Burns credit to the
extent of £543 17s. 4d., so that the sum due to the plaintiff was the
balance of £231 2s. 8d.   This account might have been settled, but
M'Clure, without adequate legal justification, as has now been
proved, had already gone further, and had taken out a warrant of
sequestration against the whole stock at Lochlie.   This was executed
on 17th May 1783, cattle, agricultural implements, carts, the produce
in the barns and the crops still in the fields being seized.   That
William Burns should have attempted, in spite of this public pro-
clamation, to dispose of part of the sequestrated property in an
underhand way, does not seem credible.   His opponents are our
only witnesses that he acted thus; but even though their suspicions
were not wholly unfounded, we should bear in mind the spiritual
distress of the proud and now broken man, before we pass judgment upon him.   Necessity does not only teach men to pray, it
also teaches them to sin.   And more we shall not say, than that we
should have liked to see a life so full of care, but yet so full of high
endeavour, granted a more peaceful ending.

In the late autumn of 1783 Robert and Gilbert had to be ready
for the worst.   Realizing that it would be impossible for them to
stay on at Lochlie after their father's death, an event which was now

---

[29] See Lowe, "Burns's Passionate Pilgrimage," from p 154; for Tait's lines
see Snyder, pp. 499-501.

[30] John M'Vie, "The Lochlie Litigation," *B. Chr.*, 1935, pp. 69-87.

imminent, they accepted the offer of Robert's patron, Gavin Hamilton, and leased the farm of Mossgiel from him, thus making sure of a sheltering roof, at least, for themselves and the rest of the family. At Lochlie disaster could no longer be averted, and death alone saved the father from the imprisonment for debt with which he knew himself threatened.

William Burns is said to have followed his eldest son's development with a certain amount of apprehension, not unmixed with pride and occasional amusement. That he was able wholly to understand or to approve of the passionate impulses or the restless, volcanic emotions of the young genius is scarcely conceivable. In the end his misgivings must have gained the upper hand, for he belonged to a harder generation, and had grown up in a sterner faith, where self-discipline was an inexorable law; and when the life of this fighter was drawing to a close, he feared for the moral and spiritual welfare of the son whom he would no longer be able to guide and to protect.

His youngest daughter, Isobel, has described to Chambers a scene which she says took place by her father's death-bed, and the truth of which we have no reason to doubt. At a certain hour on that last morning she had been alone with her brother Robert at the bedside of the dying man, who with his remaining strength exhorted her to follow the path of virtue and to shun vice. After a pause, he said that there was one member of his family about whose future conduct he was troubled, and he repeated the phrase. Then Robert came to him and asked: "Father, is it me you mean?" The old man replied that it was. Robert turned away to the window, the bitter tears streaming down his bronzed cheeks, and his breast heaving as though it would burst under the restraint which he had to impose upon himself.

William Burns died on 13th February 1784. His body was laid to rest near the spot where, with his own hands, he had built the home to which he brought his bride, and which he had left, for his children's sake, to tread the weary path of disappointment of his last years. He was buried in the churchyard of Alloway, in the shade of the now famous old church, the maintenance of which had ever been dear to him. His son's epitaph describes him as the "friend of man, to vice alone a foe," and concludes with Goldsmith's words:

"Ev'n his failings lean'd to virtue's side."

Chapter IV

MOSSGIEL AND MAUCHLINE

1784-1786

It was at Mossgiel that the floodtide of Burns's genius burst its bounds and began to sweep irresistibly onward. The farm, owned by the Earl of Loudoun, was leased by Gavin Hamilton, who had fitted it up with some degree of comfort as a summer residence for himself and his family. Situated on a high ridge not far from the little town of Mauchline, near the spot where two roads cross, the one leading west to Tarbolton, the other north-west to Kilmarnock, it has a fine clear view of the surrounding country. The poet, whose senses eagerly craved such stimuli, now had the prospect of the bustle of town life, wider interests, and the possibility of a more varied social existence, all of which put him—true to his favourite quotation—in a position to "study men, their manners and their ways," while he himself, however, not merely observed their activities, but mingled in them to his heart's content. The moment had come when every restricting influence fell from him, and mind and body, careless of consequences, prepared to follow the passionate urging of the inward voice. After the death of his austere and imperious father, Robert was the recognized head of the family, which consisted of five members—three sisters and two brothers—besides his mother, his brother Gilbert, and himself. In spite of the catastrophe at Lochlie, they were still not quite destitute when they moved to the new farm. Under the pretext that they had been employed by their father, the older brothers and sisters put forward a claim for wages due to them. This claim was allowed and thus they saved a little from the general *débâcle*. They came to Mossgiel with the best of resolutions. Burns's words: "Come, go to, I will be wise!"[1] burned in all their hearts. Burns himself, in his autobiographical letter, gives a short and striking account of how the venture turned out:

"I read farming books; I calculated crops; I attended markets;

---

[1] *Cf.* Eccl., vi, 23.

and, in short, in spite of 'The devil, the world and the flesh,' I believe ¬
I would have been a wise man; but the first year, from unfortunately
buying in bad seed, the second from a late harvest, we lost half of
our crops: this overset all my wisdom, and I returned 'Like the dog
to his vomit, and the sow that was washed to her wallowing in the
mire.' "

The sentence which follows this pithy biblical quotation[2] runs:

"I now began to be known in the neighbourhood as a maker of
rhymes."

Poetry and constant bad luck are thus brought into causal relationship. The poet, fully conscious of the creative power of his genius,
now rose up in proud, defiant opposition to the depressing penury
of his home. From now on his genius no longer found expression
only in isolated songs, epigrams, or short descriptive poems, but
broke forth, particularly in the years 1785 and 1786,[3] like the storm-
wind, or like a rhythmical tidal-wave, that swept everything,
including himself and the limitations of his environment, irresistibly
before it. His genius rose over Mauchline in splendour, like the
great morning sun, radiating warmth, and illuminating every
corner.

In his poem, "The Vision,"[4] Burns has given expression to the
conflict between his miserable position and his inward doubts, and
the inspiration which brought him deliverance. He describes how
one winter evening, tired out by the work of threshing, he is resting
pensive and alone beside the open fireplace in the parlour or
"spence." The only light is that given out by the logs, from
which the dense smoke rises—the only sound, that of the rats
scurrying to and fro in the rafters. Irritated by the "reek" from
the fire, the toil-weary, discontented poet lets his gloomy thoughts
dwell remorsefully on his past life. Squandered youth, good advice
thrown to the winds, making silly rhymes for the lips of fools, have
brought him to this state, where he may truly be described as
"half-mad, half-fed, and half-sarkit." At this point he starts up,
raising his hand to swear that henceforth till his last breath he

---

2 2 Peter ii, 22.
3 *Cf.* the chronological list in Ch. W., iv, 571-574, or in Cleghorn's edition
of the Kilmarnock Poems, Oxford, 1913, 271-274.
4 H. H., i, 74-87, probably written in 1786.

will be rhyme-proof, when suddenly the' door opens, and in the
flickering light from the ingle-nook he beholds a maiden, the sight
of whom makes the oath die on his lips.   It is his native Muse,
Coila.   A wreath of holly crowns her brow, and on the green
mantle which flows about her limbs are depicted familiar scenes
of his native country.   She greets Burns as the "rustic bard" con-
signed to her special care, telling him how since his childhood
she has watched him with hopes for his future, in the blast of the
north wind, in the blossom-laden spring, under the azure firmament
in autumn, in love and passionate transgressing: even then, she
says,

> "the light that led astray,
> Was light from Heaven."

She assures him that his fame will grow, and that though he may
not hope to equal Thomson, Shenstone, or Gray, he is more
fortunate in his humble sphere as "rustic bard" than if he owned
riches or enjoyed a king's favour.   She advises him to remain
true to poetry; to "preserve the dignity of Man, with Soul erect";
to trust the Creator's Universal Plan; and, finally, she bids him
wear the holly wreath which she binds round his brow, while its
polished leaves and red berries play rustlingly against each other.
Then "like a passing thought" she flees "in light away."   The
poet's consecration is complete.

The glow of inspiration—the companionship of his native Muse
—did not desert Burns during those joyous and exuberant years,
even when, as not infrequently happened, he descended into the
depths of life.   It finally led to the compiling of the Kilmarnock
Edition of the "Poems," with the publication of which his career
reached its zenith.   We must now examine more closely the events
which led up to this climax.

Burns's family moved to Mossgiel in March 1784.   In the
summer of the same year the poet seems to have had another violent
attack of the physical and spiritual suffering which he had first
experienced in Irvine, and a small group of piously meditative
poems is generally attributed to its influence.   Although some of
these poems, which have little merit in themselves, appear among
the entries made in the Common-place Book during August 1784,
it is possible that they belong to the end of the Irvine period, when

his life was darkened by moods of depression.[5] The autumn, always a favourable season for him, restored his strength and courage. He was now a frequent visitor to Mauchline, where his great gifts and his rhetorical power were soon recognized, and, according to his listener, admired or feared. He did not mind the long journey to and fro, when he wished to be present at the meetings of the Tarbolton Freemasons' Lodge, where he was depute master; and as he now saw possible subjects for his Muse in everything with which he came in contact, he brought away with him from there also many a fruitful inspiration.

To such an excursion to Tarbolton the poem "Death and Dr. Hornbook"[6] owes its origin. The original Hornbook was a certain John Wilson, a schoolmaster in Tarbolton, who endeavoured to eke out his frugal income by keeping a small grocery store and country chemist's shop, announcing that "in common disorders"—this much conscience he had, at least!—advice and help could be had at his shop, gratis, as well as, naturally, the corresponding medicines, ointments and plasters—these, however, to be paid for. Apparently one evening at the lodge Wilson had boasted of his medical skill, and had thereby roused the mockery of Burns, who was present, and who immediately set up a monument *ære perennius* to this Tarbolton Dr. Eisenbart. In the poem Burns describes how he was with difficulty—for he was somewhat intoxicated—making his way home to Mossgiel. He had successfully negotiated Hood's Hill, near Tarbolton, round which so many stories are woven, and found himself in the vicinity of Willie's Mill (Willie being William Muir, a man who was friendly both with the poet and the poet's father), when in the pale moonlight Something uncanny and of a bony thinness appeared before him: Death with his scythe and "three-taed leister." After greeting each other in jovial fashion, the two sat down on a stone by the roadside—the stone may still be seen!—and Death at once broke out into a woeful lamentation about his opponent, Dr. Hornbook, who had such skill in medicines. Who can do anything, asked Death, against such remedies as *sal-marinum* of the seas, the *farina*

---

[5] "A prayer in the Prospect of Death," H. H., i, 135-136; "Stanzas written in Prospect of Death," *ibid.*, 229-230; "Paraphrase of the First Psalm, *ibid.*, 232-233; "The Ninetieth Psalm Versified," *ibid.*, 234-236. The first-named poem appeared in the Kilmarnock Edition, the three others in the first Edinburgh Edition.

[6] H. H., i, 191-200; first published in the Edinburgh Edition, 1787.

of beans and peas, *aqua-fontis* or perchance *urinus spiritus* of capons? "Wae's me for Johnie Ged's Hole now," interpolated the listener (Johnie Ged being the gravedigger). But Death answered with "an eldritch laugh" that that was not the way of it at all: where he helped one to a natural death, Hornbook with his pills and physic put a dozen underground. And he proceeded to give examples. Just when Death was about to outline a plan of revenge against Hornbook, who snatched his lawful prey from him and, instead of leaving his victims in Death's care, did the greatest harm with his "d——d dirt," the clock on the church tower gave the warning note—"some wee short hour ayont the twal"— and each went his way. This satire does not appear to have prevented John Wilson from carrying on his business—indeed, he is even said to have remarked that the poem, on the whole, was rather complimentary to him! Nor does it seem to have affected the relations between him and Burns, in the long run at least. When Wilson was contemplating a change, he asked the poet's assistance, and the latter furnished him with a letter of introduction to a writer in Edinburgh.[7] Wilson died in 1839 in Glasgow.[8]

Burns also seems to have paid frequent visits to an older friend, John Rankine, who lived at his farm of Adamhill, not far from Tarbolton. The poet valued this rough, hard-drinking man, who was always up to some witty or audacious joke, as a sympathetic boon-companion and as a reliable confidant, whose sense of humour did not fail him even in the most painful situation. In such a situation Burns found himself towards the end of the year 1784. It was the first of a considerable number of cases of this sort in which Burns was involved during the course of his life, but as it *was* the first, it affected him deeply.

While at his father's farm of Lochlie, Burns had made the acquaintance of a servant named Elizabeth Paton, of whom his niece, Isabella Begg, later sketched a realistic portrait in a letter to Robert Chambers, describing her as a well-developed, plain-featured peasant girl, industrious, frank and independent, and for these reasons a special favourite with her mistress, Burns's mother; but incredibly ignorant and endowed with a strong "masculine understanding" and a sovereign contempt for anything that savoured of

---

[7] Letters, 420 and 421. *B. Chr.*, 1930, 19-21.
[8] Letters, ii, p. 376.

culture.⁹ She loved Burns with heart-felt devotion, and that he
returned this affection in his own way, which was certainly more
physical than spiritual, is made clear by the fact that he continued
to visit her steadily even after the household at Lochlie had been
broken up. At that time Elizabeth was living at her home at
Largieside, near Rankine's farm of Adamhill, and the latter must
have sent Burns word, somewhere about November 1784,¹⁰ that
her condition was beginning to attract public attention. The first
reply to this news was two stanzas expressing astonishment: "To
John Rankine in Reply to an Announcement."¹¹ The misdemeanour demanded and received expiation in the form of a
reprimand by the local minister and the payment of a guinea into
the poor-box. In addition, it called forth the "Epistle to John
Rankine Enclosing some Poems" (1785), which were included in
the Kilmarnock Edition, in spite of the scarcely veiled obscenities
in stanzas VII-XIII.¹² The epistle is witty and pithy, openly gives
vent to his ill-humour at the humiliation and the penalty inflicted
upon him by the Kirk, and culminates in his avowed intention,
expressed with somewhat frivolous boastfulness, of making up,
when the time comes—"as soon's the clockin-time is by"—for the
gold piece which he has forfeited, by having another affair with
Elizabeth. But when the expected event became a reality, and a
daughter was born to him on 22nd May 1785,¹³ he found other
and more worthy strains in the emotion of first paternal happiness
and pride. The result was "The Poet's Welcome to his Love-
begotten Daughter,"¹⁴ in which he tenderly bends over the child,
the image of his "bonie Betty," and hopes that it may inherit his
virtues without his vices:

> "Gude grant that thou may aye inherit
> Thy mither's person, grace and merit,
> An' thy poor, worthless daddy's spirit
>   Without his failins!
> 'Twill please me mair to see thee heir it
>   Than stocket mailins."

⁹ Ch. W., i, 119-120.
¹⁰ Burns's letter to Orr, dated 11th Nov. 1784, points to this date. See
Letters, 19.
¹¹ H. H., ii, 70.
¹² H. H., i, 176-179. Kil. Ed., 218-222.
¹³ This is the date discovered by that distinguished Burns authority, J. C.
Ewing of Glasgow. All other dates hitherto quoted should be corrected from it.
¹⁴ H. H., ii, 37-39. These are three different MS. versions of this poem, which
was first published in 1801.

It was always one of Burns's principles never to hide anything he had done, but, heedless of gossip, to own up and take the consequences manfully upon himself. Here we have in addition such a lovable touch of pure joy in fatherhood, such a naïvely happy satisfaction with this "sweet fruit" of his amorous adventure, that we can only rejoice at the beneficent warmth which finally radiated from this wild-fire. Elizabeth Paton later married a ploughman, and is said to have become a model housewife. Burns's daughter, who was given her mother's Christian name, lived in the household at Mossgiel until the poet's death, after which she returned to her mother's care, and likewise married, but died young, in her thirty-second year.

The poet's welcome to the new-born child belongs to the middle of the most prolific and most important period in his literary life— a period which was a direct reflection of his connection with Mauchline and its prevailing conditions and noteworthy personalities. It was the realities of the many-sided life in Mauchline and its immediate vicinity that first gave the right direction to his powers as champion, satirist, and eulogist of certain circumscribed "sets" and social customs. His poetry, which at all times strove to express what was of universal significance, had its roots in the sphere of interest of a small community. The magic of his genius enabled him to grasp and to formulate its eternal values.

To-day, Mauchline,[15] in contrast to the impoverished and more remote Tarbolton, is a peaceful, flourishing, friendly little country town with broad, well-kept streets and a visibly growing colony of villas on its outskirts. It is healthy, clean, and well provided with public buildings. The inhabitants are for the most part employed in quarries and sawmills, the houses now, as in Burns's time, being constructed of beautiful red sandstone which is quarried in the immediate vicinity, at Ballochmyle, and from which emanates the homely, warm glow peculiar to this material, especially in clear sunny weather. In spite of the remains of a Cistercian monastery— a square, crenellated freestone structure called "the Castle"—once the centre of the original ancient settlement, and an almost direct link with more dangerous and more turbulent times, the last echo of which has long since died away, it would be difficult to imagine

---

[15] *Cf.* J. Taylor Gibb's excellent little book, "Mauchline, Town and District," Glasgow, 1911, with numerous good illustrations.

anything farther removed from the poet's storm-tossed, undisciplined spirit than the peaceful atmosphere of the Mauchline of to-day, that Mecca and Medina of every Burns pilgrim. The frictions from which he drew fire have been smoothed over; the factions and festivals in which he took part no longer exist; the evil-smelling taverns which offered shelter to the "drucken gangrel bodies" have become models of respectability and cleanliness; even the old parish church, with its many memories (some of them very painful for Burns!), has entirely disappeared, the miserable, barn-like house of God which dated from pre-Reformation times and was, as someone once said, "as ugly a lump of consecrated stone as ever cumbered the earth," having been replaced in 1829 by the present handsome though perhaps unimposing building. For all these changes, however, it is not difficult to conjure up a picture of Mauchline, its inhabitants and its environs, as they were about 1785. If the church has gone, the churchyard, the scene of the "Holy Fair," remains, with its grave-stones beneath which rest Burns's friends and foes.[16] Here lie several of his children; the Armours; "Daddy" Auld; the Kirk elder Holy Willie (William Fisher); John Richmond and Gavin Hamilton, unswerving in their loyalty to the poet; Mary Morison, who died young and who is the heroine of one of Burns's finest early poems; Agnes Gibson, alias Poosie Nansie, and her·disreputable daughter, Racer Jess; Nanse Tinnock, in whose tavern, just behind the graveyard wall, Burns, according to himself, occasionally studied politics over a glass of "gude auld Scotch drink";[17] members of the families of Whitefoord and Alexander of Ballochmyle; and many others, who appear in his letters and poems in more or less identifiable form. Nor can the appearance of the town itself have altered fundamentally, for there are still numerous houses (though they are for the most part modernized, and in 'particular robbed of their inflammable thick thatch roofs), which keep alive the memory of Burns and his frequent visits to Mauchline. These houses are all situated in the immediate vicinity of the church and the old churchyard. They are Nanse Tinnock's "howff," and, a few steps away, Dr. Mackenzie's house and the house in which Burns took up residence

---

[16] B. Chr., 1927, p. 159-160.
[17] See stanza xxi of "The Author's Earnest Cry and Prayer," with Burns's footnote to it.

immediately after his marriage to Jean Armour; Poosie Nansie's lodging-house, in which the "jolly beggars" forgathered; and on the opposite side of the "Cowgate," John Dove's trim public-house, "The Whitefoord Arms," where, with Burns as president and his friends James Smith, John Richmond and William Hunter as his assistants, in various offices, a sort of bachelors' club held its meetings. It carefully watched and registered sexual frivolities in the little town, and occasionally inflicted severe punishment on unrepentant offenders. The house where the Armours lived was quite close by, only a narrow lane dividing it from the back of the Whitefoord Arms. It has not been preserved, but Gavin Hamilton's hospitable home still leans inviolate against the old wall of "the Castle." A few miles south and south-east of Mauchline, on the banks of the Ayr, the tourist reaches Barskimming and the steep slopes of Ballochmyle, the place where the Lugar meets the Ayr, and the village of Catrine, close to which the celebrated professor of moral philosophy, Dugald Stewart, had his summer residence. It was there that Burns, on what was for him a memorable day, in October 1786 for the first time sat down at table with a lord, the eldest son of the Earl of Selkirk, and with a representative of the highest culture of his country. Somewhat farther on, in the village of Ochiltree and at the farm of Glenconner, lived friends of humbler rank, who were equally devoted to him.

On a high ridge to the north, on the Kilmarnock road, stands Burns's farm of Mossgiel, which is still being cultivated—with more success, be it said, than could be achieved under the hand of the poet. The present spacious steading probably contains little of the more modest buildings of his time, the dwelling-house then consisting only of two rooms on the ground-floor and a few garret rooms reached by means of a ladder. Burns and his brother Gilbert slept in one of these attic apartments, which was lighted by a sky-light window. Here, at a small table underneath that window, Burns used to write down the impressions of the day, which had often already taken definite shape during the work in the fields, and been imparted to his brother. All this has disappeared, the sole remaining relic being a dense thorn hedge which encloses the yard and is said to have been planted by the two brothers. In spring time the meadows near the house are a mass of daisies, and now, as then, the eye sweeps over undulating hills, fields and hedgerows, and is charmed and uplifted by the far, free vista of immeasurable distance. The details have gone, but the general picture cannot have altered perceptibly, and through a thin veil of clouds the poet's world rises before us, with the peace and tribulations which Mossgiel held for him, and the noisy, exuberant pleasures which he sought in Mauchline; we see his friends, his patrons, his love-affairs and his enemies. In these fairs, carousals, and disputes there was an infinite wealth of scenes and figures, the close inter-linking of which was grasped by his keen eye and penetrating intelligence, and transformed by his creative genius, which was seldom idle in those days, into an imperishable, living picture of the times.

At Mossgiel poems dealing with scenes from country life followed each other in swift succession, from the description of the field-mouse's flight to the farmer's New Year's greeting to his old mare and the solemn stanzas of the "Cotter's Saturday Night," that favourite poem of Burns's in which he reverently exalted the virtues of the peasantry. It was from Mossgiel that he sent those friendly epistles which are so full of the joy of living and of creating; it was there that he composed reflective poems, rhythmical expressions of certain ideas carefully thought out beforehand, such as "Man was Made to Mourn" (1785), or the epistle containing much good advice (which the poet followed but imperfectly himself!) sent to a young friend, Andrew Aiken, in Ayr (15th May, 1786); and, finally, it was there that he poured out his sorrow over disappointments in love-affairs in sentimental verses such as "The Lament" and the "Ode to Despondency" (both belonging to the spring of 1786). The rhythm of labour stimulated his creative powers, and many of his best lines, Gilbert tells us, came to him at the plough. In Mauchline, however, he was swept into the maelstrom of life. It was Mauchline that decided his destiny: it is there that we must now follow him.

At that time the population of Mauchline consisted of about a thousand inhabitants, who were engaged either in agriculture, weaving or trade. Twice a year a great concourse of people assembled in the town: in the spring on the occasion of the races, which were held in the immediate neighbourhood of Burns's farm; and in the second week of August, for the fair and the sacrament of the Lord's Supper. Invited and uninvited, folk came flocking from all sides, and gave the keen watcher at Mossgiel just and welcome opportunities for social pleasures, for critical observation, for the widening of his experience, and for the extending of his intellectual horizon. But he also found plenty of stimulating material in Mauchline in the quiet routine of daily life. The wave of progress which about the middle of the eighteenth century gradually began to sweep away the patriarchally narrow and in some ways incredibly primitive conditions prevailing in the country, had affected Mauchline too, and had evoked the characteristic and almost always optimistic unrest which generally lays hold upon men's minds during such transition periods. The Rev. William Auld (1709-91) wrote just before his death the following description of the state of affairs in the parish for Sir John Sinclair's "Statistical Account of Scotland":

> "The manner of living and dress, is much altered from what it was about 50 years ago (when Auld entered upon his charge). At that period, and for some time after, there were only two or three families in this parish, who made use of tea daily, now it is done by, at least, one half of the parish, and almost the whole use it occasionally. At that period, good two-penny, strong-ale, and home-spirits were in vogue: but now even people in the middling and lower stations of life, deal much in foreign spirits, rum-punch, and wine. In former times, the gentlemen of the country entered into a resolution to encourage the consumption of their own grain, and, for that purpose, to drink no foreign spirits: But, in consequence of the prevalence of smuggling, and the heavy taxes laid on home-made liquors, this patriotic resolution was either forgotten or abandoned.—As to dress, about 50 years ago, there were few females who wore scarlet or silks. But now, nothing is more common, than silk caps and silk cloaks; and women, in a middling station, are as fine as ladies of quality were formerly. The like change may be observed in the dress of the male sex, though, perhaps, not in the same degree."[18]

There is one contrast which Auld does not mention here: whereas in earlier generations, in the country at all events, Calvinism exercised its authority in its strictest form, with unopposed ruthlessness, the number of free-thinkers, sectarians, and scoffers was at that time assuming shocking dimensions. "Polemical divinity

---

[18] ii, 113-114. With regard to the question of dress, Burns himself corroborates this account when he says of the "Belles of Mauchline":
"Their carriage and dress, a stranger would guess
In Lon'on or Paris they'd gotten it a'."

about this time was putting the country half-mad," wrote Burns with reference to the early years'of his life spent at Mount Oliphant. In Mauchline he was swept into the midst of these controversies. Whereas he had formerly only let his light shine forth in "conversation parties, on Sundays, between sermons, or at funerals," (thereby, even in those days, alienating some of his strictly orthodox listeners), indignation now inspired him to write verses of overwhelming power, which reveal him for all time as one of the bravest champions of humanity and liberty of conscience as opposed to ecclesiastical narrow-mindedness and hypocrisy. Not that it was he who started this great fight in Scotland: on the contrary, he found the whole trail blazed for him; but he brought to his side the full, irresistible force of his temperament, the gay assaults of his utterly fearless satire, and the rich and pithy idiom of his speech. More than that: being a great poet, he was able to raise this purely local dispute about dogma between individuals in a little Scottish town to the level of something that concerned the whole of humanity; and in this cause his voice must gain a hearing as long as there is a possibility of self-satisfied autocrats and inquisitors uniting with obscurantists of any kind to give the *coup de grâce* to freedom of speech and the sincere regard for the higher glory of God. It was close personal contact with these controversies that first loosened Burns's tongue, and brought forth the stream of poetry which probably did not begin to flow in full flood until the winter of 1784-85.

We must also emphasize the fact that it took more than these differences on matters of dogma between the two conflicting tendencies in Scottish church life, known as the "Auld Lichts" and the "New Lichts," the "Evangelicals" and the "Moderates" (when they did not call each other by more insulting names), to exert such a strong and stimulating influence on Burns. Poets of his calibre do not take problems but individuals as their starting-point, though, in their hands, the individual may often be exalted to a symbol of the universal. The individual case around which the greater part of Burns's anti-orthodox poetry[19] is grouped was

---

[19] To this group belong: "The Twa Herds, or The Holy Tulzie" (perhaps written at the end of 1784?), H. H., ii, 20-25; "Holy Willie's Prayer" (beginning of 1785), H. H., ii, 25-30; "The Holy Fair" (autumn, 1785), H. H., i, 36-47; "Address to the Deil" (winter of 1785-86, before Feb. 1786), H. H., i, 47-53; "The Ordination" (spring, 1786), H. H., i, 210-215; "To William Simpson of

the bitter quarrel between the Kirk Session of Mauchline and the
poet's landlord, patron, and friend, the Mauchline lawyer Gavin
Hamilton: "The poor man's friend in need,
                    The gentleman in word and deed."

Roughly, this is what had happened: previous to the time in
question, relations between Gavin Hamilton's father, John
Hamilton, who was likewise a lawyer, and William Auld, seem to
have been somewhat strained. The chief reason for this may have
been a hereditary tendency of the Hamiltons towards Episcopacy:
at the time of the Restoration Gavin's great-grandfather is said to
have inflicted heavy and permanent damage on the Presbyterians.[20]
The distrust continued from generation to generation, and was
expressed with particular fervour with regard to the free-thinking
and outspoken Gavin Hamilton, when at the end of the 'seventies
he was accused by the Kirk Session of negligence in the management or disbursement of a poor-rate. William Fisher, an elder of
the Kirk, is said to have played the unedifying rôle of informer
against Hamilton even then. We have no information as to how
this strange controversy developed, but from July 1784 veiled attacks
on Hamilton on the ground of his failure to carry out his duty to
the Kirk began to appear in the session minutes.[21] He and some
others not mentioned were reproached with Sabbath-breaking and
continued inattendance at church, even when in excellent bodily
health; and it was resolved first of all to send those concerned a
mildly worded private admonition. Hamilton did not react to this
until several months had elapsed. In a violent letter dated November 1784, he forbade the insertion in the books of the Kirk Session
of the entries derogatory to him, saying that the gentlemen need
have no doubt that these accusations were unfounded and based on
personal animosity or malice. Though this sharp thrust was keenly
resented by the Kirk Session, it led to conciliatory measures, these,
however, being frustrated by Hamilton's obstinately hostile
behaviour, which was obviously supported by a good conscience.

Ochilree" (May 1785), H. H., i, 167-175; "To John Goldie" (August 1785),
H. H., ii, 70-73; "To the Rev. John M'Math" (17th Sept. 1785), H. H., ii, 76-81.
To complete our list, we may mention "The Kirk's Alarm," which belongs to a
later period (July 1789), H. H., ii, 30-37.

[20] See Lockhart (ed. Ingram), 47, and H. H., i, 379.

[21] Reprint of the documents given in "Robert Burns and the Ayrshire
Moderates," 1883, 36-47. See also Ch. W., i, 185-186, 464 (Appendix iv).

A detailed complaint by Hamilton to the Presbytery of Ayr made the quarrel more bitter. On 20th January 1785, the Kirk Session in its turn summed up the reasons for its displeasure under the following heads: unnecessary absence from the church service on two Sundays in December and on three Sundays in January; setting out on a journey to Carrick on the third Sunday in January; habitual or total neglect of religious observances within his family; and an abusive letter to the Kirk Session. Hamilton's former servants and those actually in his employment at the time were summoned as witnesses. The document shows how the rulers of the church tried to exercise control over its members by vexatious interference and tyrannical aspersions, and by the unscrupulous manufacture of evidence against suspected persons. Meanwhile Hamilton was man enough to offer resistance. His interests were successfully represented before the Presbytery by a friend, Robert Aiken, an able writer, and by 26th January 1785, it was decreed that the compromising minutes should be erased. An appeal to the Synod of Glasgow failed, and on 17th July 1785, the Kirk Session was ordered to furnish Hamilton with a certificate to the effect that he was "free from public scandal or ground of church censure known to them." The peace thus unwillingly established was not of long duration, but the resumption of the conflict is of no great importance to us.

When we consider Hamilton's respected and prominent position in Mauchline, we can understand how the various phases of his controversy with the "Auld Lichts" under the leadership of the Rev. William Auld and his henchman, the elder William Fisher, would be followed by the inhabitants with eager attention and that mixture of satisfaction and malicious joy which is generally displayed on such occasions. On Hamilton's side, apart from Aiken, were Dr. John Mackenzie, who had attended Burns's father during his last illness and who had followed the poet's career with keen interest and growing sympathy; a group of liberal ministers, such as Dalrymple and MacGill of Ayr, MacQuae of St. Quivox, Dr. Peter Wodrow and his assistant (who later became his successor) John McMath of Tarbolton, and above all, his devoted and admiring tenant, the poet of Mossgiel himself. With caustic, flaming satire Burns took part in the already passionately heated dispute, and his verses, as he says in his autobiographical letter, "with a

certain description of the clergy, as well as laity, met with a roar
of applause."

Burns's first satire on the orthodox clergy, "The Twa Herds:
or The Holy Tulzie,"[22] was directly inspired by a ridiculous
incident, in which those concerned revealed themselves in an
utterly farcical light, so glaringly was their behaviour at odds with
their precepts and calling. Two ministers of uncompromising
orthodoxy, shining lights of the faith, powerful preachers and
supervisors of morals, John Russell of Kilmarnock and Alexander
Moodie of Riccarton, from being friends had become bitter enemies
through a quarrel over parish boundaries, and now directed the
knife-edge of their tongues, not against careless church-goers or
adherents of socinian and arminian doctrines, but against each
other, at a time when, as Burns says in one of the MSS. of his
poem,[23] "the hue and cry against patronage had reached its height."
Further details have not been handed down to posterity, but according to Lockhart[24] the two antagonists were obliged to appear before
the Presbytery in Irvine, in order that their quarrel might be settled.
There the storm broke in full fury. The reverend gentlemen,
heedless of the presence of a considerable crowd of listeners, lost
every vestige of self-control, and "abused each other, *coram populo,*
with expressions such as have long been banished from all popular
assemblies, wherein the laws of courtesy are enforced by those of a
certain unwritten code."

Burns's satire consists of ironical lamentation over this incident,
which was so humiliating for the Auld Lichts. What is to become
of the good sheep, he wonders, now that even their faithful and
incomparable shepherds have lifted up their staves against each
other? The godless New-Licht herds will rejoice at the insulting
words hurled at each other by the two opponents, and will say
that both are right!

> "Sic twa—O, do I live to see't?—
> Sic famous twa sud disagree't,
> An' names like villain, hypocrite,
>   Ilk ither gi'en,
> While New-Light herds wi' laughin' spite
>   Say neither's liein!"[25]

---

[22] H. H., ii, 20-25.
[23] Egerton, 1656.
[24] p. 50.
[25] Stanza ix.

The two adversaries must agree, for the number of those unreliable in the doctrines of faith is legion. The flocks must join forces and take away from the lairds the right to choose the herds; only then will Orthodoxy flourish, "that fell cur ca'd Commonsense" be banished over the sea to France, and the liberal clergy reach the end of their eloquence, their psychology, their free-thinking, and their independent spirit.

With "Holy Willie's Prayer"[26] Burns then threw himself directly into the quarrel between Hamilton and the Kirk Session of Mauchline, the poem about the two shepherds, Moodie and Russell, having already, of course, served as a background for his part in the controversy. "Holy Willie" was none other than the Kirk-elder William Fisher, whom we have already mentioned several times. He had held this honorary office since 1772, was the Rev. Mr. Auld's right-hand man, and, as we have already said, acted as informer against Hamilton. Burns hated him as an individual and as a representative of a class of human beings abhorrent to him: the sanctimonious hypocrite. When he included the satire on him in the collection of his poems intended for his friend Robert Riddell, he provided it with a bitter character-sketch of its "hero," contrasting, in a few striking sentences, the untruthfulness and drunkenness of this elderly bachelor with the uprightness of Hamilton. The poet's *saeva indignatio* does not seem to have overstepped the bounds of truth. Fisher was reprimanded before the Kirk Session in 1790 for drunkenness, and there was a rumour —unproven, to be sure—that he had tampered with the "plate." He finally perished miserably, in February 1809, in a ditch by the wayside, as he was making his way home from Mauchline in a snowstorm. Burns's poem shows us Holy Willie at prayer, while under the influence of the victory which Hamilton had won over the Kirk Session in July 1785, by the decision of the Presbytery of Ayr. "Lord," he prays, "I thank Thee for choosing me from among the thousands who must suffer the pains of damnation, and for allowing me to stand as a pillar of Thy temple, 'strong as a rock, a guide, a buckler and example' to Thy flock, for I am unworthy, in that the flesh often gains the victory over the spirit; but perhaps Thou leavest this thorn in me so that I may not grow too proud

---

[26] H. H., ii, 25-30; *cf.* the notes, 320-321. The editors knew six MSS. of the poem.

and arrogant in the fullness of grace which Thou hast conferred
upon me.

> 'If sae, Thy han' must e'en be borne
> Until Thou lift it!'

I pray Thee, therefore, to bless Thy chosen one, and to confound
the blasphemers, such as Gavin Hamilton, the Presbytery of Ayr,
and the glib-tongued Aiken, who have brought mockery and
embarrassment upon us:

> 'But, Lord, remember me and mine,
> Wi' mercies temporal and divine,
> That I for grace an' gear may shine,
>   Excell'd by nane:
> And a' the glory shall be Thine—
>   Amen, amen!' "

The fearlessness, the force, and the piled-up humour of this satire
have still to find their match. Referring, like "The Twa Herds,"
to a particular incident, it surpasses the earlier poem by the universal
validity of its characterization. The squabble which revealed the
two pastors in such an ungodly light has become meaningless to
us, however willingly we may join in the poet's satisfied laughter
at seeing his ecclesiastical enemies take part in such an unworthy
scene. But Holy Willie did not live only in Mauchline, or only
at the end of the eighteenth century: however closely Burns has kept
his picture to the original, William Fisher, elder of the Kirk and
Gavin Hamilton's opponent in the law-suit, he is for us the type
of the officious ecclesiastic and hypocrite known to every age but
rarely unmasked with such courage and power. No wonder the
Kirk Session of Mauchline of that time mustered all its holy
artillery in several successive meetings, to see if it could not find
some weapon to point against "profane rhymers!"

A few weeks later, in the autumn of 1785, when the excitement
over the lawsuit had died down, Burns wrote a third great satire,
"The Holy Fair,"[27] describing the scenes which used to take place
every year in Mauchline in the second week of August, when people
came flocking from far and near to the Sacrament of the Holy
Communion. The communicants were bent equally upon edifica-
tion and merry-making: they looked forward to the sacrament with

---

[27] H. H., i, 36-47.

anxiety and remorse of conscience, but they also looked forward with eager curiosity to seeing and hearing the celebrated ministers of the district and to criticizing their appearance and delivery, while the younger folk saw in the occasion an opportunity for friendly encounters and amorous adventures such as seldom came their way. The Fair and the Holy Sacrament were inextricably woven together. The people crowded together in the open, in a churchyard situated in the centre of the little town. The only seats under cover were those for the notabilities, the country gentry, and the preachers. The latter took it in turns to give the crowd edifying addresses from pulpits like sentry-boxes, before the sacrament was dispensed. The service in the open air probably still held memories of the great time of the religious wars of the seventeenth century, when the brave covenanters worshipped in inaccessible moors and on remote hillsides. The assembly must have presented a lively, colourful picture, full of variety and contrasts, at that time presumably already tainted by many dubious symptoms which must have struck Burns forcibly as he mingled with this rich, full life, and may have spurred him on to give a faithful account of his impressions: for the essence of his "Holy Fair" is critical. The introductory six stanzas are unmistakably influenced by Fergusson's "Leith Races,"[28] and describe the splendour of the early summer morning and the poet's meeting with three allegorical female figures, Fun, Superstition and Hypocrisy, one of whom, Fun, offers to accompany him to Mauchline Holy Fair. "There," she says, "we shall spend a happy hour or two, and laugh to our heart's content at the 'runkl'd pair,' Superstition and Hypocrisy." The corresponding figure in Fergusson's poem is named Mirth, and this very difference in the nomenclature of the two guides reveals the deep-seated difference in the treatment of the theme. Burns does not look with Fergusson's harmless joy at the throng of people about him: the imp of mockery is at his heels. Apart from this, Burns imitates Fergusson in so far as he, like the latter, dispenses with the expedient, technically so promising, of finding his companion again in the crowded Fair. Fun is, and remains, forgotten in the depicting of the scenes which the poet observes around him. These pass before us in unconnected episodes: the lads, bold and braw

---

[28] Works, ed. by Grosart, 1879, 84-92.

in their Sunday clothes, the lasses barefoot, but dressed in silks and scarlet, throng past; beside the plate an elder with a "greedy glower" keeps watch, to see that no one passes without contributing an offering; at the place where the holy ceremony is held there has been erected for the gentry a weather-proof wooden shelter, at whose entrance a crowd of loose women stand gaping, among them Poosie Nansie's ill-famed daughter, nicknamed "Racer Jess." The humour of the poem lies in the contradiction between the sacred nature of the function and the profane bearing of the participants, and is expressed with epigrammatic pungency in the tenth stanza, which successfully contrasts these differences:

> "Here some are thinkin on their sins,
>   An' some upo' their claes;
> Ane curses feet that fyl'd his shins,
>   Anither sighs an' prays:
> On this hand sits a chosen swatch,
>   Wi' screw'd up, grace-proud faces;
> On that a set o' chaps at watch,
>   Thrang winkin on the lasses
>   To chairs that day."

Then follow characteristic peculiarities of the ministers who take it in turn to preach: Alexander Moodie with "lengthen'd chin and turn'd-up snout," wild with wrath, stamping and fuming, to the delight of devout hearts; George Smith, during whose cold, highly erudite harangues the benches empty and the refreshment places fill up; Alexander Millar, who preaches orthodoxy only half-heartedly, but—"the birkie wants a manse"; and, finally, when the young folks have given themselves up to totally different joys, John Russell, "the Lord's ain trumpet," ascends the pulpit, and with a voice of thunder describes to his horrified audience "Hell, where devils dwell,"

> "A vast, unbottom'd, boundless pit,
>   Fill'd fu' o' lowin' brunstane,"

painting the picture so vividly that the half-asleep start up, as though they already heard the roaring of the Evil One—but it turns out to be nothing but the snoring of a slumbering neighbour! The last stanzas describe the busy scenes in the inns directly adjacent to the churchyard wall, where hearts grow warm with drink and love, till Clinkumbell, the bell-ringer, warns them that

it is time to be off home. They depart, some "fou o' love divine,"
and some "fou o' brandy":

> "An' mony jobs that day begin,
>   May end in houghmagandie
>   Some ither day."

Burns's satire is said to have contributed to the removal, or at least
to the modification, of the long-recognized and deeply felt evil conditions which accompanied the dispensing of the sacrament. His
attack, while strong, is free from exaggeration, and the truth of
the picture he gives adds to its greatness. The open letter of an
anonymous blacksmith to the ministers and elders of the Church
of Scotland,[29] published the very year Burns was born, corresponds
so closely in its description of these practices, and occasionally also
in its wording, to the poet's stanzas, that some writers have thought,
without adequate grounds, that it was one of Burns's sources.[30]
The continual influx of the multitude, thus swelling the
congregation to intolerable dimensions;[31] the obvious hypocrisy
of many who took part in these praiseworthy demonstra-
tions of religious zeal; the nervous excitability of others, and the
disgusting scenes of drunkenness and immorality which were cease-
lessly occurring, evoked the criticism of the unbiassed, and added
a keener edge to Burns's pen than any printed treatise would have
done. In obeying the instinct of his genius and describing the
multi-coloured bustle of the Fair, he was indulging his own sense
of fun and at the same time with ruthless, formidable hand firmly
sketching the portrait of that bigotry which he abhorred, its intellectual darkness being an insult to his own bright, pleasure-loving
spirit.

Neither "The Holy Fair" nor the far more biting satires written
under the influence of Hamilton's lawsuit can justify the charge
of irreligion or frivolity in spiritual matters which has been levelled
against Burns. It is true that he had laid aside the naïve faith

[29] "A Letter from a Blacksmith to the Ministers and Elders of the Church of
Scotland"; London, J. Coote, 1759. The letter itself is signed "Inverary, May 8th,
1758." Extracts from it are quoted by Ch. W., i, 357-358.

[30] See, for instance, W. A. Craigie, "A Primer of Burns," and Ritter,
"Quellenstudien," 134-135.

[31] In 1786 the number of communicants in Mauchline was 1400, of whom 400
belonged to the congregation. Cf. H. G. Graham, "Social Life in Scotland in the
Eighteenth Century," London, 1906, 302-314.

which had dominated him up to the Irvine period, and, under
masonic and liberal influence, had begun to formulate for himself
a religion of benevolence, love, and atonement, basing his views
upon the writings of Dalrymple, MacGill, John Taylor and John
Goldie.   This religion had nothing in common with Calvinism
and its grim doctrines of effectual calling, predestination, and
original sin.[32]   It appealed to him as the child of an avowedly sentimental age, to whom, as to Faust, feeling was everything; it
satisfied the demands of his keen intellect; and it gave him the
faith which he needed, a faith in a Supreme Being who, if a man's
soul were worth saving, would be willing to overlook even manifold transgressions.   In his "Address to the Deil"[33] he lets a gentle
ray of hope of redemption fall upon the Prince of Hell himself,
thus echoing, perhaps unconsciously, ideas already expressed by
Origenes.   To him religion was and remained a sacred, indispensable consolation, to which, in spite of occasional leanings
towards scepticism, he turned with an ever increasing confidence,
the more plainly he realized the discords and failings of his own
earthly pilgrimage.   His theology is extremely clear and simple:

> "A man," he writes to Robert Muir,[34] "conscious of having acted an
> honest part among his fellow creatures; even granting that he may have
> been the sport, at times, of passions and instincts; he goes to a great
> unknown Being who could have no other end in giving him existence
> but to make him happy; who gave him those passions and instincts, and
> well knows their force."

And in an important confessional letter to Mrs. Dunlop, written
on New Year's morning 1789 in which he sets down his religious
convictions, he says:

> "Still I am a very sincere believer in the Bible; but I am drawn by
> the conviction of a Man, not the halter of an Ass."[35]

He bore no brief for any of the dogmas then current in the country,
and it has rightly been pointed out by Chambers that, in spite of

---

[32] *Cf.* in particular Ch. W., i, 166-169 and 455-462; Henderson's "Robert
Burns," 64-68; "To John Goldie" (Aug. 1785), H. H., ii, 70-73. For the religion
of Burns *cf.* amongst others *B. Chr.*, 1926, 70-77 (D. M'Naught), and *B. Chr.*,
1932, 80-93 (James Muir), which gives the most pertinent illustrative quotations.

[33] H. H., i, 47-53 (especially verse xxi).

[34] Letters, 221.

[35] *Ibid*, 293.

nis passionate campaign against Orthodoxy, he cannot be reckoned as belonging unreservedly to any particular liberal or modernist party.[36] In the *Postscript* to his Epistle to William Simpson of Ochiltree (May 1785)[37] he characterizes the quarrel between the "Old and New Lights" as "moonshine matter," adding:

> "I hope we bardies ken some better
> Than mind sic brulzie."

It was not against religion that the sharpest arrows of his satire were directed, but against the sanctimonious hypocrisy of the clergy and the laity, against calumniators and agitators, who have God's words on their tongues, but falseness and selfishness in their hearts, a class which we shall always have with us so long as it is profitable for men to act in this sinister way. Burns hated them and fought against them all his life with the same acrimony as animated Shakespeare, Molière, and Ibsen, when they tore the mask from the face of dissimulation, falsehood, and narrow-mindedness, and thus fulfilled that high judicial function, the exercising of which has been regarded by the greatest poets of all times and nations as a sacred duty to themselves and to their fellows.

On 17th September 1785 Burns sent a copy of "Holy Willie's Prayer" to John M'Math, a minister of the more liberal school of thought, who afterwards came to an unedifying end; and in the accompanying poetical epistle,[38] an extremely high-spirited piece of writing, he took the opportunity of once more explaining his motives for taking part in the quarrels of the Kirk. The personal element—his reason for espousing the cause of the unjustly persecuted Gavin Hamilton—is clearly revealed (v and vi); his own weakness is frankly confessed (viii and xii); and homage is paid, with humility and fervour, to Religion, the "maid divine" (xi and xii); but, he says in stanza viii, he would rather be an atheist than hide behind the Gospel as behind a screen, talking of Mercy, Grace and Truth, and at the same time hard-heartedly and pitilessly ruining an unfortunate man in the name of religion. Those who act thus are his real enemies:

---

[36] *Ibid.*, 352.

[37] H. H., i, 167-175 (stanza xxxi).

[38] H. H., ii, 76-81. The poem was first published in Cromek's "Reliques" in 1808.

"But I gae mad at their grimaces,
Their sighin' cantin, grace-proud faces,
Their three-mile prayers, an' hauf-mile graces,
    Their raxin conscience,
Whase greed, revenge, an' pride disgraces
    Waur nor their nonsense."

The reader of these verses, which are written with such verve and such aggressive joy, will be in no doubt as to the true motives which drove Burns to satirize Orthodoxy, and will applaud the undaunted courage with which he carried his weapon, no less than the skill with which he handled it.

Meanwhile, the time was not far off when the poet's passionate nature, with its craving for sensual joys, was to offer the desired target to his sorely exasperated opponents, who lay in wait behind their artillery. The road from Mossgiel to Mauchline did not always lead Burns to the upper classes of society, to which men like Hamilton, Dr. Mackenzie, and their clerical and professional friends belonged. He at all times felt himself one with the man of humble standing, and as an observer of life in its entirety studied the latter's emotions and utterances with no less interest than he did the more cultured habits of those in a higher station. In an entry in the "Common-place Book," dated March 1784, he remarks that even among the outcasts (the "blackguards") of life he has often met with the noblest virtues in the highest perfection, and has for this reason sought their acquaintance "farther than has been consistent with the safety of his character."[39] The thought of one day having to wander about the country as a beggar, like these people, poor but free and unbroken in spirit, the victim of his own unbridled passions, was not unfamiliar to him and held no terrors for him. Between these two extremes stood the band of happy cronies in Mauchline, among them John Richmond, Hamilton's assistant; James Smith, the cloth-merchant (both born in 1765 and both censured by the Kirk Session because of a transgression similar to that of Burns); and William Hunter, the currier, concerning whom we have no further information. They were not, as in Tarbolton, held together by an interest in intellectual debates and rules of strict discipline and order, but, with Burns as their leader and bard, met to indulge in exuberant fun and frolic. At these

---

[39] Ch. W., i, 105.

long-drawn-out meetings, held in taverns of good and ill repute, the poet's genius flashed forth with glorious freedom, never averse to the greatest coarseness, but at the same time never far from sublimity. Outside this inner circle, there were probably many listeners whose names we do not know, who saw to it that the news of the reckless conduct and speech of the company did not remain confined to the four walls of the inn concerned. The two poems in praise of whisky, "Scotch Drink"[40] and "The Author's Earnest Cry and Prayer,"[41] probably both written in the winter of 1785-86, were composed in Nanse Tinnock's respectable public-house, already mentioned as being directly adjacent to the scene of the "Holy Fair." Nine times in the week, as he put it in stanza xxi of the second poem, Burns would drink to the Prime Minister's health "in auld Nanse Tinnock's," if only the people might have easier access to the noble barley-juice, by means of more favourable conditions of taxation—a conception of the drink question which would meet with less applause in our day and age. But behind the poet's patriotic joy in drinking it is not hard to recognize his harassing financial worries and love problems, which these festive carousals were intended to stifle and drown. The motto to "Scotch Drink," a paraphrased version of Solomon's Proverbs, chapter xxxi, 6-7, expresses this thought in no uncertain terms:

> "Gie him strong drink, until he wink,
> That's sinking in despair;
> An' liquor guid to fire his bluid,
> That's prest wi' grief an' care:
> There let him bouse, an' deep carouse,
> Wi' bumpers flowing o'er,
> Till he forgets his love or debts,
> An' minds his griefs no more."

This same sentiment is clearly re-echoed in not a few lines of both poems.

About the same time, in the late autumn of 1785, Burns took note, in a "doss-house," of incidents and figures which inspired him with the idea of his humorous cantata, "The Jolly Beggars."[42] That numerous literary works served as models for the poem as a whole and for particular parts of it, both as regards forms and

---

[40] H. H., i, 19-25.
[41] *Ibid.*, i, 26-35. Both poems were published in the Kil. Ed.
[42] H. H., ii, 1-19.

contents, has been proved,[43] while several songs in the cantata
have obviously led a separate existence outside the general frame-
work of the piece;[44] but the compact unity of the whole poem and
the realistic clearness of the types presented, which meet, quarrel,
and are reconciled, finally—carried away by love, drink, and
enthusiasm—joining in the bard's concluding song against the laws
of Church and State, are in no way impaired by the fact of this
dependence upon preceding efforts. Never since Shakespeare's
Autolycus have vagabond figures been created in English literature
with such frank and convincing sincerity. The background of the
scene is the ill-famed lodging-house of a certain Mr. and Mrs.
Gibson, for the management of which the hostess, Mrs. Agnes
Gibson, commonly known as Poosie Nansie, seems to have merited
special credit. Her daughter, known as Racer Jess, because among
other things she hired herself out as an express messenger (she is
mentioned under this name along with other loose women in
stanza ix of the "Holy Fair"), shared her mother's unsavoury
reputation. Mother and daughter had already been censured by
the Kirk Session on account of drunkenness and reset, on which
occasion Poosie Nansie announced her intention of "continuing
in the sin of drunkenness."[45] In this atmosphere, while a late
autumnal storm is raging outside, tramps of both sexes meet and
indulge in unbridled carousal. Among them are a discharged
soldier and his "doxy," who "once was a maid, tho' she could
not tell when"; a crippled fiddler; a stout beldame, relict of a
Highlander who had been hanged, and a successful pick-pocket to
trade; a hot-blooded tinker, far-travelled, and, true to the tradition
of his race, fond of trafficking in love—and, lastly, a Bard, whose
proud, freedom-loving heart—it is Burns himself who speaks!—
refuses to be daunted by Fate's hard blows. These are the figures
which emerge singing and dancing from the semi-darkness of the
room and from the chorus of unnamed beggars. Eight recitatives,
describing the players and developing the plot, link up the songs,

---

[43] Cf. H. H. ii, 292-304; Ritter's "Quellenstudien," 84-93; Raske, "Der Bettler
in der Schottischen Dichtung," Berlin, 1908, 62-69.

[44] The song of the soldier's "doxy" and the first song of the strolling singer
appeared in "The Merry Muses of Caledonia" (see Archiv, 130, 59). The latter
also appeared in a slightly different form, in the third volume of Johnson's
"Museum" (No. 290).

[45] H. H., ii, 308.

each of which is in keeping with the character by whom it is sung. In these songs, sung throughout to familiar airs and modelled on older poetical forms, we can already clearly see the later technique of the reformer of the Scottish folk-song. The subject-matter is held together and the dramatic climax gradually achieved by the introduction of a little descriptive action: the charms of the Highlander's widow inflame the pigmy fiddler who is no higher than her waist, and he "woos her in an arioso key" with the melody "Whistle owre the lave o't"; but at once he has a dangerous rival in the tinker, before whose wild threats he has of necessity to withdraw. He recompenses himself with one of the companions of the poet, who consoles himself, without regret, with the remaining two:

> "I've lost but ane, I've twa behin',
> I've wife eneugh for a' that."

Peace and harmony are restored, they "toom their pocks an' pawn their duds," and the good-natured bard must crown the festive scene with the best he can find in his well-filled repertoire. Supported by his two Deborahs he rises and, with the steaming punch bowl before him, strikes up a song in praise of a roving life, social freedom, and lawlessness, the attendant throng, triumphant over the immediate ills of their lot, joining eagerly and enthusiastically in the chorus.

It is significant of the consummate ease with which Burns wrote at this period, that the beggars' cantata, so bold and masterly in every stanza and so overwhelming in its general effect, seems completely to have escaped his memory. In September 1793 he wrote, in reply to a question by Thomson, that he had forgotten the cantata—in fact, that he owned no copy of it and that he was even unaware that a copy of it still existed.[46] And yet two MSS. of the work have come down to us. One of these is in Edinburgh University Library, and bears what is possibly the original inscription, "Love and Liberty." The cantata first appeared in print 1799, three years after Burns's death.[47]

Just across from Poosie Nansie's inn stood the third of the public-houses most frequented by Burns and his friends. This was the Whitefoord Arms. An excellent epigram by Burns

---

[46] Letters, 55.
[47] H. H., ii, 306-307.

describes the host, John Dove, as being a man more concerned with
the goodness of his liquor than with the future of his soul.[48]

His son Alexander, or Sandy, who drove the coach between
Mauchline and Kilmarnock, was dear to Burns as a masonic brother.
The respectability of the house, which was carried on after John's
death by his widow, is shown by the fact that on a certain occasion
even ecclesiastical gentlemen partook of a modest dinner there.
Further poems written by Burns during the spring of 1786 mark
it as the place where he loved to meet his friends;[49] and it was
there, with Burns as chairman, that the curious court of justice,
which called itself the "Court of Equity," was held. This court
was probably instituted in the autumn of 1785, and consisted of a
committee of bachelors belonging to the little town, who were
skilled in affairs of the heart, and who felt it incumbent upon them
to keep watch, to a certain extent, over irregular relationships. The
court consisted of the fiscal, James Smith; the clerk, Richmond; and
the "messenger at arms," William Hunter, in addition to Burns,
who was chairman. It is hard to determine whether there was any
extensive organisation behind this committee, or whether it was
really possible for it to execute a kind of rustic lynch-law against
sinners of both sexes. We know, indeed, from the poem "Adam
Armour's Prayer,"[50] that a servant-girl employed by George Gibson,
Poosie Nansie's husband, was, to Poosie Nansie's intense anger,
"stanged" (i.e., carried on an unbarked pole) through Mauchline by
the local youths as a punishment for her immorality; but though we
may conjecture that this incident was connected with the ruling of
the Court of Equity, we cannot prove it. We do, however, possess
a document relating to its work in the racy poem entitled "Libel
Summons,"[51] various MSS. of which have been preserved but which
have up till now either been omitted from the official editions or
given only in a mutilated form. In it "Coachman Dow" (= Dove)
and "Clockie" Brown are summoned before the tribunal, both for

---

[48] *Ibid.*, 267.

[49] "To John Kennedy," H. H., ii, 83-85 (3rd Mar. 1786); and "To Gavin
Hamilton," H. H., ii, 85-86 (3rd May 1786).

[50] H. H., ii, 44-46 (Jan. or Feb. 1786); Armour later became Burns's brother-
in-law.

[51] The form given in *Archiv*, 130, 65-72, is based on the three MSS. hitherto
known, in preference to the printed editions, which are unreliable. The date lies
between May and June 1786. It has lately been reprinted by Mrs. C. Carswell in
her "Life of Robert Burns," as an Appendix, on pp. 457-462.

having denied the paternity of their illegitimate children. As a freemason, Brother Dow is let off with a straightforward but mild admonition. The lines addressed to him (93-125) state the case with all Burns's characteristic force, and soar high above the somewhat coarse description of the misdemeanour in the introductory passages. With "Monsieur Brown" a more threatening tone is adopted: if he does not confess, he shall be bound naked to the village pump and exposed to the mockery of the populace and the grace and mercy of his victim, Maggie Mitchell, for as long as shall be determined by the court of morals. "Adam Armour's Prayer" and "The Court of Equity" go far to prove the existence in Scotland of an institution known to have existed in many nations, though not in England, and extremely interesting from the point of view of folk-lore—namely, the "Knabenschaften" or "Bachelors' Associations."[52] The judicial organisation, the duties of the office-bearers and the carrying-out of the punishments at the pump or well, force us, in spite of considerable deviations from the original type in question, to this inevitable conclusion, so that both these racy poems may be considered to possess some importance as documentary evidence of forgotten popular customs.

The poet's relations to the loose folk in whose company he was often seen were little conducive to preserving his good reputation, which had already been undermined by his rebellious attitude in Kirk matters, and by growing rumours that things were not going well with him at Mossgiel. A union with him seemed, to any respectable citizen, most undesirable and compromising. It is said that his sweetheart's father, the master-mason Armour, "hated him, and would raither hae seen the deil himsel' comin' to the hoose to coort his dochter than him."[53] The clash was inevitable. It led Burns through months of unspeakable misery to the very edge of a dangerous abyss: and yet this experience resulted in what was best for him and for his fellow-countrymen—the triumph of his genius in the shape of the first edition of his poems. The threatened catastrophe brought him another blessing in the person of his quiet, devoted wife, Jean Armour, the daughter of the above-mentioned master-mason, Armour of Mauchline.

[52] Cf. E. Hoffman-Krayer's essay: Knabenschaften und Volksjustiz in der Schweiz." Schweizerisches Archiv für Volkskunde, viii, 81-99 and 161-178.
[53] Account given by Burns's former herd-boy, William Patrick (1776-1864). Cf. W. Jolly, "R. B. at Mossgiel," Paisley, 1881: not too reliable a source.

Burns's acquaintance with Jean, who was born on 25th February 1765, began doubtless soon after his arrival at Mossgiel. He mentions her in his lines on the "Belles of Mauchline" as "the jewel o' them a'," and in all probability he also refers to her in the stanzas of "The Mauchline Lady,"[54] written in the same year (1784), and entered in his "Common-place Book" in August 1785:

> "But when I came roun' by Mauchline toun,
> Not dreadin anybody,
> My heart was caught, before I thought,
> And by a Mauchline lady."

In the "Epistle to Davie, a Brother Poet,"[55] written in January 1785, his love is already burning brightly: (viii-xi): she is his darling Jean, dearer to him than his life-blood, and the thought of her brings him relief, solace and poetic inspiration. We have no reason to doubt the sincerity of this passion, the powerful assault of which the girl was quite unable to resist. On 17th February 1786 Burns wrote to his friend John Richmond, now settled in Edinburgh, giving him an impressive list of new poems he had composed, and telling him that he had "some very important news with respect to himself, not the most agreeable," to impart to him.[56] A few lines to James Smith, written about June 1786,[57] reveal nothing more than his natural agitation at his sweetheart's condition, which could no longer be concealed. Once more, in spite of his straitened circumstances, he did not shrink from the consequences of his actions, but gave Jean a written acknowledgment of marriage, thinking that by so doing he had legally ratified his marriage with her and protected himself and her from scandal.[58] At the same time he decided to emigrate to Jamaica in order to earn the necessary means for the upkeep of a family. While he was away, Jean was to stay with her parents in Mauchline and await his return under more favourable circumstances. This plan, which Burns believed to be an adequate solution for all the difficulties of the situation, was wrecked by the attitude taken up by the other

---

[54] H. H., iv, 12.

[55] H. H., i, 117-123; Davie = Davie Sillar.

[56] Letters, 21.

[57] Ibid., 37.

[58] There is some doubt as to the legal validity of such a document. See Ch. W., i, 313 (note). The church authorities recognized it in many cases, but *not* in Mauchline!

side, especially by the behaviour of Armour, the deeply affronted father, who, according to Gilbert, fell down unconscious when apprised of the state of affairs. Heedless of his daughter's condition, he declined a union with Burns, saying that a husband in the West Indies was not much better than none at all, and that, in spite of all that had happened, he still dared hope for a better future for his daughter than marriage with her poverty-stricken, dissolute seducer. Towards the end of March, Jean was sent to relatives in Paisley. Previous to this she had yielded to her parents' entreaties and had handed over to her father the document that was to make her Burns's wife. After consulting Pastor Auld and Aiken, the Ayr lawyer (a man who had the poet's welfare at heart), Mr. Armour caused it to be mutilated or destroyed by having the names taken out. Aiken's share in this affair cannot be entirely proved, but apparently he believed he was doing his friend a service by giving him back his freedom and his independence.[59]

To Burns the destruction of the document was like a slap in the face. He was indignant at the submissiveness and the faithlessness of the girl whom he considered to be under an obligation to him, and outraged at the Armours' insult to his honour. He was equally wounded in his pride, his self-respect, his love—and in his good conscience. He went "stark, staring mad," and felt himself nine-tenths ripe for Bedlam. "This was a shocking affair," he wrote in his autobiographical letter, "which I cannot yet bear to reflect upon." A letter to an otherwise unknown John Arnot of Dalquhatswood, illuminating despite its unnaturally stilted phraseology, describes the unchained tempest of his emotions and his gradual subsidence into the dull calm of the sorrowing widower, "who, wiping away the decent tear, lifts up his grief-worn eye to look—for another wife."[60] The woman with whom Burns sought and found consolation for the insult he had suffered was, according to a firmly rooted, sentimental tradition, Mary Campbell, the Highland lassie, the never-forgotten, immortal sweetheart, the transfigured lover of the song "Thou Lingering Star," written in the autumn of 1789. But who was this Mary, that "white rose" among the poet's "passion-flowers"? We know nothing either of her personality or of her life. Some say she was the daughter of a

[59] Cf. "R. Burns and the Ayrshire Moderates," 31-35.
[60] Letters, 29.

Clyde master-mariner, and that she had served as a nurse in the household of Gavin Hamilton in Mauchline. The episode of which she is the central figure must have developed within the space of a few weeks, beginning in April 1786. It has been expanded into a stirring romance with a tragic ending. Mary Campbell has been made into a kind of rival of Jean Armour, the latter being represented as a wanton creature of earth, the former as a figure of light, who stooped down to the forsaken poet in his hour of darkness and poured healing balm upon his wounded heart. Somewhere on the banks of the river Ayr, where it is joined by the Mauchline burn, or at Coilsfield,[61] a touching scene of betrothal and farewell, accompanied by special rites, is said to have taken place, on "the second Sunday in May." After this Mary is said to have returned to her family in the Western Highlands, to prepare for the journey which she and the poet were to make together to the West Indies; but in October she was snatched away by a malignant fever in Greenock, where she was to have joined Burns. This version of the story, given by Cromek,[62] and adopted by Lockhart, has met with sceptical criticism,[63] and rightly so. It lacks that documentary basis which is necessary if the incident is to have the importance traditionally ascribed to it. In Burns's correspondence there are a few vague, reserved sentences here and there, hinting at a love-affair ended by death before his intended emigration to the colonies, the Christian name Mary being used without any surname.[64] Currie[65] and Thomson[66] have heard of it, but likewise restrict themselves to vague references. The autobiographical letter and Gilbert's narrative make no mention of it, neither does Heron in his "Memoir." Moreover, the note in the commentated copy of Johnson's "Musical Museum" which Burns prepared for Riddell—"My Highland Lassie, O"—on which Cromek based his story and which Henley

---

[61] See Burns's song: "Ye banks and braes and streams around The Castle o' Montgomery," 1792. H. H., iii, 255, 480.

[62] "Reliques of R. B.," 237.

[63] See H. H., iii, 309-311, iv, 285-292 (W. E. Henley's "Essay"); Ch. W., i, 470-479. Snyder (pp. 129-144) discusses the available material, but his reconstruction of the affair does not convince me.

[64] To Mrs. Dunlop, 13th Dec., 1789, Dunlop Corresp., 230, Letters, 374; to Thomson, 26th Oct. 1792, Letters, 511, and to the same, 14th Nov. 1792, Letters, 518.

[65] "Works of R. B.," i, 125.

[66] To Burns, Nov. 1792, Ch. W., iii, 367.

and Henderson took for genuine, is no longer extant,[67] the page in question being missing. Nevertheless the entry may have existed: Cromek's sentences bear the unmistakable mark of Burns's style and temperament. Verses 2 and 3 of "Thou Lingering Star" confirm the essential part of his story, unless the story itself has been reconstructed out of these verses:

> "Can I forget the hallow'd grove
> Where by the winding Ayr we met
> To live one day of parting love?" &c.

But they do not bring us any nearer to the facts which Burns may have intentionally concealed. Mary Campbell, about whose existence it is not permissible to doubt, remains in herself and in her real or imaginary relationship to Burns a shadowy female figure which glided through the life of the passionate poet during this period, and whose death later became to him the subject of melancholy memories. That is all. The star that ruled the hour was named Jean, not Mary.

At the beginning of June, in spite of her submissiveness to her parents' wishes, and in spite of certain reports about her fickleness, which seems to have reached Burns in an exaggerated form,[68] Jean, the passionately beloved, was back in Mauchline. Burns called upon her, but did not find her as penitent as he had expected. Her mother forbade him the house, and the Kirk demanded its rights: public atonement in sackcloth and ashes on three consecutive Sundays. Burns submitted to this penalty, because the minister had promised him a bachelor's certificate if he obeyed. Auld also let him off a little of the severity which his sin deserved: instead of being obliged to appear on the dreaded and detested "cutty stool" in front of the pulpit, facing the assembled congregation, he enjoyed the privilege of standing in his own place, apart from his fellow-delinquent, and being censured and admonished from there. These humiliating and painful scenes reached their conclusion on 6th August.

Meanwhile his plans for emigrating had assumed a more definite form. Friends in Ayr had found him a post as book-keeper in Port Antonio in Jamaica, at £30 a year. Burns had accepted it,

[67] See Dick, "Notes on Scottish Song," pp. 72 and 122, and D. Cook, "Annotations of Scottish Songs by Burns" in B. Chr., 1922.
[68] To David Brice, 12th June 1786; Letters, 31.

the ship on which he was to sail lay ready at Greenock—but its departure was postponed from week to week. Amongst the arrangements that Burns made at that time, those which he set down on paper on 22nd July 1786 and had publicly proclaimed two days later in Ayr, are of special significance: in them he appointed his brother Gilbert his chief heir, bequeathing him not only his share of Mossgiel, but also whatever profit might accrue from the publication of the volume of poems then in the press, on condition that Gilbert undertook to clothe and educate the poet's natural daughter, Elizabeth.[69] The absence of any settlement in favour of Jean Armour's expected issue can only be interpreted as a hostile gesture directed against the Armours, and as such it was treated by them. Old Armour took out a warrant of arrest against Burns, but he, learning of the impending danger, probably through Jean herself, fled from "one friend's house to another" until, a wretched and embittered fugitive, he at last found hospitality and shelter in the vicinity of Kilmarnock, under the roof of his mother's half-sister, Jean Allan. It was under these circumstances that his volume of poems left the press. As a result of this event, the purifying and liberating effect of which we shall discuss in our next chapter, Burns was able to return to Mossgiel, and when the news was brought to him on Sunday, 3rd September, that Jean Armour had borne him twins, he wrote, exultingly triumphant over all the tempestuous hours through which he had passed, to his faithful friend John Richmond in Edinburgh:

"Wish me luck, dear Richmond! Armour has just brought me a fine boy and girl at one throw. God bless the little dears!
Green grow the rashes, O,
Green grow the rashes, O,
A feather bed is no sae saft
As the bosoms o' the lasses, O."[70]

---

[69] See the Deed of Assignment in Letters, 35. (Original in the Sheriff-Clerk's office, Ayr.)

[70] Letters, 45.

Chapter V

THE KILMARNOCK POEMS

1786

FROM the vertigo of dissipations and conflicts which gripped the poet during his life in Mauchline and its environs, we now turn to the achievement, the artistic result, of these rich and varied experiences. "Poems, Chiefly in the Scottish Dialect" proved to be the one work to which Burns was privileged to apply the finishing touches; the contents of which he was able, after painstaking consideration and selection, to lay before the public entirely on his own responsibility. It was also the poetical emanation of a considerable and very important part of his life.

It is not easy to determine when exactly Burns formed the plan of appearing before a larger public with a collection of his poems, which had long been praised and possibly also abused by a large circle of acquaintances, but we shall not be far wrong if we name the autumn of 1785 as the decisive period. The strong though unsystematic increase in production points to this; a reference made by the poet, who by the way was not always reliable in details of a chronological nature, likewise suggests the end of 1785;[1] and due weight should also be given to Scott Douglas's suggestion[2] that the breaking-off of the "Common-place Book" (begun at Lochlie and several times mentioned in these pages) with Burns's avowed intention of displaying his creations in "guid black prent,"[3] must have some connection with this idea of publishing. The last short entry is dated October 1785. The events of the first months of the year, Jean's pregnancy, the quarrel with the Armours, the emigration plan, and the immediate need of money engendered by it doubtless influenced him very strongly. The persuasions of his friends in Mauchline, Kilmarnock, and Ayr, and the energetic support promised by them, encouraged him and spurred him on,

---

[1] See note to the collection of letters in the Glenriddell MSS., Ch. W., i, 321.
[2] iv, 98.
[3] To James Smith (1786), vii, 2; H. H., i, 61.

with the result that an invitation to subscribe to the proposed
publication was sent to the printers at the beginning of April 1786.
The poet himself fully realized the great literary responsibility
involved in this decisive step. In one of the concluding passages
of his autobiographical letter he expresses himself as follows :—

> "Before leaving my native country for ever, I resolved to publish my
> Poems.—I weighed my productions as impartially as in my power; I
> thought they had merit; and 'twas a delicious idea that I would be
> called a clever fellow, even though it should never reach my ears a poor
> Negro-driver, or perhaps a victim to that inhospitable clime gone to
> the world of Spirits. . . . To know myself had been all along my con-
> stant study.—I weighed myself alone; I balanced myself with others; I
> watched every means of information how much ground I occupied as
> a Man and as a Poet; I studied assiduously Nature's DESIGN where
> she seem'd to have intended the various LIGHTS and SHADES in my
> character.—I was pretty sure my Poems would meet with some
> applause; but at the worst, the roar of the Atlantic would deafen the
> voice of Censure, and the novelty of west-Indian scenes make me forget
> Neglect."

The proposals, which appeared on 14th April 1786,[4] announced
the publication of the "Scotch Poems, by Robert Burns," elegantly
printed in one volume octavo, stitched, price three shillings, as
soon as the number of subscribers necessary to cover the expenses
of printing would be forthcoming. The reader is assured that the
author has not the most distant mercenary view in mind. An aptly
chosen stanza from Ramsay speaks of poetic pride and the desire
for fame. In June and July, amid the greatest internal and external
confusion, while the poet was vainly trying to forget his disappointment about Jean in dissipation, masons' meetings, and drinking bouts, the poems, to which he had constantly added new productions during the year, went through the press of John Wilson,
a printer in Kilmarnock.

> "It is the last foolish action I intend to do," wrote Burns to David
> Brice in Glasgow, "and then turn a wise man as fast as possible."[5]

The well-got-up volume, containing 240 pages, was published on
31st July 1786.

---

[4] Reproduction of the only known copy given (inaccurately) by Ch. W., i, 316.
(See facsimile in Memorial Catalogue of Burns Exhibition, Glasgow 1898.) The
book, at that time offered for three shillings, could not be bought for less than
£250 in 1914; the excellent copy in the Museum at Alloway was purchased in 1908
for £1000. Since then the monetary value of good copies has again risen.
[5] 12th June 1786; Letters, 31.

The Preface (pp. iii-vi), like the greater part of Burns's prose, suffers from the affectations of the eighteenth century. Its style, with its carefully rounded periods, its studied literary phraseology, and the free use of circumlocution and personification, seems rather artificial and insincere. As for the subject-matter, it cannot be denied that there is a certain tendency to pose, to which Burns was prone to yield in his life as well as in his writings. He stresses the deficiencies of his education compared with that of such poets as "look down for a rural theme, with an eye to Theocrites or Virgil" more strongly than seems justified, when we consider the lines along which his mind had actually developed; he speaks of the "obscure, nameless Bard, who appears with fear and trembling in the public character of an Author," shrinking at the thought of adverse criticism; and he repeatedly reminds his readers that he, a peasant, is "unacquainted with the necessary requisites for commencing Poet by rule." At the same time his pride, the consciousness of possessing poetic genius, and the realization of his peculiar literary position are by no means lost to view behind these phrases. He feels that he belongs to a definite school, the chief representatives of which he justly recognizes in Ramsay and Fergusson. He has often, he says, looked up to their works, but—and in these words his attitude to his predecessors is clearly and accurately defined—"rather with a view to kindle at their flame, than for servile imitation." The inheritance which he gratefully receives from them flows into the main stream of his own forceful personality: it is his own life, his own outlook, his own experiences and convictions that have loosened his tongue.

> "To amuse himself with the little creations of his own fancy, amid the toil and fatigues of a laborious life; to transcribe the various feelings, the loves, the griefs, the hopes, the fears, in his own breast; to find some kind of counterpoise to the struggles of a world, always an alien scene, a task uncouth to the poetical mind; these were his motives for courting the Muses, and in these he found Poetry to be its own reward."

Even if, as he expressly points out, none of the poems contained in the Kilmarnock Volume "were composed with a view to the press," that is, with deliberate literary intentions, yet Burns was fully conscious, while compiling the contents, of appearing before a wider and more exacting public, and no longer before a circle of

admiring friends, on whose instant appreciation and sympathy
he could count. Accordingly, there is no question of mental sloven-
liness or carelessness on the part of the author. It is important
that we should remember this criticism to which Burns subjected
his own work, when we come to consider the mass of his later
poems, especially the songs, to which he did not have the opportunity to give the final touches. We shall have occasion to discuss
this later on. Just as he sometimes, to the point of insincerity,
suited the contents and tone of his letters to the social standing
and educational level of his correspondents, so in selecting his poems
he never lost sight of the question of the responsiveness or sensibility
of whatever readers he might have to expect. "I hold it a piece of
contemptible baseness," he wrote later to Mrs. Dunlop, "to detail
the sallies of thoughtless merriment or the orgies of accidental
intoxication, to the ear of cool Sobriety or female Delicacy."[6]
Consequently, the poems in the Kilmarnock Volume are not in
every sense representative of Burns's work. The extremes are
absent: the cantata of "The Jolly Beggars," probably because of
the low sphere in which its action is laid; the satires on Dr.
Hornbook and Holy Willie, as going too far in personal invective;
"The Twa Herds" from similar considerations, and doubtless also
because Burns did not wish to incense the clergy beyond measure;
while poems like the verses on his first-born daughter, "Libel
Summons," and others of a similar nature, however vigorous, witty
and effective, have been omitted out of regard for the proprieties.
The volume contains only a very few of the earliest youthful poems,
belonging to the period preceding Mossgiel—namely, "The Death
and Dying Words of Poor Mailie" (pp. 62-65), "Winter, a Dirge"
(pp. 166-167), "A Prayer in the Prospect of Death" (pp. 168-169),
perhaps "To Ruin" (pp. 174-175);[7] and, lastly, two of the three
songs included: "It was upon a Lammas Night" (pp. 222-224), and
"Song, Composed in August" (pp. 224-226). All the rest, apart
from a few of the epitaphs, which are not of much account, belong
to the period from January 1785 till June 1786. He did not mean
to publish tentative efforts, but poems of full maturity, especially

---

6 Letters, 310.

7 The date is uncertain. Its form places it near "Despondency" (1786), while
its contents would rather suggest the melancholy poems of the Irvine period (1782).
Cf. H. H., i, 376, and Ritter, 141.

the fruits of the rich harvest gathered during those happy months of creative activity which began in the autumn of 1785.

A further question concerns the order in which the poems are given in the book. There is nothing to indicate that Burns tried to impress his readers through following a definite artistic plan, such as, for instance, the gradual transition from the humorous to the tragic, from the subjective description to the objective picture of contemporary life and manners, or by a peculiarly effective arrangement of the satires. Instead of this, the magnificent Dedication to Gavin Hamilton is characteristically placed somewhere near the end of the second third of the volume (pp. 185-191). I suppose that the poet's original intention was to make this delightful poetical confession, this flaming beacon of loyalty to "his friend and brother," the final item in the volume. In that case it would be eminently suitable that the verses on "A Scotch Bard gone to the West Indies," a poem by the poet in memory of himself, should immediately precede it. The Dedication was meant to be the last poem in the book. What follows it—"To a Louse," the Epistles to John Lapraik, William Simpson of Ochiltree, and John Rankine, the three songs, the "Farewell to the Brothers of St. James's Lodge," and the Epitaphs—was probably added later as the result of further consideration, chiefly on account of the Epistles, the inclusion of which seemed to Burns indispensable, although their tone is different in many respects from that of the greater part of the contents. "A Bard's Epitaph" (pp. 234-235) forms the second ending. Before the Dedication to Hamilton, too, it is possible to divide the poems into at least two distinct groups. It is certainly not by accident that the crowning of the poet by his native Muse and the three poems glorifying Scottish peasant life ("Hallowe'en," pp. 100-117, "The Auld Farmer's New-Year Morning Salutation to his Auld Mare, Maggie," pp. 118-123, and "The Cotter's Saturday Night," pp. 124-137) are placed in the very centre of the book —at its apex, as it were. "The Vision" and the three poems just mentioned in praise of the men and women, the manners and customs most familiar to him, are related to each other as promise to fulfilment. With these poems the dream which from the earliest stirrings of poetic power had spurred Burns on to become the singer of the world around him—that world with which he was in daily contact—and to spread abroad the fame and beauty of Coila,

became a reality. A second group re-echoes his experiences with
Jean Armour. To this group belong "The Lament" (pp. 150-155),
"Despondency, an Ode" (pp. 156-159), probably also the premoni-
tory greeting "To Ruin" (pp. 174-175), whose influence he had
already begun to feel, and—inserted between these pieces or following them—a number of seriously reflective or didactic poems, partly
from recent, partly from earlier times, the reason for their appearance together in this part of the book being that they are all
animated by the same rather gloomy spirit. Here we have the
famous address "To a Mountain Daisy" (pp. 170-173), the lament
"Man was Made to Mourn" (pp. 160-165), and, striking a somewhat lighter note, the "Epistle to a Young Friend" (Andrew Aiken,
pp. 176-180), full of wise precepts, the value of which Burns had
learned from his own life—through disregarding them. The prevailing tone of the whole group is clearly discernible, despite the
humorous style, in the last poem belonging to this section—the poem
on the Scotch Bard gone to the West Indies:

> "A jillet brak his heart at last,
> Ill may she be!"

Apart from this, there is no evidence of any fixed principles
governing the arrangement of the poems. Social and political
themes play an important, if not predominant, part in the first
four pieces: "The Twa Dogs" (pp. 9-21), "Scotch Drink" (pp.
22-28), "The Author's Ernest Cry and Prayer" (pp. 29-39), and
"The Holy Fair" (pp. 40-54), as well as in the ninth, "A Dream,"
written on the occasion of George III's birthday, in June 1786, and
one of the latest in the collection (pp. 79-86). Mention of the
Epistles to James Smith (pp. 69-78, early 1786) and David Sillar
(pp. 141-149, January 1785), and the more vigorously worded
counterpart to the address to the daisy, namely "To a Mouse" (pp.
138-140, November 1785), exhausts the review of the contents of
the Kilmarnock Volume. Its effect depends not on the carefully
planned structure of the whole, but on the irresistible qualities of
its individual parts.

In our last chapter an account has been given of the circumstances under which a considerable number of the poems belonging
to this volume—or at least to this period—were written; but even
when this has not been the case, there should be no difficulty in

proving a direct connection between the poems and the poet's reactions to certain definite events and stimuli. Gilbert's testimony that certain poems were composed in order to give expression to some favourite idea of the poet's must not be taken to mean that Burns was a purely intellectual poet who strove to give poetic form to philosophical concepts. The following sentence of Gilbert's makes the meaning clear:

> "Robert used to remark to me that he could not conceive a more mortifying picture of human life than a man seeking work."

To this thought the poem "Man was Made to Mourn" owes its origin. Gilbert goes on to say that his brother frequently remarked that he thought there was something peculiarly venerable in the phrase "Let us worship God," used by the worthy head of the family in introducing family worship. It is to this sentiment of the author's that the world owes "The Cotter's Saturday Night."[8] It is clear that in both cases there lies behind the thought a very concrete reality: in the one case social distress, which Burns himself had experienced oftener than he liked, in the other the customs of a large number of peasant families with whom he associated—above all, the customs of his own family, as long as his father was at the head of it. Not that the intellectual element in Burns should be underestimated: anyone who expects his poetry to be purely impressionistic, in the sense in which this word is used in later periods of literature, does not understand him. Trained from his early youth in debating and discussing, a brilliant, eloquent talker, and a man who had not only read a great deal but whose reading was firmly fixed in his memory, he does not, as a poet, hide these gifts under a bushel. He is fond of teaching. He obviously rejoices when he finds the exact phrase in which to clothe a striking thought, but these thoughts are full of his own vitality; the pulse of his stupendous temperament beats in them. Living force is the distinguishing feature of the Kilmarnock volume, and no more is needed to account for the permanency of its influence.

To his contemporaries the revelation of this poetic achievement was like a great miracle, to be joyfully and gratefully accepted as such. Carlyle's arguments in his review of Lockhart's "Biography

---

[8] Currie's "Burns," iii, 382.

of Burns" have always rightly been considered as representative of this standpoint. "An educated man," he says in that essay, "stands, as it were, in the midst of a boundless arsenal and magazine, filled with all the weapons and engines which man's skill has been able to devise from the earliest time; and he works, accordingly, with a strength borrowed from all past ages. How different is *his* state who stands on the outside of that storehouse, and feels that its gates must be stormed, or remain for ever shut against him! His means are the commonest and rudest; the mere work done is no measure of his strength. A dwarf behind his steam-engine may remove mountains; but no dwarf will hew them down with a pickaxe; and he must be a Titan that hurls them abroad with his arms. It is in this last shape that Burns presents himself."[9]

Literary history has felt itself in duty bound to rectify this conception, which, indeed, cannot be defended from a historical point of view. At the same time, however, we must note that Carlyle's statements have not always been quite justly criticised by those whose conclusions are based upon intensive study of the sources. As early as 1797 Robert Heron pointed out more or less accurately the line of communication between the poet and Scottish national literature on the one hand and English literature on the other.[10] Gilbert Burns recognized these connections in part at least, and the poet himself, as we have seen, sometimes with exaggerated modesty, most emphatically stressed the important influence of his English and Scottish predecessors upon his own work. Above all, he felt plainly and clearly that he himself, in common with the lesser contemporary spirits who had taken the care of Scottish folk-poetry upon them—men like Sillar, Lapraik, Tait, John Rankine, and William Simpson in his immediate vicinity, and John Mayne, Skinner, Alexander Ross, and Alexander Geddes in remoter counties of Scotland—was in the grip of a national literary tradition, and that the masters from whom *they* had learned their speech and style were *his* masters too. Is it possible that Carlyle failed to grasp this fact? It seems incredible. Carlyle, however, was not a literary historian in our sense of the term. When he was dealing with a genius such as Burns's, the problems which claimed his attention were other than those of modern research. He, like many

---

[9] Standard Edition, v, 236-237.
[10] "Memoir," pp. 5-9. See our Appendix, p. 249.

others even at the present day who have meditated upon the nature
of creative activity in a genius, laid less stress upon these relationships, they explained less to his own productive mind than to the
learned, detailed research of our own time. And yet, on the whole,
the points of view are not wholly contradictory: rather do they
supplement each other in many things, and both sides are open to
correction. In referring even to the two most talented poets in that
stream of national literature—Allan Ramsay (1686-1758), who in
many different ways was its pioneer and founder, and the artistically
more refined Robert Fergusson (1750-74), who had a greater gift
of originality, both of whom were very closely bound up with the
life of the city of Edinburgh, and belonged to a circle which was
keenly interested in literature and delighted in music and poetry—
Carlyle speaks of "models of the meanest sort." They seem so to
him—compared with Burns. It is not so much his appreciation
of the poet, which was founded on strong faith,[11] that is at fault,
as the fact that he under-estimated the importance of the poet's predecessors.

Burns, as has been pointed out several times already, and proved
by a characteristic sentence from the preface to the Kilmarnock
Volume, took up quite a different attitude. It is not going too
far to say that he himself laid the foundation of the modern com-
parative study of his work, and that it receives valuable support
and justification from his own statements. This is particularly
true with regard to "the glorious dawnings of the poor, unfortunate
Fergusson."[12] In him he recognizes his master, and his own
creative work was definitely influenced by the collected poems of
Fergusson, of which he owned a copy of the second edition, published in 1782.[13] Unmistakable traces of this influence can be found
in the poems of the Kilmarnock Volume. Burns, looking back at
the depressing months of the Irvine period, writes in his autobiographical letter:

   "Rhyme . . . I had given up; but meeting with Fergusson's Scotch

---

[11] Carlyle passes the following striking comment on Currie, with reference to
his biography of Burns: "His fault was not want of love, but weakness of faith."
   [12] Preface to Kil. Ed.
   [13] Burns's copy, with an "Apostrophe to Fergusson," is now in the Rosebery
Collection (H. H., ii, 211, 408-409). The edition contains a sketch of Fergusson's
life by T. Ruddiman, and an idiotic portrait of the poet by Birrel. See John A.
Fairley, "Bibliography of R. Fergusson," Glasgow 1915, pp. 9-11; 25 (No. 12).

Poems, I strung anew my wildly-sounding, rustic lyre with emulating vigour."

This "emulating vigour" is the connecting link between Burns's "Scotch Drink" and Fergusson's "Caller Water," between his "Holy Fair" and Fergusson's "Leith Races" and "Hallow Fair," between "The Cotter's Saturday Night" and "The Farmer's Ingle," and between "The Brigs of Ayr" (in the Edinburgh Edition of 1787) and "The Mutual Complaint of Plainstanes and Causey." He was more closely related to Fergusson than to any other poet of the native Scottish School. Characteristically, there is a purely human element in this relationship, quite apart from the literary interest. Burns esteemed Allan Ramsay, but did not hesitate on occasion to subject his poems to criticism. Fergusson, on the other hand, he loved and looked upon as his model, not only in his works, but in his destiny. Fergusson's life showed him the poet's irresistible craving for the joys and pleasures of the world, with care, deprivation, and early ruin as the answer to his passionate desires: the true picture of his own earthly pilgrimage. No Scot, not even Stevenson, has done so much for Fergusson's memory as Burns, and if the present generation begins to turn again with increasing interest to the literary legacy of that fine, ardent spirit, Burns's warm-hearted championing of the Edinburgh city poet, too early fallen into decay, must never be forgotten. It was not through Fergusson alone, however, that the influence of the Scottish literary revival of the eighteenth century was brought to bear on Burns: he experienced the full force of its influence by reason of his wide reading, and it determined to a very large extent the choice of material, the style, and the metrical forms of the Kilmarnock Volume.[14] The popular, half-humorous elegy, in the manner of the lament for "poor Mailie," goes back to the seventeenth century. The honour of precedence belongs to Robert Semphill of Beltrees, Renfrewshire, who died about 1665, and whose elegy on Habbie Simson, the town-piper of Kilbarchan, is said to have been written as early as 1640. It was widely circulated as a street-ballad, printed in 1706 in the first volume of Watson's

---

[14] *Cf.* the excellent account of Scottish Literature (mediæval and modern) by T. F. Henderson, "Scottish Vernacular Literature," Edinburgh, 1910; the same author's essay, "Scottish Popular Poetry before Burns," 14th chap. of 9th vol. of "Cambridge History of English Literature," 1912, with comprehensive bibliography to this chapter by H. G. Aldis, *ibid.*, 542-568.

"Choice Collection of Comic and Serious Scots Poems,"[15] and by reason of its form, contents, and treatment won considerable renown as a model for subsequent efforts. Among the imitations which were based upon it special mention must be made of "The Last Words of Bonny Heck, a Famous Grey-Hound in the Shire of Fife," by William Hamilton of Gilbertfield (1665?-1751). This is the first example of the lament being transferred from man to an animal which, as it lies at the point of death, looks back over its past life and praises the advantages of its early days. This poem also appeared in the first part of Watson's "Collection."[16] To these models we must add Allan Ramsay with his elegies on "Maggy Johnstoun," who sold good small-ale in the neighbourhood of Edinburgh; on "John Cowper," the Kirk beadle; on "Lucky Wood," hostess of an ale-house in the Canongate of Edinburgh; and on "Patie Birnie, the famous fiddler of Kinghorn."[17] Robert Fergusson followed his example, and we have three elegies of this kind written by him: "On the Death of Mr. David Gregory," "On the Death of Scots Music" and "On John Hogg," beadle of the University of St. Andrews.[18]

A second poetic form in great favour with the national school was that of the poetic epistle or friendly letter. Here again Allan Ramsay and William Hamilton head the list, for as far as we can see, it is they who set the ball rolling in their correspondence, which comprises six letters written in this form.[19] From the point of view of the contents, these letters are extremely simple: the correspondents vie with each other in expressions of reciprocal admiration, and generally end with the hope that they may meet and, over a flowing glass, revel in the joys of To-day, with no thought of the unrevealed To-morrow. We find exactly the same thing in Fergusson's poems: a certain J. S. addresses Fergusson, acknowledging his indebtedness to the latter and inviting him to Berwick, where, he says, Fergusson will find all sorts of attractions, especially pretty girls. Fergusson replies evasively, modestly refusing to accept his correspondent's flattering comparison with Ramsay,

[15] pp. 32-35.
[16] pp. 68-70.
[17] "Works of Allan Ramsay," London, &c., 1851, 287-304.
[18] "Works of Robert Fergusson," ed. Grossart, 1879, 1-2, 7-110, 107-111.
[19] Ramsay's "Works," as above, iii, 24-46. *Cf.* also his Letter to John Gay. *ibid.*, 73-77.

and saying that there are pretty girls in Edinburgh too. He, in
turn, summons his admirer in Berwick to come and have a good
time in the capital.[20] Two further letters are addressed by a
certain Andrew Gray—the name is fictitious!—to Fergusson, who
replies to the first. Here again the letters consist of flattery, gratitude, and the mutual hope that the writers will soon be personally
acquainted with each other.[21] John Skinner, minister of the Episcopalian Church at Longside, Aberdeenshire (1721-1807), a man for
whom Burns had the highest regard, wrote several letters of this
kind. One of these was composed after the appearance of the
Kilmarnock Volume, and, in response to a lady's wish, subjected
the somewhat jarring poem "To a Louse, on Seeing One on a
Lady's Bonnet at Church" (pp. 192-194), to a well-meaning but
rather severe criticism.[22] Even the grave James Beattie (1735-1803),
who avoided the use of the dialect in his other works, must be
mentioned here because of a little masterpiece: his letter to
Alexander Ross (1699-1784), school master at Lochlea, Forfarshire.[23]
The stereotyped form is in this case handled with gratifying freshness, the vivacity and spontaneity of the diction reminding one of
Burns himself, who, by the way, knew this epistle and quoted it in
a letter to Mrs. Dunlop.[24] A definite style had been developed in
these epistles, as well as in the elegies—a style well suited to the
intimacy of their character and utilized by Burns to its full extent.

Similarly, Burns cannot be regarded as the first poet to describe
those scenes from Scottish country life, to which a great part of
the Kilmarnock Volume is devoted. Elements of such descriptions
already existed in many of the elegies and epistles; the folk-song
and the street-ballad are full of them; and Middle-Scottish literature
had produced poetry of this kind, which Watson's "Collection"
and Allan Ramsay's literary flair had handed on to the eighteenth
century. We must here mention Ramsay's "Evergreen" (2 vols.,
1724), a collection of numerous pieces by the old masters, contained
in the Bannatyne MS., now in the Scottish National Library in
Edinburgh. The poem, "Christis Kirk on the Green," generally

20 Works, as above, 19-25.

21 Ibid., 71-77.

22 Skinner's "Poetical Pieces," Edinburgh, 1809, 92-108.

23 Beattie's "Works," Aldine Ed., 241-244.

24 7th March 1788. Dunlop Corr., 47-48; Letters, 219.

ascribed to James I (1394-1437), which describes a wild brawl that took place on the occasion of a country fête, justly attained the celebrity of a classical work, its influence remaining undiminished through many generations. Even Pope had heard of it:

"A Scot will fight for Christ's Kirk o' the Green,"

he says on one occasion.[25] It heads the list in Watson's "Collection" (1, 1-7). Ramsay brought out an edition of it and wrote two supplementary and concluding cantos for it.[26] It inspired Fergusson to write "Hallow Fair," "Leith Races," and "The Election."[27] Skinner knew it by heart before he was twelve years old, later translated it into Latin, and modelled one of his earliest and longest poems, "The Monymusk Christmas Ba'ing,"[28] on it. The description by John Mayne (1759-1836) of the competition for a silver gun taken part in by the Dumfries Corporations (first version in 1777, then altered and enlarged several times till 1836[29]), is influenced by it in spirit, though not in form: it bears on the title-page, as a motto, the first four lines of "Christis Kirk." Animated by the same spirit, Ramsay's pastoral comedy, "The Gentle Shepherd" (1725),[30] which ran into numerous editions, achieved a memorable success by its sequence of scenes from rustic life, free from the taints of grotesque coarseness which are prevalent in "Christis Kirk." Alexander Ross's "Helenore, or, The Fortunate Shepherdess" (first edition 1768, second 1778, and frequently reprinted)[31] is, in spite of its epic form, one of the best-known and most popular of the imitations of Ramsay's comedy. There are many other poems, all probably composed under the influence of Ramsay and Fergusson, in which scenes from Scottish life are variously depicted. These include a "Hallowe'en," a poem perhaps known to Burns;[32] but it is neither possible nor necessary to augment the references already given by further examples.

25 "Imitations of Horace," (Bk. II, Epistle i) Globe Ed., p. 306, l. 40.

26 1715 and 1718, cf. "Works," i, 304-332.

27 "Works," 33-37, 84-92, 98-103.

28 See "Poetical Pieces," 1809, 41-52.

29 "The Siller Gun, A Poem in Five Cantos." London and Edinburgh, 1836.

30 "Works," ii, 37-147.

31 Ed. by Longmuir, Edinburgh, 1866.

32 Fragments from it, quoted by Ch. W., i, 209-210, appeared in 1780 in *Ruddiman's Weekly Magazine*. Cf. Ritter, p. 78, note 1, who rightly estimates the influence on Burns of this poem as being very slight.

In assimilating the style and the particular line of thought of
this school of poetry, Burns also took over its metrical forms. The
Kilmarnock Volume does not contain a single stanza-form which
had not already been used for a similar purpose by his predecessors
and contemporaries. He was no pioneer as far as metre was concerned. The eight-syllabled lines, rhyming in pairs, of "The Twa
Dogs" and the "Dedication to Gavin Hamilton" may be found in
Ramsay's "Fables" and in Fergusson's "Auld Reikie"[33]—to give
two examples instead of many. Burns's favourite six-lined stanza,
which he uses in "Scotch Drink," in most of the elegies and epistles,
and in numerous satires and descriptive poems, is known to have
existed in England since the fourteenth century and had been in
common use in Scotland since the sixteenth century.[34] The eight-
lined stanza of the "Holy Fair," with its two-beat refrain "that
day" (varied in "Hallowe'en" to "that night"), is a simplified and
frequently applied form of the metre of "Christis Kirk on the
Green," which Burns has used in "A Dream" in its more complicated form, each verse containing only two rhymes.[35] The nine-
lined stanza of "The Cotter's Saturday Night" goes back to Spenser
and was used by Burns in the simplified form to which Thomson,
Shenstone and Beattie had reduced it. It differs from that used in
Fergusson's "Farmer's Ingle" in its somewhat modified rhyme-
scheme.[36] The complicated fourteen-lined stanza of the "Epistle to
Davie" occurs frequently in Scottish poetry from Montgomery to
Ramsay.[37] As the eight-lined and four-lined stanzas are the
common property of Anglo-Scottish poetry, we may dispense with a
comparison of the sources from which they are taken.

The reader will now have some idea of the extent and importance
of that vernacular tradition of which, as must always be recognized
by the student of literary history, Burns was not only the heir,
but also the finisher and the crowning glory. If we have not dealt
with it at all exhaustively, we have at least pointed out its principal features as far as is necessary. There can be no doubt about
it: the poems in the Kilmarnock Volume are intimately inter-

---

[33] H. H., i, 319.
[34] H. H., i, 336-342: an exaustive investigation.
[35] *Ibid.*, 328-330.
[36] *Ibid.*, 362.
[37] *Ibid.*, 366-367; see also Ch. W., i, 465-466: "The Metres of Burns," and
Henderson, "Scottish Vernacular Literature," 438-443.

woven with the past; generations of poets prepared the ground on which they were raised; a whole people filled them with the peculiar quality of its spirit. Is Carlyle's phrase, then, about the miracle of Burns's appearance a fallacy? Research has placed stanza after stanza, line after line, under the microscope—has it succeeded in explaining the apparently inexplicable, in making this miracle comprehensible, nay obvious, according to the laws of cause and effect? The answer to both questions must be in the negative.

Realization of the fact that a great tradition is being carried on by a poet endowed with the highest creative faculties only brings us to the starting-point of his genius; once we have passed that threshold we are dominated by transcendental and therefore incalculable forces. It was so with Shakespeare—it is so with Burns. Research reaches a limit when the possibilities of explanation are exhausted, and even the demonstrable tradition can only be regarded as a kind of historical foil or a welcome unit of mental economy. The spirit which fills the work of genius can and will bear evidence of the influence of this tradition, but it must be stronger in itself than the legacy inherited from the past: it will give more light than it receives, and in every case where decisive manifestations of supreme art are demanded, it will soar upwards from the foundation of the realities of the many-sided life around it to the eternal symbols of existence. Looked at from this point of view, Burns's Kilmarnock Poems, as a collection of poetry, are the greatest event in English literary history of the eighteenth century. In no other collection, not even in the "Lyrical Ballads" of 1798, is the irresistible force of inspiration felt so directly as in this: it is as obvious and as powerful as a natural phenomenon.

> "Among those secondhand acting-figures, *mimes* for most part, of the Eighteenth Century, once more a giant Original Man; one of those men who reach down to the perennial Deeps, who take rank with the Heroic among men: and he was born in a poor Ayrshire hut. The largest soul of all the British lands came among us in the shape of a hard-handed Scottish Peasant."[38]

That was the miracle which Carlyle, in spite of, or perhaps because of, his under-estimation of the remarkable conditions which bring it into line with its time, rightly appreciated.

If we try to define the inmost spirit of the Kilmarnock Poems,

---

[38] "On Heroes, Hero-Worship," &c., Lect. v, Standard Ed., vol. iv, 155.

we must give it a name familiar to us to-day: "Heimatkunst," i.e., "home" or "regional" art, in the strictest sense of the word, meaning that these poems aim at describing the personalities and conditions of a narrowly compassed area, with every detail of which the poet himself is most intimately acquainted. The "Alemannic Poems" of Burns's contemporary, Johann Peter Hebel[39] and the "Quickborn" of Klaus Groth, who was in many ways influenced by Burns, may be named as parallel examples of this species of writing from the South and North of Germany respectively. The Kilmarnock Poems are also "Heimatkunst" in the specific sense that they take as their theme country life and not the life and spirit of the great cities: the word is very apt here, for it is in God's open spaces that man seeks his home. Burns was, of course, far removed from the literary culture of London, and even the intellectual life of Edinburgh had as yet left him untouched, in striking contrast to Fergusson, who had his roots in it, and who paid but fleeting visits to the country, about the liberating· influences of which he wrote so yearningly. Apart from a few scattered poems dealing with the poet's past life and his future prospects, the whole contents of the Kilmarnock Volume are connected with Mossgiel, its meadows and fields; with Mauchline, its taverns and fairs; or with the homesteads of neighbouring farmer-folks, of whom we know little or nothing. Men, animals, and plants belonging to this small area live and flourish in his pages; manners and customs long fallen into disuse are depicted gaily, satirically, or sentimentally, with obvious knowledge of the subject and irreproachably faithful observation; we are shown the peace of domestic life, and the squabbles of the Kirk. But in all this there is nothing sufficiently outstanding to account for the triumphant greatness of the book. Fergusson—and before him, Ramsay—had done very nearly the same for Edinburgh. Anyone familiar with the city of Edinburgh and the customs of its inhabitants will appreciate the delightful, pleasantly sarcastic sketches written by those two poets about the life of the Scottish capital, while the uninitiated will admire the originality of their technique; but spiritually they will impress no one. The danger for all "regional art" lies in the indifference of the many whose native haunts are elsewhere. After all, what

---

[39] See the little publication by that excellent Burns authority and translator, Aug. Corrodi, "Rob. Burns und Peter Hebel," Berlin, 1873.

matter to us the adventures of the doddering City Guard who patrolled Edinburgh in the eighteenth century? But the glow of immortality rests upon Burns's modest farm. The mouse which he startled with the ploughshare in November 1785, the daisy which he had to crush "amang the stoure" while working in the fields in April 1786, will live transfigured through the ages. Wherein does the compelling force of this art consist?

To answer this question we must take various factors into account. The first is that the poet's personality is never lost to view behind the scenes depicted in the Kilmarnock Volume. This personality is so great, so discerning, so courageous, so sincere, and inwardly so gripped by the subjects which it sets out to describe, that a wave of warmest life passes from it to them. The poet sets down not only what he has observed, but also what he has experienced, and so what he writes acquires a vital strength corresponding to the keenness with which these experiences were felt. The volume contains a wealth of autobiographical detail: the scenes of terror at Mount Oliphant, when the threats of the pitiless factor reduced his whole family to tears; his spiritual desolation in Irvine; the glorification of his own domestic circle; the joy and sorrow of his relation with Jean Armour; his consecration to poetry; his friendships; his conflict with Orthodoxy; the dread with which he faced the prospect of an eternal farewell to his native land; and, lastly, his epitaph on himself, honest alike in stressing his good points and his failings. Every page makes us feel that we are in direct contact with the poet, whose inward riches, whose fine and all-embracing humanity have lost nothing of their irresistible force since the days when he recited his poems in their earliest form to his brother at the plough and to friends in the tavern or in their homes, and by so doing lifted himself and them out of the cares of the moment into the realm of the eternally significant.

This brings us to the second fundamental quality of the Kilmarnock Poems to which we have already referred in passing— their universal applicability, their value as symbols of human life. The figures of the father, the friend, the flower, the animal, do not seem exclusively confined to the furrows of Mossgiel and the stones of Mauchline, but are seen by the poet as symbols of what has been from time immemorial and will be again while ages run; and yet they have lost nothing of the strong earthy flavour of their own individual existence. Burns arrives at this effect by the simplest means: passing easily from the particular to the general, he gives the poem a happy, epigrammatic turn, adding a philosophic reflection or a moralizing conclusion. The high level of the execution, the pathos without which neither Burns nor his poetry is conceivable, correspond to the greatness of the conception. It is therefore unjust, or at any rate not in keeping with Burns's spirit, to speak condescendingly of a poem like "The Cotter's Saturday Night." Burns refers to it in one of his later letters (to Thomson)[40] as being his favourite poem, and there can be no doubt that the sincerity and intensity of the patriotic sentiments expressed in it justify the prominent position it occupies at the apex of the volume (although its language is at times too strongly influenced by English classical models). In "The Cotter's Saturday Night," with its ideal picture of the Scottish peasant family, Burns wishes to immortalize the fountain from which a nation draws its strength. The portrait of the cotter is in striking contrast to that sketched in the poem immediately preceding it, where we have the pensive, slightly humorously conceived individual figure of the old farmer bringing "the accustomed ripp of corn" to his faithful, worn-out mare Maggie on New Year's morning. It is only by combining these two poems that we arrive at the distinguishing characteristic of the Kilmarnock Volume: that sense of steady progression from the particular to the general, by strongly elaborating the intervening personal experience.

Next, the linguistic-technical side of the book must be taken into account. That power of intense perception and of vivid reproduction which is the gift of the greatest artists belonged to Burns to such a degree that his power of speech may be placed beside Shakespeare's—this is the only point in which I should like to maintain the oft-drawn parallel. To reinforce his power of expression, his native dialect, with its wealth of vocabulary, its flexible phraseology, and at times its utterly fearless coarseness, came to his aid. Whenever Burns makes use of it, he reaches his zenith as an artist in words, and content and form are blended into an ideal unity. In utilizing the dialect, however, he has wisely confined himself to certain limits, thus avoiding the dangerous extreme of "regional art"—namely, use of the dialect to the point of

---

[40] Letters, 625 (May? 1794).

fatiguing or alienating the reader or hearer who is ignorant of that form of speech; and in this way he assures himself a greater influence on a wider public, without sacrificing any of the permanent values of his work. This mixture of speech extends to the individual stanzas—nay, to individual lines: the dialect clings to the humorous and satirical poems, and to works of purely local interest, while for what is solemn, pathetic, or of general import he uses literary English, with its not always desirable accompaniments of excessive sentimentality, affectation, uncertainty of expression, and too obvious dependence on literary models of the classical-sentimental school—points on which modern research has laid too much, rather than too little, emphasis. And yet it cannot be denied that this literary compromise was necessary and that it may even be defended from the point of view of style, when we consider the varied nature of the contents of the volume. It enriches the composition, it increases the number of items to be put in the list of contents, and makes possible certain effects, with which Burns, who kept his public firmly in his mind's eye while he was compiling his volume of poems, believed he could not afford to dispense.

Lastly, it must be emphasized that in the varied contents of the book neither the satirical nor the world-weary element predominates. We know Burns's fearless joy in attacking what offended him, and the peculiar keenness of his mind and his pen when he was bent on exposing hypocrisy and arrogance. His poems also reflect the bitterness of the moods of depression brought on by his own wrong-doing, by constitutional weakness, and by the heavy burden of conditions around him. He was no stranger to the struggle for existence. Animal and plant spoke to him of it. He saw it in the discord between his own highly-strung mind and the place to which life had assigned him—a discord of which he was only too fully conscious; he saw it in the unsolved social and other problems which came thronging upon him with the mutterings of the approaching revolution. But neither criticism nor negation obtained the mastery in the Kilmarnock Poems. On the contrary, they proclaim great joy, deepened by sympathy, in the whole world, in friendship and love, in poetic creation, and above all, in his native land, to sing the praises of which he felt himself called and predestined. When a friend slipped the Kilmarnock Volume into the hands of a noble lady, Mrs. Frances Anna Dunlop, who had suffered grievously in body and soul, she felt the fire of the work so refreshing, so purifying, and so healing, that the sense of oppression fell from her mind and she was restored to the friendly use and wont of her life. From that day forward she was Burns's warmest and most faithful friend, grateful to the poet for the richest blessing which human power can dispense: the gift of comfort and healing to a sick heart!

The success of the Kilmarnock Volume corresponded to the unusual nature of the event. It was instant and universal. If we let figures speak, Wilson, the printer,[41] calculated that of the 612 copies printed, only thirteen remained to be disposed of on 28th August, that is, four weeks after their appearance. Burns himself had only taken three; the remainder were dispersed by his friends, Robert Aiken of Ayr taking no less than 145 copies. Burns names the sum of £20 as his net profit. If Wilson's statement is correct, more than double that amount should have accrued to him; but we have now no clue as to what happened to the balance. In any case, it was a small fortune to him, with which he intended, in the first place, to meet the expenses of his journey to the West Indies.

In his "Memoir," Robert Heron describes the reception of the poems, telling how they were greeted everywhere with admiration and delight:

> "Old and young, high and low, grave and gay, learned or ignorant, all were alike delighted, agitated, transported. I was at that time resident in *Galloway,* contiguous to *Ayrshire* : and I can well remember, how that even ploughboys and maid-servants would have gladly bestowed the wages which they earned the most hardly, and which they wanted to purchase necessary clothing, if they might but procure the works of BURNS. A copy happened to be presented from a gentleman in Ayrshire to a friend in my neighbourhood. He put it into my hands, as a work containing some effusions of a most extraordinary genius. I took it, rather that I might not disoblige the lender, than from any ardour of curiosity or expectation. 'An unlettered ploughman, a poet!' said I, with contemptuous incredulity. It was on a Saturday evening. I opened the volume by accident, while I was undressing, to go to bed. I closed it not, till a late hour on the rising Sunday morn, after I had read over every syllable it contained."[42]

The literary society of Edinburgh also showed itself immediately

---

[41] Ch. W., i, 468-470.
[42] See Appendix (p. 17 in the original text).

susceptible to the powerful influence of the "Poems." The first—
and for Burns, the most important—sign was a letter from the
venerable blind poet and friend of literature Dr. Thomas Blacklock
(1721-91), a man of whom Heron, who occasionally acted as his
amanuensis, says that "there was, perhaps, never one among all
mankind whom you might more truly have called an angel upon
earth." Blacklock's letter, dated 4th September 1786,[43] was
addressed to the minister of Loudoun, the Rev. George Lawrie,
who took a keen interest in Burns and sometimes received him
in his manse, which was beautifully situated on the Irvine.
Blacklock speaks in this letter of the deep impression made upon
him by the reading of the book. Dugald Stewart, the well-known
professor of philosophy at Edinburgh University, had, he said,
formerly read to him three of the poems:

> "Many instances have I seen of Nature's force or beneficence exerted
> under numerous and formidable disadvantages; but none equal to that
> with which you have been kind enough to present me."

Since, as he had heard, the first edition was exhausted, he thought
it would be to the young poet's advantage to have a second, more
numerous edition printed at once. Burns, to whom this letter was
forwarded by Gavin Hamilton after a delay of several weeks, was
encouraged by it to try his luck with one of the more enterprizing
publishers in Edinburgh, for, as he wrote in the autobiographical
letter, "the doctor belonged to a set of critics for whose applause I
had not even dared to hope." For Burns to suggest, however, as
he does, that his journey to Edinburgh was the direct outcome of
this letter, is poetic licence, but the fame of being the first to
direct Burns's hopes to the capital, by calling down to him from
the larger stage of life there, remains with Blacklock: the few
lines of his letter to Lawrie have won for the Doctor a longer lease
of fame than all his poetic works put together.

Dugald Stewart, whose early interest in the poems of the Kilmarnock Volume is evident from Blacklock's letter, was also the first
representative of the best intellectual society of Edinburgh whose
personal acquaintance Burns made. Their meeting took place in
October of that year at Catrine, in the neighbourhood of which
Stewart had a country house. Dr. John Mackenzie of Mauchline

---

[43] Ch. W., i 417.

brought it about, Lord Daer, son of the Earl of Selkirk and a pupil of Stewart's, also being present. Burns has commemorated the great event in the humorous "Lines on Meeting with Lord Daer";[44] and in a letter to Mackenzie enclosing the poem he passes following judgment on Stewart:

> "I think his character, divided into ten parts, stands thus—four parts Socrates, four parts Nathaniel, and two parts Shakespeare's Brutus."[45]

The philosopher, on his part, was struck with Burns's natural, frank and yet modest bearing, the poet speaking only when he thought he had something to say, and then expressing himself clearly and originally, in pure English. A certain stubbornness in his disposition did not escape Stewart, who correctly ascribes it to the dominating position to which Burns was accustomed in his usual circle of friends.

A few days after Burns had dined at the celebrated philosopher's table, the first review of the Kilmarnock Volume appeared in the October issue of *The Edinburgh Magazine, or Literary Miscellany*. It was written by Robert Anderson, a friend of the publisher James Sibbald. The reviewer could not conceal his astonishment and honest admiration at the achievement of a poor farmer who knew no other language than his own and had not viewed humanity through the spectacles of books. At the same time, however, he felt it his duty to point out that the poet had at his command neither the Doric simplicity of Ramsay nor the dazzling imagination of Fergusson! In criticism, as in other matters, discretion is the better part of valour. But even if a little more stress than was necessary was laid upon the poet's unschooled mind, the prevailing note of the article was flattering to a high degree. The faults disappeared behind countless beauties, and the reader was assured that he would find enjoyment to suit his personal taste. The review concluded with an imposing list of quotations, which were continued in the next number of the *Magazine*.[46] Finally, the December issue reproduced an essay

---

[44] H. H., ii, 49-51.

[45] Letters, 52.

[46] This interesting review has unfortunately never been reprinted. In J. D. Ross's "Early Critical Reviews of Robert Burns" (Glasgow and Edinburgh, 1900), where one would have expected to find it, there are only a few sentences from it in the preface.

by Henry Mackenzie, which had already been published in the ninety-seventh number of *The Lounger,* and under the influence of which the poet Burns and his unusual gifts were spoken of with noticeably greater appreciation in the brief preliminary sentences. His fame, according to these remarks, was rapidly spreading, and the merit of his works was being acknowledged by all who had had the opportunity of perusing them, even the very wise and erudite no longer being excepted.[47]

Meanwhile the plan of publishing a new edition of the poems in Edinburgh among the intellectual élite of his native land was slowly maturing, and as this idea advanced, the thoughts of emigration—those very thoughts which had actually provided the stimulus for the publishing of the Kilmarnock Volume—gradually receded into the background. It must be reckoned as a happy accident for Burns and for the Scottish nation that the departure of the vessel on which he was to sail was postponed from week to week. While the time was passing, the number of reasons which might induce him to stay in Scotland was increasing. The Armours had stopped their proceedings against him. An understanding had been reached regarding the care of Jean's twins, whereby the boy was to remain at Mossgiel, while the girl was to stay with her mother's relatives in Mauchline. But Burns's feeling of paternal responsibility could not be eliminated by this arrangement; more powerful than all opposing considerations, it held him fast to his native land. Blacklock's flattering letter and the ideal and material success of the Kilmarnock Volume helped to strengthen his decision. His friends, too, seem to have conceived a project which offered a more desirable solution to his difficulties than the uncertain chances of emigration. A letter from Burns to Aiken (October 1786) discusses for the first time a plan, obviously emanating from Aiken, to find a position for the poet in the Excise Office. Burns was at that time still averse to the idea, for grave reasons. He refers in his letter to the "uncertainty of getting into business," his own inward restlessness, and the general wretchedness of his position, which will, he fears, yet drive him abroad.[48] In the verses to William Logan, dated 30th October 1786, he still contemplates without aversion the idea of a life in the West Indies.[49] It was not until

---

[47] See *B. Chr.*, 1927, 89-94: Burns's "Poems," Reviews of the first Edition.
[48] Letters, 53.
[49] H. H., ii, 99-103 (see stanza xii).

November that he finally made up his mind. On the 15th of that month he wrote to Mrs. Dunlop that he meant to set out for Edinburgh in a week or, at the latest, a fortnight, to arrange for a new edition of his poems.[50] During the next few days he acquainted Robert Muir of Kilmarnock, Miss Alexander of Ballochmyle and John Ballantyne of Ayr with his intention. On 27th November he left Mossgiel on a borrowed pony, and spent the evening and the night in happy social intercourse with admirers at Covington Mains, Lanarkshire, whither his fame had preceded him, and where he was greeted as a conquering hero. On the following day, 28th November, he reached Edinburgh, worn out with the manifold vicissitudes of the journey, and welcomed by one friend, the ever-faithful John Richmond, with whom he was to share a room and a bed in the Lawnmarket. When he entered the royal city, it seemed to him that the "baneful star" which had so long ruled over his destiny had at last set and given place to more propitious aspects. A new and larger world, full of hopes and possibilities, opened up before him. Care and sorrow lay behind him, vanquished by his own strength, by the triumph of his genius. The way which had oft-times led to the edge of the precipice had suddenly swerved upwards, and the farmer's son from Ayrshire dared prepare to take his fitting and passionately desired place at the table of life, beside the best of his fellow-countrymen.

---

[50] Dunlop Corr., p. 3; Letters, 55.

PART TWO: EDINBURGH

1786-1788

CHAPTER VI

THE SOCIAL BACKGROUND

HIDDEN among the enticements, stimulating influences, and honours which the capital held in readiness for Burns, there lurked many grave dangers—dangers even greater for the poet than for the man.

Looking back, we realize to-day with perfect clarity the artistic mission which it was incumbent upon Burns to fulfil. It was his vocation to preserve and to glorify the Scottish national spirit in description, story, and song, and through the medium of his own now scathingly satirical, now sentimentally emotional, compassionate, highly-strung individuality to give it new and powerful expression; but to accomplish all this he needed the contact with the soil. On the other hand, his urge to emulate the English or English-writing classicists, to follow the famous models of the elegant style, to whom he looked up with natural admiration, had from the first been strongly developed, and was capable of being disastrously encouraged by his meetings with the representatives of literature in the Scottish capital, with men like Blair, Home, Blacklock, Mackenzie, and their friends. There was never any lack of such encouragement. Thus, to quote a characteristic example, his well-meaning patron Dr. John Moore, the novelist and writer on travel, then resident in London, wrote to him on 23rd May 1787:

> "You ought . . . to deal more sparingly, for the future, in the provincial dialect—why should you, by using *that*, limit the number of your admirers to those who understand the Scottish, when you can extend it to all persons of taste who understand the English language? In my opinion, you should plan some larger work than any you have as yet attempted. I mean, reflect upon some proper subject, and arrange the plan in your mind, without beginning to execute any part of it till you have studied most of the best English poets, and read a little more of history. The Greek and Roman stories you can read in some abridgement, and soon become master of the most brilliant facts, which must highly delight a poetical mind. You *should*, also, and very soon *may*, become master of the heathen mythology, to which there are everlasting allusions in all the poets, and which in itself is charmingly fanciful. What will require to be studied with more

attention, is modern history; that is, the history of France and Great
Britain, from the beginning of Henry the Seventh's reign," &c.[1]

No one could be further from realizing that to turn genius aside
in such a way must rob it of its greatest strength, that for a poet of
Burns's peculiar gifts to deny his connexion with the soil was
tantamount to insincerity. During the first months of his sojourn
in Edinburgh, as it happens, the danger from these influences did
not amount to much, for the task which it was his first duty to fulfil
and which had brought him to Edinburgh stood clearly before
him and admitted of no delay: that task was to see to the publishing of a second edition of his poems. Once that was done, however, the poet must have been faced with the important question
of a new work. As a matter of fact, Moore's advice had been
called forth by his perusing of the Edinburgh Edition.

When Burns arrived in Edinburgh, the wave of vigorous, varie-
gated town-life immediately carried him to its crest. He proved
himself fully able to cope with the situation, however, and con-
fronted the enthusiastic crowd that surged about him with the
tranquil pride and the clear-sighted disillusion of his self-reliant
manliness. Never was the power of his intellect more astonishingly
revealed than during those first months when honours were heaped
upon him, and he was invited to one salon after another, high and
low receiving him with every conceivable sign of interest and
admiration. He was the lion of the winter season of 1786-87, *the*
curiosity worth seeing in the capital, a rôle in which he felt rather
uncomfortable. He never lost consciousness of the fact that he was
like a meteor, which bursts upon the view with dazzling brilliance
and quickly fades away again. The letters of this period clearly
reveal his conviction that the triumph which he enjoyed must be
ephemeral, and that it must be followed sooner or later by a
reaction; but at the same time, they display the indomitable pride
of the poet who knows the value of his work, and they contain
many spirited protests against the literary criticism of his patrons.

> "I have the advice of some very judicious friends among the
> literati here, but with them I sometimes find it necessary to claim
> the privilege of thinking for myself,"

he writes on 22nd March 1787 to Mrs. Dunlop. Correspondingly,

---

[1] Ch. W., ii, 94-95.—H. Blair adopted a similar attitude, but Burns met his
efforts with passive resistance. *Cf. B. Chr.*, 1932, pp. 94-99.

the question "What is to happen when all this is over?" crops up
continually in the letters. And the answer which he instinctively
gives is always: "Back to the plough!"

> "I guess that I shall clear between two and three hundred pounds
> by my Authorship," he says in the same letter to Mrs. Dunlop. "With
> that sum I intend, so far as I may be said to have any intention, to
> return to my old acquaintance, the plough, and, if I can meet with
> a lease by which I can live, to commence Farmer.—I do not intend
> to give up Poesy: being bred to labor secures me independance,
> and the Muses are my chief, sometimes have been my only enjoy-
> ment."[2]

He had other vague plans besides this, especially that of entering
the excise or the army, and even the thought of possible emigration to Jamaica does not seem to have been wholly eliminated from
his mind, in his anxious efforts to solve the problem of his future.[3]
    While thus shrewdly and conscientiously envisaging what inevit-
ably lay before him, Burns gave the present its due. The eye which
had found so much to interest it upon the little stage of life in
Mauchline turned with even more intense eagerness to the crowded,
animated scene which met its gaze in the fascinating capital—
"Auld Reekie," as Fergusson, its gifted, unfortunate son, loved
to call it, "Edina, Scotia's darling seat," as Burns, riding towards
it from Ayrshire, more emotionally had addressed it. The room in
which Burns had found a modest lodging with Richmond, at the
low rent of three shillings a week, was situated in the first storey
of a house in Baxter's Close, one of the narrow courtyards formed
by towering, over-populated buildings, which were reached from
the broad, busy Lawnmarket by narrow passages running in a
northerly direction. From his window he could see the adjacent
Lady Stair's Close with the handsome residence from which that
block of buildings got its name.[4]
    The fact that Richmond and Burns had settled in the first
storey and not, as one might have supposed, in the more airy
heights befitting a poet, need not surprise us. The nearer the
ground, the cheaper the dwellings were, for there the poorest

---

2 Dunlop Corr., 14-15; Letters, 90.

3 Letters, 113 (to J. Smith) and 210 (to Clarinda).

4 The house of Lady Stair (who died in 1731) was acquired in 1895 by the
Earl·of Rosebery, excellently restored and in 1907 presented to the town, to whose
most notable buildings it now belongs. Cf. "The Book of the Old Edinburgh
Club," iii, 1910, 243-252.

people, with their countless swarms of children, were crowded together; and there, too, one was nearest the famous Edinburgh night-smells that were wafted abroad when about ten o'clock the windows of the gigantic houses opened and, after the hasty warning cry of "Gardy loo!" (*gardez l'eau*), slops and rubbish of every sort rained down on street and courtyard. When in August 1773 Samuel Johnson, in company with Boswell, was walking up the High Street towards James's Court, where Boswell was then living, the moralist, whose attitude to conditions in Scotland was extremely critical, could not refrain from remarking to his companion: "I can smell you in the dark!" Whoever could manage it, moved higher up. Captain Topham in his "Letters from Edinburgh" (1774-75), tells a characteristic story of a Scottish gentleman who had gone to London for the first time, and having found lodgings in the top storey of a house, was agreeably surprised to find that he was being charged the cheapest rate for the "genteelest" position. He met the explanations of his friends with persistent incredulity, saying that he "ken'd vary weel what gentility was and he had not lived all his life in a sixth storey to come to London to live upon the ground." Each of these tremendous tenement houses or "lands" sheltered a world of its own: scavengers and runners lived in the lowest flats, artisans and labourers dwelt in the attics; doctors, judges, clergymen and noblemen on the middle floors; while dancing masters, merchants and clerks would settle immediately above or below them. However strictly class distinctions were observed in general, the direct contact of these widely varying social elements with each other resulted inevitably in a strong feeling of unity and a lively and natural amalgamation of the whole population. The walls of the overcrowded city seemed to enclose one large family, whose life was passed on the long, steep street leading up from Holyrood Palace to the Castle, enthroned on its precipitous rock; in the Cowgate and in the countless little lanes, alleys, and closes branching off from those thoroughfares. Just before Burns's arrival, a little after the beginning of the 'seventies, the congestion among the population had forced the inhabitants, especially the upper classes, to open up new quarters beyond the Nor' Loch, which filled the hollow in which Princes Street Gardens now lie, a bridge having been built across the valley in 1772. Princes Street, George Street, and Queen Street were slowly developing to the West, whilst in the Old Town middle-class people and artisans gradually were moving into the dwellings deserted by the rank and intellect of society. This change, however, which the old-established residents of Edinburgh viewed with interest, aversion, or superstitious anxiety, according to their mentality, did not affect Burns. The Old Town still formed the undisputed centre of all commercial, intellectual, and social life. It was there that the publishers and booksellers lived. There were situated the printing works on whose services he was to depend. There, too, were the High Court of Justice, the University, and St. Cecilia's Hall, famous for its concerts; and, lastly, there were to be found the oyster-cellars and the taverns whose narrow rooms, shut off from the bustle of traffic, and scarcely touched by the light of day, were filled morning, noon, and night by a motley crowd drawn from all ranks of society and from every profession. In the inn the doctor received his patients, the merchant his customers, and the provost his guests, for the narrow flats rendered the discharge of social duties impossible save in the rarest cases: it was usual for the lady of the house to receive and entertain friends in her bedroom. In the taverns, several of the best known of which were situated in the immediate vicinity of Parliament House, lawyers forgathered with their clients, and judges exchanged legal opinions and discussed interesting cases with their colleagues; and the conversation at these meetings sometimes became so absorbing that it led to such scenes of riotous intoxication as Scott in "Guy Mannering" makes Paulus Pleydell Esq. take part in. It was there, too, that eccentrics such as George Paton and David Herd met for a quiet drink in the evenings, and that countless clubs, with names as queer as their practices, held their meetings: of these clubs we shall have more to say later on. It was a hard-drinking society, from whose activities even the ladies of the highest classes did not wholly exclude themselves. Captain Topham has described the national dances which were performed in the oyster cellars, in the dim light of tallow candles, by members of both sexes of the Edinburgh aristocracy, after liberal indulgence in shell-fish, pots of porter, and punch. It must all have looked rather fantastic. Topham found it astonishing but by no means displeasing.

While there is no doubt that Burns did not close his mind to these appealing but—for a man of his temperament—dangerous allurements, it is no less certain that his heart and soul were fully alive to the historical greatness, the inexhaustible romance, of the captivating city, and that they were permeated by these influences. Because of the elevated position of the city, the wind sometimes seems to blow from every quarter at once: it sweeps through the chimney, it shrieks in every key, and in stormy autumn and winter weather drives smoke and flames into the rooms; but it makes bright eyes and clear heads. Its austere strength steels the nerves, braces the muscles, and heightens the receptive faculty; and even the coolest and most critical person acquires, under its stimulus, a keener sense of the heroic history written in the stones of Edinburgh, and becomes more responsive to the magic of the legends which cling like ivy round the grey walls of its houses (piled up in some cases to a height of twelve storeys), or flutter like bats from the dark corners of its closes and alleys. Much that was wonderful has to-day been sacrificed to the demands of city hygiene and the need for space for new buildings: the eye looks in vain for the quaint row of houses known as the "luckenbooths,", which at St. Giles Cathedral split up the stately breadth of the High Street into little lanes; the old city prison, the Heart of Midlothian, has fallen; Libberton's Wynd, which was the principal thoroughfare from the High Street to the Cowgate, has also vanished, and with it Johnnie Dowie's famous tavern. The ill-famed house of Major Weir, magician and boon-companion of Satan, no longer stands at the West Bow, and many other handsome and aristocratic buildings have either been torn down or—what renders them scarcely more recognizable—have been submerged in the squalor and meanness of quarters which have come down in the world.

And yet the Old Town of Edinburgh has not passed away, leaving no trace to mark its existence. On the contrary, it still dominates an austere, imposing, and extensive scene, as it rises above the cheerful elegance of the more modern parts of the city, which spread towards the Forth and the Pentland Hills. It clings grandly and almost dramatically to the long ridge of hill, the west side of which, growing out of impregnable rock, is crowned by the Castle; while to the East it gradually slopes down in a long street to the bottom of the valley, and comes to an end at that most venerable memorial of tragedy and ancient splendour, Holyrood, the palace of the Stuarts. From there the ground rises again abruptly to the barren walls of Salisbury Crags, above which towers a steep, conical peak, Arthur's Seat, a point which commands a view over a dozen counties, beyond town and sea to the Highlands in the North-west and the Braid Hills and the Pentlands in the South. This vast panorama of human achievement and natural grandeur, of idyllic loveliness and austere greatness, remains tremendously impressive.

We are told of walks that Burns was fond of taking in the immediate vicinity of the town. The top of Arthur's Seat was, according to Chambers,[5] one of his favourite goals, and we hear of excursions to that spot and to the Pentland Hills, in company with Alexander Nasmyth, the painter, and Dugald Stewart, the philosopher, who describes how fascinating the poet's conversation was on such occasions. When Stewart himself once expressed his admiration of the landscape spread out before them, Burns remarked "that the sight of so many smoking cottages gave a pleasure to his mind which none could understand who had not witnessed, like himself, the happiness and the worth which they contained."[6] The remark reveals his emotional attitude to nature, and reveals, too, his predominating interest in the power exercised over it by man. From it we can imagine with what eagerness he must have given himself up to the wealth of impressions of city life. The brilliant, colourful picture which historical fancy must paint for us anew as we look backwards—the Old Town of Edinburgh in the full swing of still almost undiminished social and intellectual activity—would meet his eyes in all its gleaming freshness the moment he stepped out of Baxter's Close and mingled with the busy throng that peopled the Lawnmarket. Each step must have been exciting, each glance around him must have shown him something of interest. Impressions would jostle each other as closely as the crowds hurrying past. If he turned to St. Giles Cathedral, the great Castle was behind him, whilst the commercial bustle of the Lawnmarket surged around him, and the many wares set out in the small open-fronted shops demanded his attention. Worthy magistrates would cross his path, among them, perhaps, the esteemed town councillor and president of the Guild of Cabinet Makers, William Brodie, who lived in a large house just opposite him. A whole close bore the name of this highly respected citizen, who moved in good society

5 Ch. W., ii, 55.
6 Ch. W., ii, 77-78.

and had access to exclusive clubs by day, but who at night, armed
with a dark lantern and a black mask, burgled the houses of his
fellow-citizens, and ended on the gallows two years later, after a
sensational trial. A few minutes' walk would bring the poet to
the centre of the town. There, neglected and sinister, stood the
Tolbooth with the guard-house of the City Guard so often and so
audaciously jeered at by Fergusson; there were the headquarters of
the goldsmiths and watchmakers; on the right was Parliament
Close with its administrative, legal, and library buildings, and the
grave of John Knox, the Reformer, who had found his last resting-
place in the old churchyard of St. Giles in 1572. The crowd of those
who intended to be present, either in an official capacity or as
audience, during the proceedings in the law courts, would stream
past, among them important individuals whose houses stood open
to Burns and held honours and excitements in readiness for him.
The principal church in the city, St. Giles, stood in the midst of
all the noisy hurry and scurry, itself not quite devoid of traces of
worldly activity: in every nook and corner of its outer wall were
stuck trading booths, often of tiny dimensions but greatly coveted
because of their favourable situation. In the luckenbooths already
mentioned a brisk business was carried on. For the poet, however,
the chief centre of attraction was a house at the east end of the
row, the front of which afforded a fine view of the Mercat Cross,
with its thronging crowds, and of the long High Street. This
house drew Burns like a magnet; for in it, for a number of years
back, had lived and worked William Creech (1745-1815), one of
Edinburgh's most influential citizens, and at that time the foremost
publisher in the town. The house had its history, which was not
unknown to Burns: Allan Ramsay had kept his bookshop there
since 1726, with a lending library, the first in Scotland, and it was
there that the literati of Edinburgh (and occasionally also distinguished visitors from London, such as John Gay) used to hold
their daily meetings and keep each other informed of the latest
publications in what was still, in the main, purely Southern-
English literature.[7] The house then passed into the possession
of the book-publishing firm of Kincaïd & Bell, and after that of
Creech, who revived the old tradition of the daily meeting of the

---

[7] Chalmers's "Life of Ramsay," in "Works of Allan Ramsay," 1851, I, p. 33
(with notes 2 and 3).

literati and brought it to a flourishing condition. Among those who frequented it were the witty lawyers Lords Kames, Hailes, and Monboddo; the philosophers Hume, Stewart, and Ferguson; the political economist Adam Smith; Blair and Beattie; Henry Mackenzie, the editor of *The Lounger* and *The Mirror;* and many others, whose works Creech published and whom he loved to gather round him, he himself being a clever, rather conceited man, heartily addicted to the joys of life. "His shop," says Chambers, "might have been called 'The Lounger's Observatory,'"[8] for the doorway was seldom free of idlers who observed and commented upon the crowd passing to and fro in front of it. Creech himself, with black silk breeches and powdered hair, was always a conspicuous member of this group, which Burns, whose poems were to be published in a second edition by Creech and printed by William Smellie, now also joined.

A few steps brought the poet from the publisher's house to the printer's office, situated at the back of Anchor Close, which branched off from the High Street to the North, and at the entrance to which stood Daniel Douglas's much-frequented "howff." Burns, who was soon on most intimate terms with the witty, jovial Smellie, was often seen at both places, where his actions were watched with interest. Daniel Wilson could point out the desk-stool with the inscription: "This is the stool on which Burns sat while correcting the proofs of his poems, from December 1786 to April 1787,"[9] and Alexander Smellie, the son of the printer, distinctly remembers the curious way in which Burns deported himself while in the composing-room: he would walk up and down the room several times, making a long whip which he carried in his hand whistle through the air, but he did not seem to take the slightest interest in the work of the compositors, who were busy with his own manuscripts. His behaviour gave the younger Smellie the impression of a certain affectation, as if Burns wished to emphasize the fact that he was a farmer.[10] From the Mercat Cross, where an English visitor of Smellie's is said to have exclaimed with admiration that here, within a few minutes, one could shake hands with fifty men of genius and erudition,[11] the poet may have pursued his way

---

[8] "Traditions of Edinburgh," 118.
[9] "Memorials of Edinburgh," 1891, ii, 26.
[10] R. Kerr, "Memorials of William Smellie"; Edinburgh, 1811, ii, 350-351.
[11] *Ibid.*, 252.

eastwards and downhill, past John Knox's house and many another building familiar to the citizens of the time and still famous in history, then through the Canongate, towards Holyrood, amid the tumult of overcrowded streets, between tall houses covered with the gaudy signs of the trades they sheltered, while from their uppermost storeys the washing fluttered in the sharp Edinburgh wind. We must pause awhile with him at one quiet corner: the cemetery of the Canongate Church, where, since 19th October 1774, the mortal remains of Robert Fergusson had found their last resting-place. Fergusson's grave was in every sense of the word holy ground for Burns. An indissoluble tie of admiration and sympathy bound him to the spot where lay the bones of "his elder brother in misfortune, by far his elder brother in the Muses." A somewhat fantastic story of Cunningham's tells us that one of the first walks Burns took after his arrival in Edinburgh was to this grave, to which at that time scarcely anyone paid any heed; and the tale goes on to describe how Burns, with a characteristic outburst of emotion, knelt there bareheaded and kissed the hallowed ground. Be that as it may, he did not let the matter rest at this ephemeral sign of his reverence, but on 6th February 1787 addressed a letter to "The Hon[ble] the Bailies of the Canongate," asking for permission to lay a stone over the grave, to "remain an unalienable property to his deathless fame, to direct the steps of the Lovers of Scottish Song, when they wish to shed a tear over the 'narrow house' of the Bard." The request was unanimously granted, "in consideration of the laudable and distinterested motion of Mr. Burns," and the memorial stone was ordered, but was not set up until August 1789.[12] The first verse of a three-stanza'd inscription which Burns wrote for it is engraved on the front of it.[13] From that time till the present day, when the name of Fergusson is spoken by an ever larger number of people with ever greater pride, and the story of his life and works studied with ever increasing interest, this simple

---

[12] Letters, 81; A. B. Grosart, "Robert Fergusson," 10-11. Text of the inscription, H. H., 268-269, and notes 451-452.

[13] See Ch. W., iii, 314, for the account of £5 10s. When Burn, the sculptor, sent it to Burns, he added the somewhat frivolous remark: "I shall be happy to receive orders of a like nature for as many more of your friends that have gone hence as you please." Burns settled the account through Hill in Feb. 1792, remarking in the covering letter that Burn "was two years in erecting it [the stone] after I commissioned him for it; and I have been two years paying him, after he sent me his account; so he and I are quits." Letters, 495.

memorial has remained the most prominent one which has been raised on Scottish soil in his honour. No worthier memorial could have been erected, and by no man better suited to the task.

We must turn from the silence of the hallowed ground and the bustle of the animated scene into which Burns stepped in November 1786, to the social "sets" and personalities by whom he was greeted and entertained during that winter. A prominent authority on the history of Scottish civilisation in the eighteenth century has rightly drawn attention to the great intimacy which existed at that time throughout the literary world in Scotland.[14] A brotherly bond seemed to unite its members; they were constantly meeting, in parties, in the daily discharge of their official duties, or in the numerous and varied clubs where they passed a considerable part of their spare time. They had the same habits, the same interests, the same amiable virtues and vices. In addition, they were in many cases closely related through marriage. This partly explains the unanimous cordiality of the reception which was accorded to Burns, the rapidity with which the numerous salons in the capital opened their doors to him, and the far-sounding quality of the echo which his poems unquestionably raised.

When Burns rode into Edinburgh on his borrowed pony, he was personally acquainted with very few men, and these extraordinarily different in social status and importance. Chief among them were the clerk John Richmond and the philosopher Dugald Stewart. Apart from these, he was assured of direct encouragement also from Dr. Blacklock. Despite this lack of friends he was able a few days later, on 7th December 1786, to send the following report to Gavin Hamilton at Mauchline:

"My Lord Glencairn & the Dean of Faculty, Mr. H. Erskine, have taken me under their wing; and by all probability I shall soon be the tenth Worthy and the eighth Wise Man, of the world."[15]

A letter of introduction to the Earl of Glencairn (1749-91) from his old patron James Dalrymple of Orangefield, who was connected by marriage with Glencairn, smoothed the way for him and won him a protector as benevolent as he was powerful. Through the marriage of his younger brother John with Lady Isabella Erskine in 1785, Glencairn was related to Henry Erskine (1746-1817), the

---

[14] H. G. Graham, "Scottish Men of Letters in the Eighteenth Century," 104-107.
[15] Letters, 62.

most prominent and the most able lawyer in Edinburgh. David
Stuart, eleventh Earl of Buchan (1742-1829), one of the founders
of the Scottish Society of Antiquaries, an insignificant person but
eager to be known as a literary Mæcenas, was a brother of Henry
Erskine's, and soon approached Burns with his shallow advice and
criticism. The capricious Duchess of Gordon, née Jane Maxwell,
one of the leaders of Edinburgh society, famous alike for her
beauty and for the genial bluntness of her speech and humour, was
closely allied to this circle, to which also belonged the amiable and
eccentric James Burnett, Lord Monboddo (1714-99), judge and
landowner (in philosophy a modest predecessor of Darwin), and
his daughter Elizabeth, who captivated everybody, Burns not least
of all. Elizabeth was the "fair Burnet" of the "Address to Edinburgh," and her early death in 1790 was lamented by Burns in an
elegy not altogether worthy of the tragic event. Adam Ferguson
(1723-1816), the historian, who until 1785 held the chair of Moral
Philosophy in the University of Edinburgh as one of its most celebrated ornaments, appears among his patrons; he was a man whose
gaunt figure and fiery temper were as well known as the banquets
to which he loved to invite his friends and admirers.

From these summits of Edinburgh cultural life many paths led
down to the literati in the true sense of the word. The blind, kind-
hearted Dr. Blacklock and the successful preacher and æsthete
Hugh Blair, to whose unctuous banalities the whole of Edinburgh
listened with reverent awe, were everywhere received as honoured
guests. Creech, who was to publish the new edition of Burns's
poems, we have already seen in his outstanding position in the literary
life of the city. People spoke of his "levées," from which no one
dared be absent who placed any value on being up-to-date in his
knowledge of literary affairs. Creech was bound to the Earl of
Glencairn by special ties of a personal nature, having in his youth,
while Glencairn was still heir to the earldom, with the title of
Lord Kilmaurs, served him in the capacity of travelling companion. Then again Creech was very closely associated both pro-
fessionally and socially with the printer, translator, and philosopher
William Smellie. Through the influence of Dugald Stewart, Burns
was introduced to Henry Mackenzie (1745-1831), the author of
"The Man of Feeling" (1771), whom the poet had long regarded

with extravagant admiration.[16] A number of other outstanding
personalities whom Burns met, such as William Tytler (1711-92),
Sir James Hunter Blair (1741-87), Josiah Walker (1761-1831), and
James Gregory (1753-1821), can only be mentioned here. Through
his own negligence Burns failed to come into personal contact with
Adam Smith (1723-90), the celebrated political economist, the friend
of Hume, the benevolent patron of aspiring talents, and the connoisseur of poetry. Smith's health was by that time very badly
shattered, and he was about to seek advice and treatment with a
medical friend in London. It is all the more noteworthy that immediately after the appearance of the Kilmarnock Poems he should
have interested himself in the most active fashion in the poet's
future, wishing to create a sinecure for him in the Government
Salt Tax Office, in order to leave him free for artistic production
by relieving him of financial worries. Mrs. Dunlop urged Burns
not to postpone the visit which he owed both to etiquette and to
himself. She sent him a letter of introduction to Smith, but the
day before it reached Burns, Smith had already set off for London.[17]

Outside this rich and elegant "set" in which he was gaped
at, wooed, and fêted for the space of one winter, and to whose
banquets he, like a fashionable virtuoso, added an indispensable
fillip, Burns had access to a wealth of social intercourse and contacts, and had many other friends who greeted his brilliant social
gifts with encouraging applause, taking up as much of his time as
they could. As we have already seen, the aristocracy of birth and
intellect lived by no means in privileged and professional exclusive-
ness. The many festive gatherings in private houses at which they
regularly met were far from satisfying their social needs. Every
day and every night the high-born and the illustrious assembled,
along with citizens, artists, artisans, lawyers, clergymen, and actors,
in countless more or less intimate societies or clubs, the importance
of whose cultural influence upon the public life of Edinburgh it is
not easy to over-estimate. Although it is evident that some of these
clubs were more aristocratic and some more democratic in spirit,
it was not possible to draw the lines of demarcation too sharply,
or, in the freedom of the taverns, to differentiate strictly between

---

[16] For Mackenzie and his connections with Burns see H. W. Thompson, "The
Anecdotes and Egotisms of H. Mackenzie," 1745-1831; O.U.P., 1927; and "A
Scottish Man of Feeling"; O.U.P., 1931.

[17] Dunlop Corr., 17, 18, 21; Letters, 94.

the various social grades. Above all, we cannot fail to notice a certain tendency toward the lower strata: no one liked to miss the merry companion, the gifted singer, the skilful story-teller—in short, anything that was original. People sought out novelty where it was to be found, and gave themselves up with boundless facilities of enjoyment to the prevailing spirit of gaiety. A man like James Cummyng of the Lyon Office, secretary of the Society of Antiquaries, was a member of no less than fifteen such clubs. In them and in the meetings of the Freemasons' Lodges, the most varied social elements mixed freely with each other, and developed that sense of common brotherhood which gives the public life of Edinburgh at this time its characteristic stamp. This fusing of the classes, this mutual contact and influence, brought much good with it: it strengthened the feeling of unity in the community, and widened the horizon of the individual; it facilitated political and social organisation; it fostered the love of literature and of music; and it developed, among other things, a consciousness of the need for a collection of the national songs. To supply that need, Allan Ramsay and, after him, the publishers of countless song-books, had already laboured successfully, but its noblest issue was to be Burns's work as a song-writer. Owing to the excessive indulgence in alcohol, however, to which the whole generation was addicted, this good comradeship also demanded heavy sacrifices. Fergusson's delicate constitution collapsed under it, and there can be no doubt that it did grievous harm to Burns, who in any case had a natural propensity for that sort of thing; he himself admitted as much in later regretful reminiscences. We must not, however, reproach the poet, as if he had been guilty of the most personal of vices, with what—as can be proved from hundreds of cases—was looked upon by contemporary society in town and country as the supreme joy of the table.

At gatherings of this kind, then, Burns's circle of friends was augmented and widened by people of lower standing as well. We learn from his own letter to John Ballantine, written on 14th January 1787, of the honours which had been accorded to him on the preceding evening at a festive and very well attended meeting of the St. Andrew's Lodge. The Grand Master Mason of Scotland, Francis Charteris, who presided at the meeting, proposed the toast: "Caledonia and Caledonia's Bard, brother Burns!" which was received by the assembly with repeated acclamations. Burns, who was thunder-struck by the unexpected ovation, "trembling in every nerve, made the best return in his power." He recovered his composure when he heard one of the chief office-bearers say in an encouraging tone: "Very well indeed!"[18] A fortnight later, on 1st February 1787, Burns was admitted with no less honour into the Canongate Kilwinning Lodge (No. 2),[19] a scene which the painter Stewart Watson perpetuated in 1846 with theatrical effect in a canvas crowded with figures. It is to the interpretation of this picture that we owe the interesting, if unreliable, little book, "A Winter with Robert Burns,"[20] in which the notabilities assembled in the canvas are introduced to us in a brief biographical survey. And here, besides the well-known representatives of the aristocracy and of learning, we meet the gifted but unstable William Nicol, one of the Latin masters at the Edinburgh High School; the writing-master and composer Allan Masterton; William Cruickshank, a colleague of Nicol's, in whose house in the New Town Burns lived for a time during the following winter; the tragedian William Woods, a friend of Fergusson's, for whose benefit performance on 16th April, 1787, Burns wrote a prologue;[21] the painter Alexander Nasmyth, a neighbour of Burns's in the Lawnmarket, whose famous portrait of the poet dates from this time; the versatile James Tytler, author, balloonist and globe-trotter, clever, full of ideas, but unfortunate in all his undertakings and always head over ears in debt, an out and out Bohemian; Peter Hill, Creech's business manager; James Johnson and Stephen Clarke, of whom we shall have more to say in connection with the *Scots Musical Museum;* the musician Johann G. C. Schetky, a native of Darmstadt, and many others, whose names are more or less loosely connected with Burns's Edinburgh period.

These same men, almost all distinguished by remarkable and often whimsical features and easy to differentiate as individuals (that delightful caricaturist John Kay (1742-1826) has included most of them in his "Edinburgh Portraits"),[22] also appear here and

---

[18] Letters, 77.

[19] See protocol of meeting in Ch. W., ii, 45.

[20] Edinburgh, 1846. The author's name was John Marshall.

[21] *Cf.* Sommers's "Life of Fergusson," 48-51. The Prologue in H. H., ii, 144-145.

[22] Collected under the title "Kays' Edinburgh Portraits," with biographies by Paterson and Maidment, cheap ed., London and Glasgow, 1885, 2 vols.; 1st ed. in 2 vols. 4to, Edinburgh, 1837.

there in the lists of members of the clubs, with which Burns's connections were probably much more extensive than can be proved
to-day. Though their grotesque formalities were many and varied,
these clubs had one common aim in view—the enjoyment of life.
They were for the most part harmless, though in a few cases,
perhaps, inclined to indulge in coarse ribaldry. The aristocratic
"Caledonian Hunt," to which is dedicated the second edition of the
poems—the club had subscribed for one hundred copies—cannot in
the strict sense of the term be reckoned among the social clubs: it
was rather a society of riding and hunting gentlemen.   "The
Crochallan Fencibles,"[23] however, was a genuine club, the leading
spirit of which was William Smellie.   Burns, introduced by
Smellie soon after his arrival in Edinburgh, spent many a boisterous,
happy night in its midst, drinking, and measuring his ready wit
against Smellie's in conversation and song. The name "fencible"
or "volunteer" has a military flavour, and reminds us of the formation of such companies of militia and volunteer corps at the time
of the American War of Independence. The titles of the office-
bearers were also of a military nature: there was a colonel, a major,
a quartermaster-general, a provost, and so on. Smellie himself acted
as quartermaster-general and recorder, but, unfortunately, it has not
so far been possible to find any of the records kept by him. The
name "Crochallan" is supposed to come from a Gaelic song which
Daniel Douglas, the innkeeper, who was known to everybody in
the city, and in whose rooms in Anchor Close the club held its
meetings, is said to have sung occasionally. The beautiful, mournful air—Crodh Chailean, "Colin's Cattle"—is still associated with
Burns's famous verses, "My Heart's in the Highlands."[24] The
list of members of the club has only very fragmentarily been preserved.[25] The legal element preponderated; we remember that
Douglas's "howff" was situated in the immediate vicinity of Parlia-

---

[23] Unfortunately there exists no comprehensive study of Edinburgh club life.
such as Nevill has made of the club life of London, and Strang of that of Glasgow.
Best consult Chambers's "Traditions of Edinburgh," particularly the chapters
"Convivialia" and "Taverns of Old Times"; and H. A. Cockburn's essay on
"Edinburgh Clubs" in "The Book of the Old Edinburgh Club," iii, 1910, 105-178.
For the "Crochallan Fencibles," cf., in addition, Kerr's "Memoirs of Smellie,"
ii, 255-259, and Henderson's "Robert Burns," 106-110; and for the "Cape Club,"
to which we shall shortly refer, see my "Songs from David Herd's Manuscripts,"
Edinburgh, 1904, 35-51, and *Archiv*, 129, 372-374.

[24] See Moffat, "The Minstrelsy of Scotland," 112.

[25] Cockburn, l.c., p. 164-165.

ment House. We come across the names of Henry Erskine, Lord
Newton and Lord Gillies. Alexander Cunningham and William
Dunbar, both closely connected with Burns, also belonged to the
legal profession. Other members were the critic and historian
Gilbert Stuart; Matthew Henderson, to whose memory a deeply
felt elegy was written in 1790; and Robert Cleghorn, farmer at
Saughton Mills near Edinburgh, like Smellie the recipient of
curious letters and poems which were considered unfit for publication, the majority of which have disappeared and probably been
destroyed. After Cleghorn's death, many of them were, thanks
to his stepson, John Allan, seen by Lord Byron.[26] We get a pretty
accurate idea, from some of the anecdotes told by Kerr, of the
sociable tone which prevailed among the Crochallan Fencibles.[27]
When new members were admitted, a definite ritual was carried out
(as was customary in many other clubs), the chief aim of which was
to test the humour and good nature of the newcomer. Once the
chieftain of a Highland clan, whose exterior was marked by a
specially prominent nose, found himself in this position. His
neighbour at table, Smellie, at once seized him by it, and trium-
phantly called upon the entire company to bear witness that he
had taken a Highland chieftain by the nose without the latter
daring to punish him for it. Burns, too, had to put up with many
a merry and provocative remark. Kerr tells us how the members
took special pleasure in inciting Burns and Smellie to a battle of
wits—combats from which the poet did not always emerge
victorious. A further interesting proof of the spirit prevalent in this
circle is the collection of fescennine songs made for it by Burns, and
published after his death by some unauthorised person under the
title of "The Merry Muses of Caledonia." A later chapter of this
book will deal with them more fully. The happy comradeship
of the Crochallan Fencibles, whose history unquestionably reached
its zenith with Burns's appearance in their midst, did not long
survive the death of their founder and indefatigable and inspiring
leader, Smellie, who passed away on 24th June 1795. The club
ceased to exist in December of the same year.

We should like to know more about Burns's connections with
similar societies. Here, however, our sources disappoint us, even

[26] *Archiv*, 129, 371-372.
[27] "Memoirs of Smellie," II, 255-259.

the records of the popular Cape Club, which were for a long time
preserved in the Library of the Scottish Society of Antiquaries and
have now (1935) been handed over to the Scottish National Library.
The majority of the members, or, as they called themselves, Knights
of the Cape, were of lower social standing than the Crochallan
Fencibles. The club consisted of minor shopkeepers, artisans, office-
clerks, seafaring men, and artists of various kinds. But other
elements were not lacking. Burns's friends almost all belonged
to it. Music and poetry were in high favour at this club: the
"Grand Cape" of the year 1769 was held in honour of the immortal
name of William Shakespeare, and on 22nd September of the same
year James Thomson's birthday was celebrated in an assembly room
suitably decorated for the event. Odes were composed by members
of the club for this occasion and a brimming beaker was emptied
"to the memory of this favourite poet, the pride of his native land,
the singer of freedom, and the friend of humanity." It could not
be unknown to Burns that Robert Fergusson, during the last two
years of his life, had been one of the most highly esteemed knights
of the Cape, and that David Herd, the careful preserver of Scottish
songs and ballads, had presided over it and was on terms of lasting
friendship with many of its members. How Burns reacted to the
complexity of this great Edinburgh life, uniform in spite of its
variety and the crowded setting of its magnificent stage, we learn,
of course, from his correspondence.[28] We possess, moreover, a few
rhymed character-sketches, dashed off with a sure hand, of personalities whose bearing and actions roused his interest. To these
belong the two witty epigrams, written during a sensational divorce
case, on the Lord Advocate, Sir Ilay Campbell, and Henry
Erskine;[29] the lines on Smellie in the Crochallan Club,[30] and the
lament for the absence from Edinburgh of Creech, composed in
Selkirk on 13th May 1787.[31] The lines "On William Creech,"[32]
written in an unfriendly mood, are of later date. Finally, we have
the song, "Rattlin, Roarin Willie,"[33] written in honour of the

[28] To Hamilton, Letters, 62; to Ballantine, Letters, 63; to Mrs. Dunlop, Dunlop
Corr., 14-15, Letters, 90.

[29] "Extempore in the Court of Session," H. H., ii, 240.

[30] Ibid., 236.

[31] Ibid., 53-57.

[32] Ibid., 235.

[33] H. H., iii, 35-36, 330-332; Mus., ii, No. 194.

colonel of the Crochallan Fencibles, William Dunbar, "one of the
worthiest fellows in the world." The most important document,
however, is a diary, known as the "Second Common-place Book,"
the entries in which begin with 9th April 1787.[34] Starting with a
remark of Gray's that "half a word fixed upon or near the spot, is
worth a cart-load of recollection," Burns declared his intention of
sketching "with unshrinking justice" any character that might rouse
his interest. The book was also to contain anecdotes, self-con-
fessions, and poems and rough drafts similar to those in the earlier
"Common-place Book." He made a start with the character-
sketches, speaking first of his patron, the Earl of Glencairn—under
the influence, as it happens, of a certain painful situation where he
has felt himself neglected for a nondescript noble blockhead, "a
fellow whose abilities would scarcely have made an eightpenny
taylor, and whose heart is not worth three farthings." Must the
son of genius and poverty, writes Burns, see such a man preferred to
himself? In the end, however, after a benevolent glance and hand-
shake from the Earl, the inextinguishable feeling of gratitude wins
the day: criticism is mute where Glencairn is concerned. "I
shall love him until my dying day!"—Next comes Dr. Blair,[35]
whom Burns respects as long as he does not hurt his (the poet's)
self-esteem by his arrogance. When that happens, respect passes
into indifference: "What do I care for him or his pomp either?"
Blair's vanity, he says, is proverbial. "Natural parts like his are
frequently to be met with." He is, says Burns, a striking example
of how far a man can get on through industry and application. At
the same time, however, Blair, too, is dismissed with expressions
acknowledging his eminent critical faculties. Burns feels more at
home with a minister of the High Church, William Greenfield,
professor of Rhetoric, a highly respected man whose career began
brilliantly but ended in disgrace. The philosopher Dugald Stewart
seems to Burns to merit the greatest praise. He calls him, somewhat vaguely, an exalted judge of the human heart, equally
capable of generosity and humanity, and then says more explicitly
that Stewart can see through anyone, and treats everyone according
to his inward worth. Externals have no more weight with him than

---

[34] MS. in the Burns Museum, Alloway.
[35] See J. De Lancey Ferguson, "Burns and Hugh Blair," M.L.N. 45, 440-46
(1930).

they will have at the Last Day. In the hour of social hilarity he lacks neither wit nor good-natured waggishness, and is unsurpassed in the art of telling a story. Last in the list comes the poet's "worthy bookseller, William Creech." Burns is at his happiest and most penetrating in his judgment of this man, who was not too far above him either socially or culturally. The picture he sketches of Creech shows the influential publisher's weaknesses and good qualities in an equally strong light. He calls him a "strange multiform character," amiable, especially among his friends on festive occasions—Creech's literary dinners were famous throughout Edinburgh—but vain and "with half a squint at his own interest." He feels it his duty, says Burns, "to take every instance of unprotected merit by the hand, provided it is in his power to hand it into public notice." He is a clever but not too profound writer, a man of the world, who feels impelled to emerge from mediocrity, and who has the capacity to do so. In the course of the next few months Burns had occasion to know the less pleasant side of Creech's nature more intimately, and considerably to modify his opinion of him, which was on the whole a favourable one.

When we come to outside evidence, the many voices which have testified concerning Burns for the most part confirm the impression which his own utterances make upon us.[36] He looked the life of fashion and its leaders frankly and fearlessly in the face. The acts of homage which were rendered him he accepted calmly and gratefully as his due, with the clear consciousness of their swift evanescence. As earlier in Ayrshire, so now in Edinburgh, the intensity of his conversation, which was intelligent and unusual in its idiom, impressive, and permeated with passion and feeling, roused the admiration of all who came in contact with him. He knew when to be silent, but never hesitated to state his views when he thought the occasion demanded it. In a few rare cases, perhaps, he overstepped the mark, when his artistic temperament carried him away. The peasant, of course, appeared, too, now and then, sometimes as a pose, as in Smellie's printing office, sometimes quite naturally. The distrust with which he watched at aristocratic functions for breaches of tact towards himself betrays the man of humble origin. A painful episode such as that with the servingmaid May Cameron, which finally led to a warrant of arrest

---

[36] See summary in Ch. W., ii, 71-83.

against him *in meditatione fugæ,* proves his weakness in sexual matters—a weakness which he never denied. His human greatness, his passionate sympathy, the power of his clear, penetrating intellect, which in moments of inspiration showed itself equal to the highest problems, was obvious to every one of his contemporaries. In a memorable sketch for Lockhart, Sir Walter Scott has left a picture of the poet's appearance and manner, which is too valuable to be omitted in any Burns biography. Scott was then in his sixteenth year, when Adam Ferguson's eldest son took him to one of the famous literary evenings that were held on Sundays in his father's house (Sciennes Hill House), when young men who seemed worthy of the honour were permitted to listen in silence to the edifying conversation of their illustrious elders. On this particular evening there were assembled, as usual, the most distinguished men in the city, among them Dr. Black and Dr. Hutton, John Home, the dramatist, and Dugald Stewart.[37] The lion of the evening, however, was Robert Burns, whom Stewart had brought to Ferguson's house. A print of Bunbury's, illustrating a few sentimental lines from a poem by John Langhorne, "The Country Justice," had roused Burns's interest and had actually brought tears of emotion to his eyes. He asked who was the author of the lines beneath the picture, and could get no answer until young Scott supplied the information. A friendly glance and an amiably encouraging word —"you'll be a man yet, sir"—were the reward, which Scott never forgot.

"His person," says Scott, "was strong and robust; his manners rustic, not clownish; a sort of dignified plainness and simplicity, which received part of its effect, perhaps, from one's knowledge of his extraordinary talents. His features are represented in Mr. Nasmyth's picture; but to me it conveys the idea that they are diminished, as if in perspective. I think his countenance was more massive than it looks in any of the portraits. I would have taken the poet, had I not known what he was, for a very sagacious country farmer of the old Scotch school: i.e., none of your modern agriculturists, who keep labourers for their drudgery, but the 'douce gudeman' who held his own plough. There was a strong expression of sense and shrewdness in all his lineaments; the eye alone, I think, indicated the poetical character and temperament. It was large, and of a dark cast, which glowed (I say literally *glowed*) when he spoke with feeling or interest. I never saw such another eye in a human head, though I have seen

---

37 For Ferguson see Ch. W., ii, 82; for Black and Hutton Graham, "Scottish Men of Letters," p. 167.

the most distinguished men of my time.   His conversation expressed
perfect self-confidence, without the slightest presumption.   Among the
men who were the most learned of their time and country, he expressed
himself with perfect firmness, but without the least intrusive forwardness; and when he differed in opinion, he did not hesitate to express
it firmly, yet at the same time with modesty."[38]

The impression of this meeting was so strongly imbedded in Scott's
memory that it was still present with him in undimmed clearness
after four decades.   Few scenes in literary history seem more noteworthy than that in which, surrounded by the most mature minds
in the country, the full-fledged genius greeted and, as it were, blessed
the boy who was to be the admired master of future generations.

---

[38] See Lockhart, "Life of Burns," 89-91.

CHAPTER VII

LITERARY ACHIEVEMENTS. TOURS.

CLARINDA AND JEAN.

MEANWHILE, the particular task which had brought Burns to Edinburgh was nearing completion. The enlarged new edition of the Poems of 1786 was almost ready. The necessary preliminaries seem to have been very quickly carried through, thanks to the energetic support of the Earl of Glencairn. Only a few days after his arrival in the capital, Burns was able to write to Gavin Hamilton (on 7th December 1786) that the "Caledonian Hunt" had one and all subscribed for the new edition and that the subscription bills were to be out next day.[1] On 9th December Henry Mackenzie's important review appeared in *The Lounger,* published by Creech. This review did substantial justice to the genius of the Kilmarnock Poems, though it was not given to Mackenzie to recognize wherein its greatness really consisted. To him, too, the use of the vernacular appeared a drawback, and one may read in his sentences the indirect advice to the poet to express himself in future in a language which will be more universally understood: "even in Scotland, the provincial dialect which Ramsay and he have used, is now read with a difficulty which greatly damps the pleasure of the reader: in England it cannot be read at all." Apart from this, however, it must be remembered to Mackenzie's everlasting credit that he really felt the peculiar quality of the poems, and in his critique, by his warm recommendation, very skilfully built a bridge from the work to the taste of its public. He did not omit at the same time to call attention to the poet's character and circumstances in a way which promised certain success to the appeal in his closing paragraph: to support the native poet and keep him from leaving the land of his birth. If further recommendation had been needed, it was forthcoming in the obvious social triumph which Burns, by his personal bearing, scored during that winter

---

[1] Letters, 62.

with every class of society in Edinburgh. The subscriptions flowed
in in such numbers that it was seen to be necessary, while the
printing was still in progress, substantially to increase the extent of
the edition, or, in Burns's words, to issue a second and third
edition simultaneously. In the end 3000 copies were printed, of
which 2800 were taken up by 1500 subscribers. On 17th April
Burns, in the house and in the presence of Henry Mackenzie,
transferred the copyright of the poems to Creech, who was to have
the right to take the London publisher T. Cadell into partnership in
the venture. This partnership took the form of a third, unaltered
edition which appeared in London, likewise in 1787.[2] The sum
demanded for the transaction by Mackenzie, as arbiter, and
accepted by the two contracting parties, amounted to 100 guineas.[3]
The subscription price was five shillings a copy, which was raised
to six shillings for non-subscribers. The volume was published on
21st April 1787, and brought Burns, after extremely wearisome and
unedifying wrangling with Creech, about £450, which included the
stipulated 100 guineas.

The edition contained as frontispiece the engraving of a bust of
Burns, an excellent piece of work by John Beugo, after the painting
by Nasmyth, but based upon repeated sittings by the poet. Then
followed the imposing list of subscribers. Headed by the "Caledonian Hunt" with one hundred copies, this took up no less than
thirty-eight pages. The poet's patrons and friends had given him
lavish support. Outside societies, such as the Scottish colleges in
Paris and Regensburg, and the Scottish Benedictine Monastery in
Maryborough, also subscribed. In place of the Preface to the Kilmarnock Edition there was a Dedication to the noblemen and
gentlemen of the "Caledonian Hunt," which in somewhat high-
flown accents acknowledged the poet's great indebtedness, duly
emphasized the independence of his character and the originality
of his art, and concluded with extravagant words of blessing for his
patrons. The most striking sentence in the Dedication was a
vigorous image, suggested to Burns by a passage in the Bible (1
Kings, xix, 19): the Muse, he said, found him as Elijah found
Elisha, at the plough, and threw her inspiring mantle over him.

---

[2] H. H., i, 313-314. According to this, the two Edinburgh impressions are
quoted as the *second*, and the London impression as the *third* edition.
[3] Reprint of the document by Ch. W., ii, 92.

A few words about the poetic contents of the volume will suffice. Although there was no' reference to this fact, all the poems of the Kilmarnock Edition reappeared in the new edition, with occasional changes, it is true, in the texts, and the addition of eight new verses to "The Vision,"[4] but, in spite of the advice of anxious friends, nothing of the first edition had been omitted, nor had the general character of that volume been in any way modified. Of hitherto unpublished poems the new edition contained a total of twenty-two, including seven songs.[5] Only three of these belong to the Edinburgh period itself: the "Address to Edinburgh," the "Address to a Haggis," and the slight dedicatory stanzas written in a copy of Beattie's poems "To Miss Logan." The fragment of a ballad on the American War, "When Guilford Good," to the tune "Killiecrankie," is assigned by most editors to the year 1784. That is possible, but certain essential facts which would fix the date are not available.[6] The principal pieces in the new edition belong to the great creative years of 1785-86, and, indeed, for the most part, to the months between the appearance of the Kilmarnock Edition and the poet's departure for Edinburgh. From the spring of 1785 dates "Death and Doctor Hornbook," from the autumn of 1786 the poem dedicated to John Ballantine, "The Brigs of Ayr," based on Fergusson's "Plainstanes and Causey" and strongly influenced by Thomson; but in spite of its external dependence on its models rich in graphic descriptions of nature and happily executed allegories. The same period also produced the jocular elegy on "Tam Samson," who was still alive and pursued the pleasures of the chase with unabated vigour; "A Winter Night," an impressive variation on the theme of man's inhumanity to man; and, lastly, the farewell song: "The Gloomy Night is Gathering Fast." The poet's satirical attitude to Orthodoxy, its adherent throng and the intolerance of sanctimonious hypocrites, was represented by the keen-edged poem "The Ordination" (composed in the autumn of 1785 on the occasion of James Mackinlay's admission to the ministry in Kilmarnock); the improvisation, "The Calf," and

---

[4] *Cf.* the letter to Mrs. Dunlop, 15th Jan. 1787; Dunlop Corr., 7-10; Letters, 78.

[5] All of them printed in H. H., i, 191-257.

[6] See "Aldine Edition," i, 51; Ch. W., ii, 63; Ritter's "Quellenstudien," 53. Burns, who seems to have set store by the ballad, submitted it to Glencairn and Erskine before printing it (Ch. W., ii, 66), and also published it in the second volume of Johnson's "Museum," No. 101.

the "Address to the Unco Guid" (both 1786). A further group
contained religious poems, composed, as we have already seen,
under the influence of deep depression at the end of his sojourn
in Irvine.   Among the lyrics in the real sense of the word we have
"John Barleycorn" (1785), "My Nannie, O" (1783), "Green Grow
the Rashes, O" (1783), "Composed in Spring" (1783), and a drinking song, written perhaps during the Tarbolton period: "No
Churchman am I."   Thus the 1787 edition struck no new chords.
The most favourable criticism we can pass on the poems printed
in it for the first time is that they maintain the standard of the
Kilmarnock Edition.   Of any further development there is as yet
no sign.   It must be particularly noted that the wealth of Edinburgh impressions and the stimulating intercourse with so many
interesting men and women seem at first to have evoked neither
poetic achievement nor, as far as one can see, any kind of literary
plan for the future.

The rest of the work produced during that and the following
winter spent in Edinburgh only strengthens the impression that
in the new environment Burns was unable to continue in the direction which he had taken in the Kilmarnock Volume. He lacked
the inspiration, the strength, and the greatness which only contact
with the soil of his country gave him, and which the capital, with
all its beauty and all its historical associations, denied him. However much he knew himself related to Ramsay and Fergusson, he
felt no urge to continue their work, in so far as they were chroniclers
of Edinburgh life. Up till the spring of 1788 he composed in
Edinburgh and on journeys undertaken from there a number of
occasional poems, such as the lines on the Earl of Glencairn,[7] the
Elegy on the death of Sir James Hunter Blair,[8] the poem on the
death of Dundas,[9] Lord President of the Court of Session, "The
Humble Petition of Bruar Water,"[10] "Castle Gordon,"[11] and the
Jacobite "Birthday Ode for 31st December 1787."[12] In none of
these poems is there much to indicate the peculiar genius of their
author.   Yet there is one exception, and as such it is rather

---

[7] H. H., ii. 217-218.

[8] Ibid., 218-220.

[9] Ibid., 221-222.

[10] Ibid., i, 295-299.

[11] Ibid., ii, 60-61.

[12] Ibid., 157-159.

important.   In February 1787 Burns received a rhyming letter
from Mrs. Elizabeth Scott of Wauchope House in Roxburghshire.
Written in the vernacular, this letter begins by teasingly expressing
doubt as to the rustic origin of the author of the Kilmarnock
Poems, then regrets that the writer cannot have the privilege of
hastening to the poet, and of spending a happy hour or two in
listening to him reciting his "sangs and sonnets slee"; and she
concludes with the ingenuous remark that she would like to send
him a "marled plaid," to keep him warm at kirk and market,
adding:

> "Right wae that we're sae far frae ither,
> Yet proud I am to ca' ye brither."[13]

The homely simplicity of this letter must have affected Burns as
the sound of his native tongue affects an exile. His heart filled.
The sincerity of his answer "To the Guidewife of Wauchope
House," dated March 1787,[14] coming as it does from the bustle of
Edinburgh life, gives one the impression that the writing of it was
to the poet like drawing a deep, refreshing breath. His native
Ayrshire rose before his eyes; he saw Mount Oliphant, his youth
with its great, unsatisfied longings, and his first love, Nelly
Kilpatrick, under whose sway the restless urge to "do something"
took on definite poetic shape.[15] It was there—and this is the
answer to Mrs. Scott's letter—that he learned to sing. The next
stanza is devoted purely to the glorification of womankind, the
fifth and last to thanking and blessing the guidwife. As for
the plaid, he will not fail to call for it and to wear it with greater
pride than if it were made of ermine or of imperial purple. It
needed only the right touch to make his lyre resound in the old,
grand way. Nor must we forget that, in spite of the apparent
unproductiveness of this period, it was in the last weeks of his
first Edinburgh winter that the seeds of a new work, worthy of his
highest art, fell into Burns's mind—a work that occupied his
thoughts from then until his death. His friendship with James
Johnson, the engraver and music-seller, who was at that time busy
with the production of one of the collections of songs which were

---

13 See the Epistle in Ch. W., ii, 48.
14 H. H., ii, 104-106. The metre is that of the 14-lined stanza of the "Epistle
to Davie."
15 See above, pp. 18-20.

so much in demand ("The Scots Musical Museum"), gave him the idea of revising, purifying, and reshaping the complete treasury of Scottish folk-song. We shall discuss this plan in detail in chapter IX, and show how it developed.

With the publishing of the volume of poems in 1787, the object of Burns's sojourn in Edinburgh was attained, and he was obliged to consider the question of his future. His instinctive answer to this question was, as we have already heard: "Back to the plough!" He thought of taking a new farm, preferably not in the immediate vicinity of the haunts which held so many painful memories for him. At this point an offer came to his aid: soon after his arrival in Edinburgh an admirer of his poems, one Patrick Miller, a well-to-do landowner, who had bought the estate of Dalswinton on the Nith, near Dumfries, in 1785, had offered him the lease of a farm under what he considered to be favourable conditions. Burns was doubtful from the very beginning. He thought that Miller was not sufficiently experienced in agricultural affairs, and that, as he wrote on 14th January 1787 to John Ballantine, it might easily happen that the proposed bargain, made with the best of intentions, would ruin him. Nevertheless he had already arranged to go to Dumfries in the following May and see the farm in question.[16] Other motives now urged him to take this journey, which promised to be both useful and pleasantly instructive. On 22nd March 1787 Burns wrote to Mrs. Dunlop that his most exalted ambition was to be the bard of Scotland, the singer of Scottish scenes and Scottish story. He knew

"no dearer aim than . . . unplagu'd with the routine of business . . . to make leisurely pilgrimages through Caledonia; to sit on the fields of her battles; to wander on the romantic banks of her rivers; and to muse by the stately towers or venerable ruins, once the honored abodes of her heroes."[17]

These sentimental travel plans were now to be realized for the space of a few weeks at least. At the last moment they were further encouraged by his newly formed resolution to collaborate in the work of collecting the national songs of Scotland. Burns wrote to Dr. Moore on 23rd April:

"I leave Edinburgh in the course of ten days or a fortnight, and,

---

[16] Letters, 77.
[17] Dunlop Corr., 14; Letters, 90.

after a few pilgrimages over some of the classic ground of Caledonia, Cowden Knowes, Banks of Yarrow, Tweed, &c., I shall return to my rural shades, in all likelihood never more to quit them!"[18]

On 5th May Burns started out on the first of the tours which were to enliven the next few months. This time he travelled on horseback, in the company of a young law student, Robert Ainslie, whose precocious intelligence and cheerful nature he probably found equally attractive.[19] The goal of this pilgrimage was the Border country, rich in tales of battle and in song. Ainslie's native place, Berrywell, near Duns, in Berwickshire, served the two as temporary headquarters and starting-point for a number of excursions, of which Burns has given a graphic and pleasant account in a diary that covers their activities till the first of June, the poet noting his impressions day by day in short but vivid phrases.[20] The two travellers crossed the Tweed at Coldstream, and Burns, stirred by strong emotions, for the first time found himself on English soil. He visited Kelso, was charmed by the romantic, delightful situation of Jedburgh, did not forget to call upon his correspondent, Mrs. Scott, and her husband at Wauchope, which was in the neighbourhood, and found that Mr. Scott had "exactly the figure and face commonly given to Sancho Panza." He then betook himself by way of the valley of the Ettrick and the Tweed to Melrose, Dryburgh, and Selkirk; saw the places celebrated in folk-song, Traquair, Elibanks and Elibraes, Cowden Knowes, and Earlston, the birthplace and home of the famous Thomas the Rhymer, with the ruins of his castle, and returned thence to Berrywell on 15th May. Other excursions brought him to the sea-coast, to Berwick, Eyemouth, and Dunbar. In Eyemouth there was a festive meeting of the local lodge, at which Burns and Ainslie were made "Royal Arch Masons." Ainslie had to pay a guinea as admission fee; Burns was admitted gratis, on account of his "remarkable poetical genius," the company considering themselves honoured by having a man of such shining abilities as one of their companions. All sorts of philandering interrupt the account of his journeys. In Jedburgh

---

[18] Letters, 97.

[19] See Marshall, "A Winter with Robert Burns," 152-154.

[20] Ch. W., ii, 102-119. MS. now in the possession of Lt.-Col. Sir John Murray, London. Cf. J. De Lancey Ferguson, Burns's Journal of his Border Tour. Publ. Mod. Lang. Assoc. of America, vol. xlix (1934), 1107-1115, and Scots Magazine, January 1935.

he was bewitched by Miss Isabella Lindsay, who benefited from being surrounded by ill-natured old women and spinsters. "I somehow or other," the diary tells us, "get hold of Miss Lindsay's arm. My heart is thawed into melting pleasure after being so long frozen up in the Greenland bay of indifference amid the noise and nonsense of Edinburgh"; and a *nota bene* adds: "The poet within a point and a half of being d—mnably in love.—I am afraid my bosom is still nearly as much tinder as ever!" The farewell from Jedburgh was, therefore, accompanied by "some melancholy, disagreeable sensations." Ainslie's sister Rachel roused similar feelings. "How well-bred, how frank, how good she is!" writes Burns. "Charming Rachel! May thy bosom never be wrung by the evils of this life of sorrows, or by the villainy of this world's sons!" (Some of these blessings which Burns called down on his fair friends strike us as being but seldom the outcome of unmitigated paternal feelings.) Numerous entries in the diary show how Burns paid the greatest attention to the state of the soil and the conditions of agriculture. He was personally affected by the experience of being present at the "roup" or auction of an unfortunate farmer's stock.

> "Rigid economy and decent industry," he exclaims on this occasion, "do you preserve me from being the principal *dramatis persona* in such a scene of horror!"

On 25th May he took leave of his friend Ainslie, and two days afterwards set out on the second part of his tour with two gentlemen named Thomas Hood and William Ker. They crossed the Tweed, visited Alnwick, with the Castle of the Dukes of Northumberland, and Warkworth, with its hermitage, celebrated in one of Thomas Percy's ballads, and then continued their way through Morpeth, Newcastle, Hexham, Wardrew, and Longtown, where Hood and Ker left Burns, who went on to Carlisle. The diary breaks off here, with the account of some frivolous love-affair, and the information that the poet rode along the coast to Annan, and so reached the Scottish border—probably on 1st June. On 4th June he was presented with the freedom of the burgh of Dumfries.[21] From there he took advantage of the opportunity to view the farms

---

[21] Ch. W., ii, 121.—We may mention here that altogether no less than six Royal Burghs conferred their "Freedom" on Burns, viz. Jedburgh, Dumfries, Dumbarton, Linlithgow, Sanquhar and Lochmaben. For last-named see Letters, 374. (Information kindly furnished by John M'Vie.)

on Miller's estate of Dalswinton, but did not come to any definite decision. Then he leisurely made his way up the Nith towards home, and on 9th June, after an absence of more than six months, reached Mauchline, his family, his friends and adversaries.

Burns had gone away poor and dishonoured. He returned famous, with money in his pocket, and was at once made the recipient, in Mauchline, of—to his mind—superabundant honours, even by those who had formerly held aloof from him. When he visited the Armours he was shown there, too, a "mean, servile compliance" which disgusted him, but which resulted in a renewed and intimate friendship with Jean, whom he had never wholly forgotten. In this case the compliance which he met with seemed less contemptible! His mood during the period that followed was on the whole melancholy, serious, and dissatisfied. The unsettled future weighed upon him. The natural aimlessness of his existence oppressed him. He was much preoccupied with Milton's "Satan," with whose "dauntless magnanimity, intrepid, unyielding independence, desperate daring and noble defiance of hardship" he would fain identify himself in mind. He felt himself antagonistic to mankind, which, as he wrote to William Nicol, he had never thought very capable of anything generous; but the stateliness of the patricians in Edinburgh, and the servility of his plebeian brethren (who formerly eyed him askance) since he returned home, had nearly put him out of conceit altogether with his species.[22]

A short excursion to the South-west Highlands, which he undertook towards the end of the month, seems to have had a beneficial effect upon him. From the very scrappy data at our disposal we gather that he visited Inveraray (where the Duke of Argyll's residence is situated), Arrochar, Loch Long, Loch Lomond and Dumbarton; but he was already back in Mauchline by the beginning of July, in a sorry state because of a fall with his mare Jenny Geddes, on whose back he had tried an impromptu race with a Highlander on Loch Lomondside. The result was that he had to postpone for several weeks a journey to Edinburgh which he had intended to make.[23] In Mauchline he lived, according to his own words, in the old way, rhyming, carefully attending to his masonic duties, idle, aimless and, consequently, reproaching himself for his

[22] Letters, 114.
[23] Letters, 117 and 119.

squandered life. It was in this mood, "to divert his spirits in this miserable fog of ennui," that he wrote the autobiographical letter to Dr. Moore which it has been necessary to mention so often in the earlier chapters of this book. Dated 2nd August, it was given to Mrs. Dunlop to revise, was sharply and strikingly criticised by her, and was not dispatched to the addressee until 23rd September.[24] A few days later Burns left Mauchline and arrived back in Edinburgh on 7th August.

If it was business with Creech that took the poet back to the capital, we have no indication as to how it was dispatched; nor was his stay in the city a long one. On 25th August, accompanied by William Nicol, he began the third and most impressive tour of this unsettled year, this time making use of a carriage. His travels took him to the Highlands, and lasted until 16th September. A diary, similar in design to the previous one, gives an account of the incidents of the journey.[25] This time there was no practical purpose to be served, such as he had had in mind when visiting Dalswinton during his Border tour: his chief aims were to study the country and the people, to seek inspiration, and to steep himself in the spiritual atmosphere of places of historical and literary interest. Observation of the nature of the soil, the conditions, and the culture of the rural population, again gives rise to various striking entries as, for example, that made at the beginning of the diary, when he was traversing West Lothian:

> "The more elegance and luxury among the farmers, I always observe, in equal proportion, the rudeness and stupidity of the peasantry. This remark I have made all over the Lothians, Merse, Roxburgh, &c. For this, among other reasons, I think that a man of romantic taste—a 'Man of Feeling,'—will be better pleased with the poverty, but intelligent minds, of the peasantry in Ayrshire . . . than the opulence of a club of Merse farmers, when at the same time he considers the vandalism of *their* plough-folks, &c. I carry this idea so far that an uninclosed, half-improven country is to me actually more agreeable, and gives me more pleasure as a prospect, than a country cultivated like a garden."

24 Dunlop Corr., 27-32; Letters, 124.
25 See Ch. W., ii, 149-176. Fascimile Ed. with Transcript, by J. C. Ewing; London and Glasgow, 1927. The MS. is now the property of Mr. Wm. K. Bixby, of St. Louis, Mo. The passages quoted on p. 163 are not in the Bixby MS They were first printed by J. G. Lockhart (1828) and are not above suspicion. *Cf.* Snyder, pp. 244 and 254, note 22. He thinks that they have been faked by Cunningham. I suspend judgment.

No wonder that the holder of such views failed to make a success of the cultivation of his own farm!

Travelling via Linlithgow and Falkirk, the poet reached the battlefield of Bannockburn, where Bruce defeated Edward II in 1314. Here Burns's patriotism burst into flame:

> "Here no Scot," he writes, "can pass uninterested—I fancy to myself that I see my gallant, heroic countrymen coming o'er the hill, and down upon the plunderers of their country, the murderers of their fathers; noble revenge and just hate glowing in every vein, striding more and more eagerly, as they approach the oppressive, insulting, blood-thirsty foe! I see them meet in gloriously-triumphant congratulation on the victorious field, exulting in their heroic royal leader, and rescued liberty and independence!"

The seeds of famous later songs, "The Song of Death" and especially "Scots wha hae wi' Wallace bled," are plainly to be discerned in these patriotic outbursts. From Stirling and its Castle he proceeded in a northerly direction through Crieff and Glen Almond, past Ossian's grave, Taymouth and Aberfeldy to Blair Atholl, where he was hospitably received in the castle by the family of the Duke of Atholl and entertained in great and brilliant society (31st August and 1st September). On this occasion he made the acquaintance of Robert Graham of Fintry, a friendship which was to be of great service to him later. The happy mood of these days found expression in a revival of his joy in writing poetry (witness "The Birks of Aberfeldie" and "The Humble Petition of Bruar Water"). On 4th September he reached Inverness, after a journey through wild Highland scenery with snow-topped mountains. The diary specially mentions the scenes with which he was familiar from "Macbeth": Castle Cawdor, where Duncan was murdered and where Burns was shown the bed in which the king fell a victim to the traitor; he was also told that the heath where Macbeth was said to have met the witches was still so haunted that the country people were afraid to pass it by night. From Inverness we can, by means of his brief notes, follow his route through the counties of Nairn, Elgin, Banff, and Aberdeen. Special mention is made of the friendly reception given him at the castle of the Duke and Duchess of Gordon: "The Duke," says the entry for 7th September, "makes me happier than ever great man did—noble, princely, yet mild, condescending and affable; gay and kind; the Duchess witty and sensible—God bless them!" To his vexation

the visit which promised so much had to be prematurely broken
off because of the resentment of Nicol, who felt himself slighted
and kept in the background. In Aberdeen a chance encounter
with Bishop John Skinner, son of the writer of several popular
Scottish songs which Burns prized very highly, led to a short but
important correspondence between the two poets. Skinner, using
the familiar stanza of the Epistles, expressed his regret at not having
seen Burns. Burns answered in prose, and this form was kept up
in the succeeding letters, which turn mainly on the supply of texts
for Johnson's "Museum."[26] When Burns reached Kincardineshire,
he was in his father's native county, where there still lived numerous
relatives of his, for instance his cousin James Burness from
Montrose, whom he met on 10th September in Stonehaven, and
two aunts, Jean and Isabel, "still alive, and hale old women." The
last stages of the return journey, Arbroath, Perth with Strathearn,
famous in song, Dundee and Queensferry, seemed to him scarcely
worth mentioning after the elevating impressions which the Highlands had left upon him. On 16th September, he was once more
in Edinburgh; on the 17th, he wrote to his brother Gilbert in a
letter summarizing the tour: "warm as I was from Ossian's
country, where I had seen his very grave, what cared I for fisher-
towns and fertile Carses?"[27] And in a letter dated 28th September
to Patrick Miller of Dalswinton, he spoke of his Highland journey
as having been "perfectly inspiring." He hoped, he said, to have
laid in a good stock of new poetic ideas from it.[28]

Thus began the autumn and the second winter in Edinburgh.
Burns now lived in the New Town with his friend William
Cruikshank, in St. James's Square. Much of his time was taken
up with tedious squabblings with Creech over what was due to
him, and his mind swayed in painful indecision between two
possible careers: entering the Excise service and taking over the
lease of a farm from Patrick Miller. We shall dispense with
giving details which, in view of the facts communicated in the
previous chapter, may appear superfluous. We can also only refer
here in passing to another short visit which Burns paid during
the first weeks of October to the district of Stirling, Harvieston, and

[26] Skinner, "Poetical Pieces," Edinburgh, 1809, pp. 23-36; Letters, 147.

[27] Letters, 137.

[28] Ibid., 139.

Ochtertyre.[29]   The poet's environment in Edinburgh had not
changed, but the lustre of novelty had worn off both for Burns himself and for the sensation-loving society which had received him
a year before with such applause. However much Burns may
have been animated by such motives, there is no evidence to show
that his second visit to the city was due to any longing on his
part for the companionship of the merry, roystering friends he had
made there. Quite apart from the question of choosing a career—
in settling which it was to his advantage to be near his patrons—
there are plenty of reasons to account for it, and in considering these
we must not under-estimate the importance of the work of collecting and preparing the songs for the second volume of Johnson's
"Museum," a work in which Burns was eagerly participating.
Nevertheless, the result of these months was unsatisfactory both
from the artistic and from the human point of view, and Creech
cannot be exonerated from the grave reproach of having, by his
dilatory handling of the financial issues that lay between him and
the poet, kept Burns in an atmosphere which for him of all people
held this particular danger: as the months passed, it alienated him
more and more from his true, natural self. Herein lies the pre-
carious and unpleasant part of his connection with Mrs. Agnes
M'Lehose (the Clarinda of numerous letters), which is the dominating feature of this period.

At the beginning of December 1787 Burns was still anxious to
leave Edinburgh, for some time at least. He paid farewell visits
to his friends, and on one of these occasions, at the house of a
revenue officer named Nimmo, he first met Mrs. M'Lehose, who,
being herself a poetess,[30] had eagerly desired to be introduced to
him. Burns accepted an invitation to tea at the lady's house, but
Fate held up her finger in warning: on the eve of the appointed
day, Burns fell from his carriage (he is said to have been the
victim of his driver's intoxication), sustained a severe injury to his
knee, and found himself chained to his room for weeks. With
expressions of regret at the postponement of the engagement, mutual
assurance of friendship, the hope of a speedy meeting, and many
fine phrases, there now began a correspondence which for a time

    29 Ch. W., ii, 187-197.
    30 See John D. Ross, "The Poems of Clarinda"; Stirling, 1929. The booklet
also contains a biographical sketch of the heroine.

monopolized the best part of Burns's mental powers, and formed, as Scott once said, "the most extraordinary mixture of sense and nonsense, and of love human and divine, that was ever exposed to the eye of the world."[31] We may add: a no less extraordinary mixture of truth and falsehood, gravity and humour, whose heterogeneous elements cannot be disentangled from one another. But though both letter-writers wore masks, as it were, when dealing with each other (they clothed themselves, under the pastoral names of Sylvander and Clarinda, in the garment of Arcadian innocence), the discerning reader cannot long remain in doubt as to the true nature of this friendship. When Burns made the acquaintance of Mrs. M'Lehose, his love-thirsty temperament had again passed through a spell of frozen inactivity, and at once flamed up like tinder; while Mrs. M'Lehose found herself in a situation in which even a less fascinating personality might have proved dangerous to her.

Born in April 1759, Mrs. M'Lehose was at that time in her twenty-ninth year, and was thus almost the same age as Burns. We are told that she was a beauty of a somewhat voluptuous type, elegant, blythe and educated, though her culture was, perhaps, not of the most profound. She came of a good Glasgow family: her father, Andrew Craig, was a surgeon, and her parentage on her mother's side also pointed to names of rank and importance. Her experience of matrimony had been unfortunate. In her eighteenth year she had, after a romantic courtship, married a frivolous but captivating lawyer, James M'Lehose, and borne him four children. As early as 1780 she found herself obliged to leave her brutal husband, whose path led rapidly downhill to the debtor's prison. After his family had liberated him from jail, he went the same way in 1784 as Burns meant to go two years later, to escape from his manifold difficulties: he became a planter in Jamaica. Though he made quite a success of the business, he took not the slightest interest in his wife and children, who were thrown upon the kindness of relatives, and who had eked out their existence in the most modest circumstances, first in Glasgow, then, since 1782, in Edinburgh. Such was the grey life of this disillusioned, free, and yet fettered woman when Burns entered it as a great new experience.

---

[31] "Letters of Sir Walter Scott," ed. Grierson, ii, 5-7 (to Lady Abercorn, 22nd Jan. 1808).

The consequences of the already-mentioned accident restricted their friendship to an exchange of ideas by means of letters until the beginning of January 1788. The tone of these letters was at first fairly calm and natural, the writers confining themselves to mutual sounding and to the business of getting to know each other better. Gentle hints of the poet's growing passion were rebuked by Mrs. M'Lehose with a reference to her wedded state, and cleverly excused by Burns as involuntary expressions of his deep sympathy with the unhappy, admirable woman. The pastoral names, Sylvander and Clarinda, first appeared about Christmas, languishing poems were exchanged, and Burns's lines contained a first clear confession of love, which his friend had called forth by a few playful stanzas.[32] It is true that the conventional character of the lyric might leave us in doubt as to the poet's true sentiments, but this doubt must disappear when we consider a passage such as appeared in a long letter of 28th December:

> "I do love you," he said there, "if possible still better for having so fine a taste and turn for Poesy.—I have again gone wrong in my usual unguarded way, but you may erase the word, and put esteem, respect, or any other tame Dutch expression you please in its place."[33]

And two days later he confessed to his old friend and confidant, Richard Brown:

> "Almighty Love still 'reigns and revels' in my bosom; and I am at this moment ready to hang myself for a young Edinr. widow, who has wit and beauty more murderously fatal than the assassinating stiletto of the Sicilian banditti, or the poisoned arrow of the savage African."[34]

No further evidence is needed. Burns, as was his way, goaded his emotions to an ever greater state of passion, he wrote and talked himself deeper and deeper into love with Clarinda, all the more so when, after his recovery in January, he was privileged to see and to converse with his beloved frequently in society and alone. For Burns, however, to love meant to desire, and to leave untried no method by which he might reach his goal, either by working cleverly on the thoughts and emotions of the woman he loved, or by the irresistible force of his personality. Of course, we must not

---

[32] H. H., ii, 112-114; 368.
[33] Letters, 166.
[34] Ibid., 168.

view the letters to Clarinda from this standpoint alone. They are
not devoid of greatness, and contain a certain amount of valuable
self-revelation. Burns speaks of Pride and Passion as the great
constituent elements of his character;[35] he makes no secret of his
hatred for presbyterian bigotry[36] but asserts his belief in religion,[37]
and in an important letter of 8th January 1788, makes a full and
formal confession of faith, according to which the pure, true, and
charitable man, though he does not *merit* Heaven, yet has the best
chance of attaining eternal happiness.[38] Though he seldom touches
upon literary questions, we do find an occasional reference to them.
He speaks of Goethe's "Werther," mentions that he is revising
Clarinda's poetical effusions for publication in Johnson's
"Museum," and expresses his love of quotations, with which his
letters are liberally sprinkled,[39] but which revert persistently and
cunningly to flatteries, avowals of pure desire, confessions of love,
and guarded passionate hopes.

As befits the social sphere in which Clarinda had grown up and
in which she continually moved, her letters sound in general easier
and less forced than those of Burns. The tone which he had to
make violent efforts to reach came naturally to her by reason of
her parentage and breeding. In her letters a slight gleam of
humour (wholly lacking in Burns on this occasion) here and there
breaks through the heavy clouds of shrewd counsel and religious
exhortation. It also seems certain that the whole experience meant
more to Mrs. M'Lehose than it did to Burns. For her it held a
new hope of life, though that hope was for the moment only too
obviously circumscribed: she dreamed of re-erecting the shattered
fabric of her happiness by the side of this man of genius, whom she
believed she could comfort and refine, and whose soul she thought
she could save. That Burns, when he talked of affinity of souls,
desired the woman in her, was not for one moment hidden from
her. On 5th January he presented her with the autobiographical
letter which he had written for Dr. Moore. In her reply Clarinda
expressed herself in the following characteristic sentence: "One

[35] Letters, 166.
[36] *Ibid.*, 176 and 200.
[37] *Ibid.*, 170.
[38] *Ibid.*, 174.
[39] See, for example, the letters of 14th and 19th Jan. 1788: 178 and 181.

thing I am afraid of: there is not a trace of friendship towards a female: now, in the cause of Clarinda, this is the only 'consummation devoutly to be wished.' "[40]   And a few days later she wrote, chiefly pointing out the dangerous position into which any thoughtless action on her part would put her and her children: "I am your friend, Sylvander: take care lest virtue demand even friendship as a sacrifice."   In the same letter she wished she could see Sylvander married: "You are so formed, that you cannot be happy without a tender attachment"; and she concluded by saying: "Be wise, be prudent, and be happy!"[41]   A good wish, to realize which no one was less fitted than the fire-brand to whom it was directed! Her difficulty was to keep Burns within the bounds of friendship without frightening him away by being too unapproachable; to remain the desired woman, interesting and inviolate, and yet to sympathize with the passionate man in all the impulses of his ardent temperament; to remain calm and to keep on writing, though well-wishing advisers already saw through the dangerous game, and trembled for Clarinda's peace of mind, which was long since gone.[42] The tone of the letters grew more and more intense and heated, and when Burns left Edinburgh about the middle of February 1788, for reasons of which he had made no secret to his beloved, Clarinda thought that she was sure of him.

For Burns, however, there had dawned an anxious time, full of important decisions that put an end to his life in Edinburgh and forced him to choose between Clarinda and Jean; and in spite of all his extravagant utterances, all his vows and all his praise of Clarinda, it was Clarinda who was sacrificed to his resolutions.

The severance began with an agitated, almost despairing letter, dated 22nd January 1788, of which only a fragment has been preserved,[43] to his intimate friend, Miss Margaret Chalmers: "God have mercy on me!" he wrote, "a poor, d-mned, incautious, duped, unfortunate fool!"   It could hardly have been his vexation alone at a repeated refusal on the part of Creech, who always promised but never kept his word, that drove him to such language; nor was it likely to have been a rumour that the latter was insolvent; but

[40] Ch. W., ii, 243.
[41] Ibid., 249.
[42] See Ch. W., ii, 250, 270, 277.
[43] Letters, 185; cf. also Dunlop Corr., 40-41 (letter written 21st Jan. 1788).

a report might have reached his ears which called the serious
duplicity of his conduct urgently before the bar of his conscience:
Jean Armour, with whom he had resumed the old relations during
the summer weeks spent in Mauchline, was again expecting to
become a mother, and had been driven from home by her parents
in the middle of winter. Life itself with its dire necessities was
preparing to put an end to the dalliance and philandering and the
unhealthy exchange (which had gone on for weeks) of half-true
sentimental outpourings, and was summoning him to action and to
duty. Two letters, one to Robert Graham of Fintry (January
1788), the other to the Earl of Glencairn (1st February 1788),
announce his resolution to seek a post under the Board of Excise.[44]
The recollection of his father's fate and the news of the bad state
of his brother's affairs at Mossgiel seem for the moment to have
unfavourably affected his thoughts of taking on the lease of a farm.
In spite of his doubts, however, he did not abandon this second plan.
On 18th February he left Edinburgh, met Brown and his own
brother William in Glasgow, reached his home at Mossgiel on the
23rd, and set out a few days later, accompanied by an experienced
friend, John Tennant of Glenconner, to Dumfriesshire, to visit
Patrick Miller. The impression which he got there was on the
whole favourable, and led, on 13th March, to his taking the lease
of Ellisland, a step that decided his whole future. A temporary
agreement with Creech seems to have been reached shortly afterwards, and Burns was finally, according to a letter of 31st March,
turned over to the Tarbolton Excise officer, James Findlay, for
instruction during a period of at least six weeks. The certificate of
proficiency thus attained allowed its holder at any time to enter the
Excise service, and meant for Burns that he had something to fall
back on if his new farming venture should fail. Apart from this,
the course of instruction kept him in and near Mauchline until
immediately before he entered his farm, and thus did its part in
severing the link which bound him to Clarinda, and in uniting
him, who could not live without the love of woman, permanently
with Jean Armour. The transition from Clarinda, the "fair
Empress of the Poet's Soul and Queen of Poetesses," to Jean, "the
bonnie Lassie, the Lassie I lo'e best," is psychologically of great
interest: it is entirely in keeping with Burns's manner of shaping

---

[44] Letters, 172 and 192.

his life, and has called forth a great deal of moral censure. To understand it, we must remember that the estimable virtue of conjugal fidelity was one of the human qualities with which Burns had not been endowed by nature. Rather did he reveal in this connection too the inconstancy of his poetic temperament. Change of air did not agree with his love. It could not stand the test of distance. It was more general than individual. It is certain that he was no less passionately in love with Clarinda than with Jean, but Clarinda suffered the disadvantage of being tied to Edinburgh, while the poet, having escaped from the city, very soon—one might almost say from sheer necessity—stripped off the mask of Sylvander and became Robert Burns again. On 23rd February, immediately after his arrival at Mossgiel, he presented his little son with a garment which Clarinda had made for him. That very same day he went in search of Jean, who, "banished like a martyr—forlorn, destitute, and friendless," had found shelter in the house of William Muir, at Tarbolton Mill. Burns described the impression made upon him by this meeting in a letter to Clarinda, in the following words:

> "Now for a little news that will please you.—I, this morning as I came home, called for a certain woman.—I am disgusted with her; I cannot endure her! I, while my heart smote me for the prophanity, tried to compare her with my Clarinda: 'twas setting the expiring glimmer of a farthing taper beside the cloudless glory of the meridian sun.—Here was tasteless insipidity, vulgarity of soul, and mercenary fawning; there polished good sense, heaven-born genius, and the most generous, the most delicate, the most tender Passion.—I have done with her, and she with me!"[45]

The next document referring to the meeting is a letter to Robert Ainslie, written on 3rd March 1788, the contents of which reveal such downright, elementary, unsurpassable vulgarity that one can understand the editors who have covered the greater part of it with the mantle of brotherly love. It describes the sensual favours the poet has enjoyed after he has extracted a promise from Jean that never and on the persuasion of no person will she "attempt any claim on him as a husband." Nevertheless, he provided for the girl, reconciled her with her mother, and established her comfortably in a room in Mauchline.[46] There, on the same day as

---

[45] Letters, 210.
[46] *Ibid.,* 215.

Burns dispatched the letter to Ainslie, Jean was again delivered
of twins, who did not survive, however. Burns did not feel that
there was˙any immediate necessity for informing Clarinda of this
event. On the other hand, in a letter written to Brown on 7th
March, thanking him for enquiring after Jean, he quotes Othello's
words:

> "Excellent   wretch!
> Perdition catch my soul but I do love thee!"[47]

Four weeks later, after another visit to Edinburgh, a few lines to
Peggy Chalmers hinted at sacrifices which certain circumstances had
obliged him to make,[48] and on 28th April he wrote to James Smith:
"Mrs. Burns ('tis only her private designation) begs her best com-
pliments to you."[49] He had made Jean his wife, in Gavin
Hamilton's presence and without the aid of the Kirk, and after the
decisive step was taken, felt a sense of relief and of satisfaction with
himself and his choice.

But what became of Clarinda and how did she bear her great
disappointment?

We learn nothing about the matter for a long time, until we see
Burns defending himself on 9th March 1789 in a calm, proud, and
outspoken letter, against the measureless reproaches of the woman
he had deserted.[50] The estrangement lasted until the late autumn
of 1791, when a meeting, and as far as was possible, a reconciliation,
took place in Edinburgh. At that time Mrs. M'Lehose, having
nothing more to expect from Burns, had decided to patch up the
fragments of her matrimonial life in Jamaica. The 6th of December
remained undyingly in her memory and in Burns's as the day on
which the poet and she took farewell of each other for the last time.
Mrs. M'Lehose, however, again found herself completely deceived
in her expectations. James M'Lehose had become hopelessly dissolute in the colonies, and the delicate woman could no more
endure his habits than she could the tropical climate of the West
Indies. She returned to Edinburgh the same year (1792) as she
had set out, but refrained from resuming her relations with Burns
in any way whatever. Two letters of the poet to Clarinda[51] and

---

[47] *Ibid.*, 220.
[48] *Ibid.*, 235.
[49] *Ibid.*, 237.
[50] Letters, 320.
[51] March 1793 and June 1794; Letters, 544 and 629.

a group of passionate songs, among them "Ae fond kiss, and then we sever!"[52] mark the end of this entanglement fraught with so many hopes and disappointments. They form the epitaph of a love which was already dead when in the spring of 1788 the spires of Edinburgh sank from Burns's sight in the mist; when he married Jean Armour, and, filled with new hope, with the balm of healing in his soul, again, after a period of rich and varied experience, put his hand to the long-neglected plough.

---

[52] Dec. 1791; H. H., iii, 105-106; in Johnson's *Museum*, iv, No. 347, to the tune "Rory Dall's Port." All Songs referring to Clarinda in Dick, *Songs of R. B.* Nos. 76-85.

PART THREE: DUMFRIESSHIRE

1788-1796

Chapter VIII

ELLISLAND

1788-1791

ELLISLAND was a poet's choice, an idyll on the west bank of the Nith. The farm buildings lay—and still lie—some few field-lengths distant from the Glasgow road, a slight rise in the ground separating them from that main artery of traffic. The dwelling-house stands on a slope above the gracefully meandering Nith, which, overhung with sturdy old trees, now glides through dense copsewood, now winds through meadows, pasture, and fields. For a short distance downstream, a shady path runs alongside it. Right opposite the farm, on the more fertile eastern bank of the river, lived Patrick Miller, the laird, on his estate of Dalswinton.[1] Up-stream, Burns could reach in about a quarter of an hour the boundaries of Friars' Carse, the estate of his friend Robert Riddell of Glenriddell, and the spacious park to which he had access at any time by means of a key which had been placed at his disposal. Coming from Ellisland, his path lay through quiet woods. A few minutes' further walk through moss and fern brought him to a hermitage, erected in the sentimental spirit of the century, and welcomed by the poet as a sanctuary in which to dream and meditate. Riddell's manor-house was situated some distance away, amid green lawns, on the banks of the Nith. To the north, the sturdy stone bridge of Auldgirth, which Carlyle's father had helped to build, forms the nearest means of crossing the river; to the south, near the mouth of the Cluden, on a slight ridge, rise the slender red ruins of the much-visited Benedictine Abbey of Lin-cluden. Ellisland is about six miles distant from Dumfries, that compact, busy town, "Queen of the South," as its inhabitants call it with justifiable pride. It is swept by the sea-breeze that drives the tide before it across the broad marshes, from the Solway Firth,

---

[1] For Patrick Miller, see C. Carswell's "Life of Burns," p. 265 and following. For her account of P. M., Mrs. Carswell had access to family papers. There is also a fine portrait of Miller, by Nasmyth, facing p. 342.

into which the Nith flows. The wider outlook from Ellisland is bounded all round by ranges of hills of moderate height. The general character of the landscape is peaceful and pastoral, without the exhilarating—and in a way disquieting—wide expanse of the horizon which we remember from Mossgiel. In one respect, however, Ellisland and its environs surpassed the poet's previous home: they were richer in historical memories. Various circles of stones of uncertain antiquity in the neighbourhood of the farm were considered by antiquarians of the eighteenth century to be Druid shrines; the monks, whose activity is recalled by the name "Friars' Carse," were friars of Melrose, belonging to the same community that owned the property in Mauchline with which Burns was familiar; the mansion-house of Dalswinton was situated close to the ruins of the castle of John of Badenoch, the "Red Comyn," who had been stabbed as a traitor by Robert the Bruce in Greyfriars Church in Dumfries; in the churchyard at Dunscore Burns could see the grave of that wild persecutor of the Covenanters, Sir Robert Grierson of Lag, of whose ungodly life and death many a grisly tale was told; the Wallaces, the Maxwells, the Crichtons, the Kirkpatricks, and the Douglases were connected with the history of the countryside; the Solway and the Cheviot Hills to the north-east of it recalled, by mighty ruins of castle and convent, fierce Border families, tragic stories and deeds of outlawry and heroism. The shade of the unhappy Scottish queen, Mary Stuart, also haunts this district, in whose mellow beauty Burns, after the exciting, and, on the whole, unsatisfactory years in Edinburgh now, encouraged by faithful friends, sought peace, security of life for himself and his family, and inspiration for new poetic production.

The terms of the agreement between Burns and Patrick Miller, who undoubtedly had his welfare at heart, seemed favourable to the poet in every respect. It was a long lease, divided, however, into four periods of nineteen years, the rent for the first three years to be £50 per annum, and £70 thereafter. Besides this, Miller undertook to furnish the sum of £300 for fencing and planting, and in particular for erecting a new dwelling-house and new farm buildings.[2] Burns, however, had grown wiser by experience and no longer based his hopes exclusively on the working of the farm.

---

[2] Documents reprinted by Snyder, App. C., pp. 503-510. Original in possession of Mr. Oliver R. Barrett.

After his course of instruction under Findlay was completed in the spring of 1788, he had the right of entry at any time to the Excise, and he had determined, if need be, to avail himself instantly of this possibility, which offered a modest but assured income. He also had in hand, after settling up with Creech, a sum of about £450.[3] This, however, was reduced by £150, lent without interest to his brother Gilbert, who was once more struggling to avert failure at Mossgiel. This good deed done to his family gave him the same inward satisfaction as his marriage to Jean Armour had done. The marriage had, by the way, been confirmed in Mauchline by William Auld, after he had duly admonished the guilty pair for their repeated transgressions. There had to be a fine, so Mr. Burns, to whose discretion the assessment was left, was pleased to put a guinea into the poor-box.

Such were the external and internal conditions under which Burns took over Ellisland. A new phase of life seemed to be beginning, and he hailed it with courage, if without exaggerated hope. He was now in his twenty-ninth year, in full possession of his mental and physical powers. The crown of fame shed a halo round him. When he again put his hand to the plough, he was fully conscious of the expectations that rested upon him. His material needs assured, he wished to do justice to them and to himself. Secure of a livelihood, he would consecrate the rest of his days to the Muses: thus he sums up his future hopes in an important letter to Moore.[4]

When Burns entered his farm in the middle of June 1788, he came alone, for confusion still reigned at Ellisland. The buildings agreed upon were being erected, and he was obliged to seek shelter in a miserable, tumble-down hovel, situated a little downstream from his property, and belonging to his predecessor at Ellisland, one David Kelly. The wretchedness of this abode throws some light on the state in which the whole farm had evidently been before Burns's arrival. Let a description which Patrick Miller himself has contributed to an account of agricultural conditions in Dumfriesshire complete the picture:

"When I purchased this estate about five-and-twenty years ago," he writes in September 1810, "I had not seen it. *It was in the most*

---

[3] Dunlop Corr., 157; Letters, 324.
[4] 4th Jan. 1789; Letters, 294.

miserable state of exhaustion, and all the tenants in poverty. . . .
*When I went to view my purchase, I was so much disgusted for eight
or ten days, that I then meant never to return to this county."*[5]

This state of things had probably not changed much in the hands
of Kelly, and the next epistolatory—and poetic—utterances of Burns
to Mrs. Dunlop, Ainslie, Beugo, and Hugh Parker,[6] reflect the dis-
comfort of his first impressions, mostly with good humour: he
writes of the smoky "spence," in which the spinning-wheel may
well be heard, but cannot be seen for peat reek; and of the Galloway farmers, who are his only companions, the one "kent" face
being that of his mare Jenny Geddes, on which he had come to the
valley of the Nith; and even she is gloomy and homesick for the
West, for dear Ayrshire, like her master's soul :

> "Wi' a' this care and a' this grief,
> And sma', sma' prospect of relief,
> And nought but peat reek i' my head,
> How can I write what ye can read?"[7]

Burns soon conquered these moods, but there is no denying that
behind them lay a serious truth, which had an important bearing
upon his poetic activity. He felt uprooted. He never got to know
the landscape and the people here as intimately as he had done in
Ayrshire. He missed the beneficent effect of close contact with his
native soil, and it is noteworthy how often, when his mind most
strongly felt the creative urge, he involuntarily grasped at events
and personalities belonging to the old familiar countryside, and
worked on them. The best example of this is "Tam o' Shanter."
We must not forget that, quite apart from his permanent personal
connections, the majority of his letters, particularly the extensive
correspondence with Mrs. Dunlop, were apt to take his thoughts
back constantly to the land of his youth and of his poetic adolescence.
Thus we find him writing the following lines, a variation of the
first verse of the 137th Psalm :

> "By banks of Nith I sat and wept,
>   When Coila I thought on;
> In midst thereof I hung my harp
>   The willow trees upon."[8]

---

[5] Ch. W., ii, 320.
[6] Letters, 247, 248, and 268.
[7] To Hugh Parker. H. H., ii, 116-117.
[8] See the already-mentioned letter to Beugo, Letters, 268.

Yet, as we have said, these feelings did not keep the upper hand; nor is there any direct expression of them in his poems and songs. What drove this manly spirit to write poetry was less a yearning for the "far away and long ago," than the moving, elevating, and exhilarating power of the passing moment and of the present event, for which his mind was ever receptive.

Burns's chief mood at the beginning of the Ellisland period was doubtless that of a man who has felt it necessary to draw a line below the past, pay off his old debts, and go forward calmly to meet the inevitable new obligations, conscious of having done his duty. He was thoughtful, inclined to discuss and to examine his position, especially with regard to the permanent form of his relations with Jean Armour, and was fond of repeating this formula to his friends: "The happiness or misery of a much-loved creature were in my hands, and who could trifle with such a sacred deposit?" Expressions of deep inward satisfaction, such as, for instance, follow these words in a letter dated 10th July 1788[9] to Mrs. Dunlop, clearly forbid the assumption that he was concealing secret regret at the decisive step behind a fine-sounding phrase. He himself realized that he had a certain tendency to "preach" at this time,[10] and this tendency found its most characteristic expression in the lines which he scratched on a window-pane in Friars' Carse Hermitage[11] in June 1788, and of which he circulated a large number of copies, along with a second, longer-drawn-out version, written in December of the same year. In these lines the poet, speaking as the hermit or "beadsman" of Nithside, addresses not only the stranger "whom chance may hither lead," but also himself, especially in the following passage, which is omitted in the second version:

> "For the future be prepar'd:
> Guard wherever thou canst guard;
> But, thy utmost duty done,
> Welcome what thou canst not shun.
> Follies past give thou to air—
> Make their consequence thy care.
> Keep the name of Man in mind,
> And dishonour not thy kind."

---

[9] Letters, 254.

[10] Cf. to Ainslie, ibid., 252.

[11] Original in Museum of Dumfries Observatory; both texts in H. H., ii, 57-58, and i, 258-260.

Each word a confession and a resolve! With this basic mood as our starting-point, we may now follow on broad lines the events of the three and a half years at Ellisland, and their effect upon Burns. Connected with this period there are a few important episodes which demand our closer attention in so far as they provide us with striking illustrations of the actions of the Man and the reactions of the Poet.

The remaining months of the year 1788 were full of bustle and unrest. Burns energetically helped with the building of the house and the work of the fields, but he repeatedly yielded to the urge to go up the Nith to his people in Mauchline and at Mossgiel, and settled down only when Jean followed him to his new home in the first week of December, this time still without her little son Robert. Two men-servants and a maid also came with her from Ayrshire, Burns's sister Agnes accompanying them. As there was still much to be done, it was several weeks before they could move into the new house; but the harmony of the poet's environment was to a great extent restored, and he felt free and happy, and in excellent trim for physical and mental labour. The months that followed were the happiest of his life. Two of his sons first saw the light at Ellisland: Francis Wallace, born 18th August 1789, and named in honour of the poet's friend, Mrs. Dunlop; and William Nicol, born 9th April 1791, and given the name of Burns's Edinburgh friend and travelling companion. A few days before the birth of this second son, on 31st March, an illegitimate daughter, Elizabeth, was born to Burns in Leith, the mother being a certain Helen Anne Park, niece of the landlady of the "Globe Inn" in Dumfries, where Burns used to call whenever business took him to the town. Jean had spent a few weeks in the summer of 1790 with her family in Mauchline, and during this time Burns's passionate temperament had succumbed to Anne's charms and to the opportunity that had offered itself. What later became of Anne Park, the heroine of the song "Yestreen I had a Pint of Wine" is wrapped in uncertainty. We are less struck by Burns's moral lapse than by the wonderful behaviour of Jean, who in her understanding kindness took the child, apparently without a word of reproach, and brought it up with her own children. "Our Robin should hae had twa wives," she is said to have laughingly remarked. There is absolutely no evidence of any disturbance of the domestic felicity at

Ellisland! No better proof can be given of the amiable and good-natured disposition which Burns valued and praised as being among the great virtues of his Jean, than her courageous acceptance of what could not be altered. Many a less noteworthy anecdote has been told of Burns's domestic life.

The chief development in Burns's career during this period consisted in his final transition from the plough to the Excise Service. This he accomplished gradually. For a time he tried to combine the two professions, but the strain of carrying on two jobs simultaneously was too much for his strength, and after a comparatively short time gave rise to a condition of nervous debility, melancholy, and that depression which was wont to render every crisis in his career almost unbearably difficult. Faced with the choice, he resolved to take what seemed the less dangerous road: hoping, as he had every human right to do, that he would get promotion in the Excise, he gave up his farm and settled in Dumfries.

The doubts with which he had originally taken Ellisland are familiar to us. Probably only the most intensive farming could have made the inferior soil yield a tolerable return. We remember Miller's description of his own property. Burns was neither suited nor inclined for such a struggle. It is quite unnecessary to blame faulty supervision and the extravagant habits of the farm hands for the renewed failure, as does a certain authority quoted by Allan Cunningham. There was adequate reason for it in the poet's personality. His many and varied interests, the demands of his extensive correspondence, the artistic obligations which it was incumbent upon him to fulfil, and, last not least, his social needs, the striving to play a part on the stage of the great world, the desire to live and to test his mental powers, were bound to bring him into conflict with the simple and severe demands of his station—the manual labour of the farmer. The ever-present feeling of responsibility towards his family only made him more anxiously conscious of his inadequacy in this respect, and caused him, as soon as the first cheerful and determined efforts began to be followed by serious misgivings, to fall back upon the carefully prepared alternative, namely, the Excise. As early as 10th September 1788 he applied to Robert Graham of Fintry, a member of the Board of Excise in Edinburgh, on whose influence he based great hopes, and who, indeed, became and remained one of his most loyal patrons and protectors. In this letter Burns refers to his commission as an officer of the Excise, his "sheet anchor" as he calls it, and then proceeds as follows:

> "My farm, now that I have tried it a little, tho' I think it will in time be a saving bargain,"—Burns did not wish his patron to get the impression that he was giving up hope too soon—"yet does by no means promise to be such a Pennyworth as I was taught to expect.—It is in the last stage of worn-out poverty, and it will take some time before it pay the rent.—I might have had Cash to supply the defficiencies of these hungry years, but I have a younger brother and three sisters, on a farm in Ayrshire; and it took all my surplus, over what I thought necessary for my farming capital, to save not only the comfort but the very existence of that fireside family-circle from impending destruction.—This was done before I took the farm; and rather than abstract my money from my brother, a circumstance which would ruin him, I will resign the farm, and enter immediately into the service of your Honours.—But I am embarked now on the farm; I have commenced married man; and I am determined to stand by my Lease till resistless Necessity compel me to quit my ground."

Burns's request, then, amounted to this: he wished to be put in charge of the Excise service for the district in which he lived, so that he might combine the farming of Ellisland with the new service. The removal of the present holder might, he said, be effected without any disadvantage to the latter; he himself was ready to enter on business in the following summer, but he would wait upon Graham about the affair in the ensuing winter.

> "When I think how and on what I have written to you, Sir, I shudder at my own Hardiesse. Forgive me, Sir! I have told you my situation.—If asking anything less could possibly have done, I would not have asked so much."

The poet did not forget to add that he also hoped to get useful hints for his art from his work as an exciseman, which would bring him into contact with the most varied characters. The letter ends with reiterated assurances of his gratitude.[12] A poetical epistle in the style of Pope was enclosed with it.[13]

Graham sent a friendly reply by return of post, and Burns answered it on the following day, his heart overflowing with gratitude:

> "Did you know, Sir, from how many fears and forebodings the

---

[12] Letters, 269.
[13] H. H., ii, 119-122 (371-73).

friendly assurance of your patronage and protection has freed me, it would be some reward for your goodness . . . you have, like the great Being whose image you so richly bear, made a creature happy, who had no other claim to your goodness than his necessity, and who can make you no other return than his grateful acknowledgment."[14]

The journey to Edinburgh, of which he had spoken, took place at the end of February 1789, but led to nothing definite. At the beginning of August of the same year, however, Burns received an appointment which suited his requirements in every respect, and afforded him that "something to fall back upon" for which he had been hoping, and which was all the more welcome because he was becoming more and more gloomily doubtful of the prospects at Ellisland. The alphabetical list of the Excise officers of 10th October 1789 contains, under the heading "Official Characters," the short note beside Burns's name: "Never tryed—a Poet,"[15] and in another somewhat later hand the remark has been added: "Turns out well." Burns gives expression to his satisfaction at this turn in his career in several letters.[16] He also manfully faces the fact of being tied to one of the best-hated professions in the kingdom. An income of £50 a year, he writes to Lady Cunningham, is, considering his bad bargain of the farm, not to be despised, and people may say what they like about the ignominy of the job:

"what will support my family and keep me independant of the world is to me a very important matter; and I had much rather that my Profession borrowed credit from me, than that I borrowed credit from my Profession."

It was about this time that he composed the following epigram:

"Searching auld wives' barrels,
       Ochon, the day
That clarty barm should stain my laurels!
       But what'll ye say?
These movin' things ca'd wives an' weans
Wad move the very hearts o' stanes."[17]

The duties which the Excise imposed upon Burns were heavy and took up a great deal of time. He had charge of ten parishes, which were to be visited in fourteen "rides." This meant that he

[14] 23rd Sept. 1788; Letters, 273.
[15] Sinton: "Burns: Excise Officer and Poet"; Glasgow and Edinburgh, 1897, 29 and 61 (Appendix E).
[16] To Graham, 31st July 1789, and 9th Dec. 1789; to Ainslie, 1st Nov. 1789; to Lady Eliz. Cunningham, 23rd Dec. 1789; Letters, 353, 373, 367, and 379.
[17] H. H., ii, 247.

had to ride thirty or forty miles a day on four or five days of the
week. He had to provide his own horse, and to report every two
months that he was "well mounted." He received no allowance for
expenses. When he returned home, he had to attend to the difficult
task of book-keeping, so that Sinton is justified in saying that there
was not much time left for dissipation.[18] The heavy demands on
his physical strength soon made themselves felt, especially when
his rides took him out in stormy winter weather, and the weight of
his official duties coincided with domestic worries and hypo-
chondriacal moods. At such times he would complain of the
pressure of business, which made it impossible for him to write
to his friends when he should, or to serve the Muses in his usual
way. At first, however, he found his rides tiring, but by no means
devoid of pleasure and inspiration. His district, as he said in his
letters, was large, but comprised beautiful and romantic country,[19]
while his calling kept him in touch with types and conditions which
he hoped to be able to use poetically;[20] and many a song must
have been thought out and put into form to the even rhythm
of his trotting horse :

> "Keinem hat es noch gereut,
> Der das Ross bestiegen!"

We have no reason to believe that, apart from the difficulties of
the work and the frequent worry which it occasioned him, Burns
found his profession a humiliating one, and we have no right here
to take up the oft-repeated reproach that Scotland could find no
better occupation for her greatest poet than that of examining dirty
beer barrels and consorting with an obnoxious crowd in the interests
of a hated piece of legislation. Rather is it the case that he made
the choice of his own accord, and he remained true to what he had
himself decreed, carrying out his obligations in such a way that
any thought of painful depression and inward repugnance must be
wholly rejected. From the time he entered upon his duties until
the day when his health gave way completely, he attended to his
work to the satisfaction of his superiors, with energy, conscientious-
ness, and cheerfulness. That in certain cases his warm, sympathetic
heart pleaded for the delinquent if he or she were really poor and

---

[18] *Op. cit.* p. 29.
[19] Dunlop Corr., 197; Letters, 359.
[20] To Lady Cunningham. Letters, 379.

of humble standing, but that he acted with inexorable sternness in cases of serious law-evading, was only to be expected. As a matter of fact, a few rather insignificant anecdotes are told which show us Burns in the execution of his duties;[21] but we shall merely refer the reader to a passage in a letter written to Graham on 4th September 1790, where Burns describes, among other things, the amount of work involved in attending to his district, which had hitherto, unfortunately, been very carelessly surveyed. His cases had kept the justices busy. He himself, he fancied, was taking rather an unusual way with his frauds: he recorded every defaulter, but at the court begged off every poor body whom he knew to be unable to pay. This procedure, he said, had made a good impression on the Bench, and had in no way hurt his own interest (he got a percentage of the fines imposed).[22] As early as March 1790 he wrote to Mrs. Dunlop concerning his hopes of a transfer to a quieter and more lucrative position in a seaport town or Port Division, where he would enjoy the further advantage of having no horse to keep up.[23] He had at that time Greenock or Glasgow in his mind's eye. His salary had already been raised by £20 in July 1790, and in the following year his name appeared in the list of persons to be considered for the higher rank of the Excise officers (examiners and supervisors),[24] posts which brought in between £100 and £200, according to their situation. Perhaps this promotion was not quite so imminent as Burns and some of his friends seemed to expect, but he had every reason to believe that it would come in the usual course of events, and it must have hovered before him as a goal worth striving for, giving him courage to go on, and influencing his decisions about other matters.

Foremost among these decisions was that concerning the giving up of his farm. With reference to this, the above-mentioned letter to Mrs. Dunlop contains sentences which clearly express—not for the first time, either[25]—what he had long ceased, in spite of himself, to doubt:

"My farm is a ruinous bargain, & would ruin me to abide by it.—

[21] See Ch. W., iii, 120 f., and Sinton, p. 30-31.

[22] Letters, 419; also the very characteristic document, *ibid.*, 418.

[23] Dunlop Corr., 245; Letters, 396.

[24] Sinton, 32 and 59-60 (Appendices B and C); Ch. W., iii, 200; Letters, 475 (To Peter Hill).

[25] See in particular letter to Mrs. Dunlop, 25th Mar. 1789, Dunlop Corr., 156-157; Letters, 324.

> . . . At Martinmas 1791, my rent rises 20£ per Annum, & *then,* I am,
> on the maturest deliberation, determined to give it up; & still, even
> *then,* I shall think myself well quit, if I am no more than a hundred
> pounds out of Pocket.—So much for Farming! Would to God I had
> never engaged in it!"[26]

To prevent misinterpretation of this passage, we must emphasise
that this *never,* as the general tenor of the letter shows, can only
refer to the Ellisland period. The dream of winning peace and
permanent subsistence by the plough, as poet of the soil, had faded
away. Burns now looked upon the Excise as his sole means of
support and from that time onward was anxious to rid himself
of the subsidiary business, which he considered as only a hindrance
to him; and, as far as his outward affairs were concerned, he
wished to devote himself wholly to his new profession, which
seemed to offer him more gratifying prospects. The transition
period, up to the late autumn of 1791, was not free from moods
of discouragement and misfortunes of various kinds, and there is
no lack of bitter complaints against the unlucky star whose evil
influence again brought his plans to nought. But the bright side is
there too. As elsewhere, so at Ellisland, it needed only the slightest
breath to make the flames of boundless humanity, benevolence, and
joy of life blaze up in his ardent soul. No personal or professional
difficulty was strong enough to alienate his ever watchful spirit and
his warmly sympathetic heart from the universally significant. As
before, he took part in everything that affected his environment,
and as a rule the incident which claimed his attention was also
strong enough to stimulate his never dormant creative faculties to
poetic production. The measure of success depended, in the true
artistic way, on the nature of the event and the influences which
happened to be prevalent at the moment, so that not only what was
really great but what was ephemeral now came almost simultaneously from the unquenchable central fire. Let us take a few
particularly typical episodes.

The first is the founding of the "Monkland Friendly Society,"
a reading circle, with a lending library, for the inhabitants of the
parish of Dunscore. Burns started it with the help of his friend
Riddell, who supplied a considerable number of books from his
own library as a nucleus. We have Riddell's testimony that Burns

---

[26] Similarly to Gilbert Burns, 11th Jan., and to Graham, 4th Sept. 1790. Letters,
381 and 419.

was the heart and soul of the undertaking, its treasurer, its librarian
—and its censor.[27] Burns was a very keen reader for a man of
his station, and found books scarcely less necessary to his happiness
than human beings. The leading English poets from Dryden
onward were familiar to him. He now read with enjoyment
difficult works such as Smith's "Wealth of Nations" and Alison's
"Essays on the Nature and Principles of Taste." In his letters he
mentions Thomas Reid's "Inquiry into the Human Mind,"
enlightens Mrs. Dunlop concerning Falconer, and plans to write an
essay on Dr. Moore's novel "Zeluco," which had just been published (1789), comparing its literary peculiarities with those of Fielding and Richardson. Unpublished works were submitted to his
judgment, as for instance, James Cririe's "Address to Loch
Lomond," the chief source of which he recognizes in Thomson's
"Seasons";[28] James Mylne's literary legacy, and the poems of Miss
Helen Maria Williams, which he subjects to a gentle but thorough
criticism, fully conscious all the while of his own mastery in the art
of poetry.[30] He expressed himself sharply with regard to the
numerous imitators who sprang up after the publication of his
Poems in 1786:

> "My success," he wrote to Patrick Carfrae, "perhaps as much
> accidental as merited, has brought an innundation of nonsense over
> the Land.—Subscription bills for Scots Poems have so dunned and
> daily do so dun the Public, that the very term, Scots Poetry, totters
> on the brink of contempt."[31]

Far from shielding his own genius against foreign influences,
which in his case were often harmful enough, Burns, like other
great writers, felt an imperative need to absorb and digest the
literary tendencies of his time. He never had the slightest doubt,
either consciously or unconsciously, of the value of tradition, or of
the importance and inevitability of the organic development in
literature. Moreover, he felt it his duty to kindle for others the
light to which he himself owed so much. He had already accom-

---

[27] Ch. W., iii, 290.

[28] To Hill, 1st Oct. 1788. Letters, 276.

[29] Ch. W., iii, 45-49; Letters, 319.

[30] Letters, 358.

[31] Letters, 333; similarly to Mrs. Dunlop, 4th Mar. 1789, Dunlop Corr., 151;
Letters, 318. Collections of this kind were published, for instance, by Campbell, in
1787; Taylor, 1787; Lapraik, 1788; Sillar, 1789; A. Tait and A. Wilson, 1790; Janet
Little, 1792; D. Crawford, 1798; G. Turnbull, 1788 and 1794; Skinner, 1809, &c.

plished a similar mission in Tarbolton, and later repeated it in
Dumfries. Burns was one of the first men to conclude, from
personal experience, that the lower as well as the higher classes
might be spiritually elevated by the reading of good books and so
raised above the purely vegetable level of mentality—that is to
say, he was one of the first to popularize and to democratize English
literature. Herein lies the more than momentary importance of
the founding of the library in Dunscore. We owe a valuable letter
by Burns, signed "A Peasant," to the fact that the parish minister,
Joseph Kirkpatrick, had omitted to give Sir John Sinclair, whose
"Statistical Account of Scotland" appeared in the years 1791-99,
a proper account of the "Monkland Friendly Society." The letter
was handed over to Sinclair by Riddell. In it Burns describes the
venture as new, beneficial, and worthy of imitation, and the
organization as extremely simple: an entrance fee of 5s. was levied
upon each member, and the meetings were held every fourth
Saturday, when each person present paid another sixpence. The
majority decided what new books should be added to the library.
All the books had to be produced at the meetings and the redistri-
bution was made according to a list, the name which was first
on the list at one meeting being moved to the foot at the next, and
so on. Finally, the whole stock was put up to auction among the
members. At the breaking-up of this little society, the library
contained 150 volumes. There was, as Burns says, a good deal of
trash among these, but, naturally, there was also some good literature, such as the periodicals (*The Spectator, The Idler, The Adven-
turer, The Mirror, The Lounger,* and *The Observer*); historical
works by Hume, Robertson, Knox and Rae; Hervey's "Medita-
tions"; a number of theological treatises, such as Blair's "Sermons,"
Beveridge's "Thoughts" and Watson's "Body of Divinity," a work
which was so popular amongst the members that one copy was
not considered sufficient;[32] and, finally, a selection of the best contemporary novels, among them being, of course, Henry Mackenzie's
"Man of Feeling" and "Man of the World," "Don Quixote,"
Fielding's works, Johnstone's "Chrysal," and others. The list is
of considerable interest. It tallies in the main with Burns's own
early reading, and shows what books were at that time gradually

---

[32] To Peter Hill, 2nd Mar. 1790; Letters, 395.

beginning to find their way into the lowest strata of the reading public. Burns concludes his report by saying:

> "A peasant who can read, and enjoy such books, is certainly a much superior being to his neighbour, who, perhaps, stalks beside his team, very little removed, except in shape, from the brutes he drives."[33]

Other chords, equally characteristic, were touched in Burns by the battle which was waging with unabated vigour between the two great Church parties, the Orthodox and the Liberal, the poet following the various symptomatic expressions of the controversy with the eager tenseness of a wild animal crouching to spring upon its prey. The parish minister of Dunscore, the Rev. Joseph Kirkpatrick whom we have just mentioned, was a strict Calvinist, and as such not to Burns's liking. This gave the latter repeated opportunities of airing his opposing views on religious questions and political events in strongly worded letters, to one of which we shall shortly give our attention. At the same time the differences of opinion did not lead to any quarrel, for Burns recognized and respected Kirkpatrick's moral qualities.[34] But Burns's interest, as we know, was constantly ranging beyond the bounds of his parish, and lingered with particular interest on events which concerned his native Ayrshire and occupied the minds of his friends and foes there. On 15th July 1789 the Presbytery of Ayr had appointed a commission to report on the doctrine of Dr. William M'Gill, minister of the second charge in Ayr, a man whom Burns had greatly esteemed from his youth. M'Gill's "Practical Essay on the Death of Christ" (Edinburgh, 1787), had, by its interpretation of Christ's atonement, given rise to discussion and to his being summoned before the Presbytery. The dispute brought a number of men well known to Burns into the arena, to fight for and against M'Gill,[35] while the public looked on with eager interest. At the critical moment the poet entered the struggle and putting forth all his strength brandished his keen blade against religious fanaticism and bigoted hypocrisy; and the good steel did not fail him. By 17th July the first draft, consisting of eleven stanzas, of "The Kirk's Alarm," to the tune of "Push about the Brisk Bowl," was dispatched to Mrs. Dunlop. The lightning plays in the accom-

---

[33] Letters, 469.

[34] To Mrs. Dunlop, 21st-22nd June 1789. Dunlop Corr., 177-178; Letters, 350.

[35] See W. L. Mathieson, "The Awakening of Scotland," Glasgow, 1910, 218-220.

panying letter. One feels with what gusto Burns attacks the old
hated enemy. The passage runs:

> "You know my sentiments respecting the present two great Parties
> that divide our Scots Ecclesiastics.—I do not care three farthings for
> Commentators & authorities.—An honest candid enquirer after truth,
> I revere; but illiberality & wrangling I equally detest.— . . . you will
> be well acquainted with the persecutions that my worthy friend, Mr.
> M'Gill, is undergoing among your Divines.—Several of these reverend
> lads, his opponents, have come thro' my hands before; but I have some
> thoughts of serving them up again in a different dish.—I have just
> sketched the following ballad, & as usual I send the first rough-
> draught to you.—I do not wish to be known in it, tho' I know, if
> ever it appear, I shall be suspected.—If I finish it, I am thinking to
> throw off two or three dozen copies at a Press in Dumfries, & send
> them, as from Edinr. to some Ayr-shire folks on both sides of the
> question. If I should fail of rendering some of the Doctor's foes
> ridiculous, I shall at least gratify my resentment in his behalf."[36]

The ballad, containing thirteen stanzas, was actually published
as a broadsheet in the year 1789, but whether at the instigation of
Burns, who according to his custom had distributed several versions,
externally widely divergent, among his friends, cannot be proved
and seems doubtful.[37] In its most complete form it consists of
eighteen verses, to which have been added two different postscripts
each containing one verse. The Orthodox party is depicted as
crying out in alarm against M'Gill and his friends, John Ballantine,
Robert Aiken, and William Dalrymple. It goes on to encourage
the Calvinist hosts:

> "Calvin's sons! Calvin's sons!
> Seize your sp'ritual guns,
> Ammunition you never can need:
> Your hearts are the stuff
> Will be powther enough,
> And your skulls are store-houses o' lead—
> Calvin's sons!
> Your skulls are store-houses o' lead."

Under the banners of Orthodoxy appear the heroes of the "Holy
Fair," the "Ordination," and the "Twa Herds": Russell, M'Kinlay,
Moodie, Auld, and Peebles, who to his sorrow had occasionally
tried his hand at writing poetry; and among the hated throng we

---

[36] Letters, 352; also 356, 354, and 379; to John Logan, 7th Aug. 1789; to
Robert Aiken, (?) Aug., and to Lady Cunningham, 23rd Dec. 1789.—Text given
by H. H., ii, 30-37, with textual notes and commentary on pp. 327-334.

[37] See letter to Logan, 356: "I am determined not to let it (i.e. 'The Kirk's
Alarm') get into the Publick."

see the best-hated one of all, the Kirk elder William Fisher, "Holy Willie."

Some hitherto unnamed representatives of the sect of the Unco Guid fare no better. Each gets his verse of scathing sarcasm thrown in his face. "Poet Burns" in person brings up the rear, striding behind his victims as with a brazen scourge, at once the avenger of intolerance and the defender of the man of good will and independent thought. We have no record of the impression produced by the poem. The affair itself came to nothing, as M'Gill consented in April 1790 to withdraw the offending sentences, with an apology, and the Synod thanked God for this happy solution to their difficulties.

With equal sympathy Burns followed the proceedings on the stage of politics both near his home and in more remote parts of the country. Thus a series of poems was inspired by the preparations for parliamentary elections and by the local elections themselves. We must confine ourselves to enumerating these poems here: "The Fête Champêtre"[38] was composed in the autumn of 1788; "The Five Carlins"[39] and "The Election Ballad for Westerha' "[40] in the autumn of 1789, in connection with the existing election campaign in Dumfries; and in the summer of 1790, after the election was over, "The Election Ballad to Robert Graham,"[41] in which we have a particularly striking illustration of Burns's intense interest in the affairs of the present, in spite of his assertion that he let them surge about him while he stood in the midst impartially "seeing and observing." Having taken up the cudgels on behalf of the defeated candidate, Sir James Johnstone of Westerhall, Burns attacks the extreme liberalism of Fox's adherents. This is all the more remarkable as the successful opposing candidate was the son of the poet's landlord, Patrick Miller, and the canvassing on his behalf was done by Burns's friends and patrons. His strong dislike for their leader, the Duke of Queensberry, added to idealistic and poetical feelings for the House of Stuart, doubtless influenced his attitude in this case. That Burns in his inmost heart favoured the extreme left and the revolutionary ideas of his time,

---

[38] H. H., ii, 174-176.
[39] *Ibid.*, 177-181.
[40] *Ibid.*, 182-183; see also Dunlop Corr., 213; Letters, 363.
[41] *Ibid.*, ii, 183-191.

in spite of his Jacobite tendencies, is obvious, and will be very plainly seen in the course of this narrative.   We can merely mention here the other political poems which were written at Ellisland: the "Ode to the Departed Regency Bill";[42] "A New Psalm for the Chapel of Kilmarnock";[43] the sketch "Inscribed to the Right Hon. C. J. Fox,"[44] all written in 1789; and the fragment "On Glenriddell's Fox breaking his Chain" (1791).[45]   Their literary interest is somewhat limited, while the events which provoked them have to a certain extent faded into the background; and Burns's treatment of the themes has done nothing to raise them into a position of universal importance: he generally aimed only at a witty epigram.

The whole weight of his personality, his love of justice and the irresistible magnetism of his temperament find expression in an open letter, signed "A Briton," to the *Edinburgh Evening Courant,* and published in that paper on 22nd November 1788. This letter was called forth by a sermon preached by Kirkpatrick in honour of the centenary of the glorious revolution of 1688. By order of the Scottish General Assembly, the 5th November was kept throughout the country as a day of remembrance, with special services.   In his laudable zeal for the existing order, Kirkpatrick had apparently gone the length of using expressions such as "the bloody and tyrannical House of Stuart."   This roused Burns's indignation, and his reply was the bold and powerful manifesto, dignified alike in speech and form, in which we may hear the rumble of the thunder not only of the revolution that was past, but of the greater revolution that was to come, mingled with the inspiring organ-music of exalted, conciliatory thoughts on man-kind, such as the Age of Feeling could inspire in the minds of its best men.   Burns begins with the Article of Faith which he always upheld, viz., that Good and not Evil is the natural heritage of man, and that even the criminal, the fallen brother, should not be shut out from the sympathy of his fellows.   He declares his adherence to the revolutionary principles of 1688, under whose dominion he was born and bred; but he goes on to say that, in spite of this,

42 *Ibid.,*   159-162.
43 *Ibid.,*   162-164.
44 *Ibid.,*   165-167.
45 *Ibid.,*   168-170.

there is something within him which keeps him from speaking scornfully or contemptuously of the House of Stuart:

> "We may," he affirms, "bless God for all his goodness to us as a nation, without, at the same time, cursing a few ruined powerless exiles, who only harboured ideas and made attempts that most of us would have done had we been in their situation."

He demands fairness in judging the actions of the Stuarts. May not the epithets "bloody" and "tyrannical" be applied to the House of Tudor or York as well? Here, as always, he rejects blind fanaticism, pointing out that what to-day gives rise to the most joyful feeling of exaltation, nay, to the most arrogant pride, may seem to future generations no less contemptible than the actions of the bloody and tyrannical Stuarts appear to his contemporaries.

> "Who would believe," he writes, "that in this our Augustan age of liberality and refinement, while we seem so justly sensible and jealous of our rights and liberties, and animated with such indignation against the very memory of those who would have subverted them, who would suppose that a certain people, under our national protection, should complain, not against a Monarch and a few favourite advisers, but against our whole legislative body, of the very same imposition and oppression, the Romish religion not excepted, and almost in the very same terms as our forefathers did against the family of Stuart! I will not, I cannot, enter into the merits of the cause; but I dare say, the American Congress, in 1776, will be allowed to have been as able and as enlightened, and, a whole empire will say, as honest, as the English Convention in 1688; and that the fourth of July will be as sacred to their posterity as the fifth of November is to us.
> To conclude, Sir, let every man, who has a tear for the many miseries incident to humanity, feel for a family, illustrious as any in Europe, and unfortunate beyond historic precedent; and let every Briton, and particularly every Scotsman, who ever looked with reverential pity on the dotage of a parent, cast a veil over the fatal mistakes of the Kings of his forefathers."[46]

Similarly, Burns raised his voice, when it was a case not of defending a royal house, but of helping an unimportant persecuted schoolmaster to obtain justice. The letter on behalf of the Stuarts belongs to the beginning of the Ellisland period. That his lofty ideals did not suffer, in spite of all his disappointments, during this time, is shown by his taking up the cause of his old friend James Clarke, a schoolmaster from Moffat, in the summer of 1791. Clarke was threatened with dismissal on the pretext that he had

---

[46] Letters, 283. See also to Mrs. Dunlop, Dunlop Corr., 112-113; Letters, 285.

inflicted cruel punishment on some of the boys in his school. After investigating the case, Burns was convinced that the accusation had been fabricated, and that Clarke was, as he put it, "falling a victim to the weakness of the Many, following in the cry of the villainy of the Few." Consequently he did his utmost to help him. He not only wrote letters himself, but he also composed a few effective letters for Clarke to send to the Edinburgh authorities, who were the patrons of the school at Moffat, and to influential people connected with them. He interested Riddell's friends in the case, which seemed all the more important to him because he recognized the Earl of Hopetoun and his "myrmidons" as his chief opponents. For him the matter became the fight for existence of the plebeian against the aristocrat and those "hellish creatures, the go-betweens," who must at all costs be overcome. He had the satisfaction of seeing his friend completely vindicated in February 1792.[47]

We have dealt with these episodes in some detail, not from mere love of relating anecdotes, but because they reveal the common roots from which Burns's human and artistic actions sprang, and which combined to give them a greater unity. His strength grew from a few strong, simple fundamental principles, which were often preached but seldom practised. Burns believed in their liberating and beneficent power, and never hesitated to carry them out effectively, even at the risk of seriously damaging his own interests. In the light of these ideas he judged the problems in which he felt called to take a part, and through them he learned to recognize what was typical in life and in art, thus acquiring that knowledge which first stamps keenness of observation and courage of bearing in a man with the hallmark of human greatness.

With the impression of Burns's varied activities and his interest in outside affairs fresh in our minds, we must now ask this last and most important question: what do the years 1788-91 mean as far as his poetic mission is concerned—that mission which, in spite of his participation in the political and religious questions of the day, we must recognize as the focus of his being? The fulfilment of his vocation as poet hovered before him, as he himself said, as the goal of "his highest ambition, his dearest wish, and

---

[47] Ch. W., iii, 262; Letters, 456, 459, 470, 496 and 498.

his unwearied study."[48] He frankly called it his "characteristical trade"[49] and felt his genius secretly exhorting him and urging him on with unabated vigour; but he was no less conscious of his responsibility. Behind him lay the great achievement of his first publication, which had appeared in 1787 in a new and enlarged edition. It was his task, if possible, to surpass that effort. How to do that caused him much thought, and in the course of his speculations he reached some interesting conclusions. Above all, it appeared to him essential not to trust blindly to the force of inspiration, but, no matter how spontaneous the production, to give a second work the benefit of a long maturing period. To see in this resolve a decline in his artistic faculties is to be guilty of a misinterpretation of the worst kind. It is only one of a number of signs of progress towards more conscious literary activity. We should rather admire him for conforming to such an ideal; and the fact that he was not privileged to give his fellow-countrymen further, carefully revised fruits of his genius, is one of the unsatisfactory things about his short earthly pilgrimage.

At the beginning of his sojourn at Ellisland he in several letters expressed his thoughts on the relationship of inspiration and technical perfection. Thus in the letter dated 22nd February, 1789, to a patron, probably Henry Erskine, he says:

> "I have no great faith in the boastful pretentions to intuitive propriety and unlabored elegance.—The rough material of Fine Writing is certainly the gift of Genius; but I as firmly believe that the workmanship is the united effort of Pains, Attention, & repeated Trial."[50]

Besides postulating perfect clearness of expression, he raises the question of novelty in the subject, in an important letter (already mentioned) to Lady Cunningham:

> "I am aware that though I were to give to the world Performances superiour to my former works, if they were productions of the same kind, the comparative reception they would meet with would mortify me.—For this reason I wish still to secure my old friend, Novelty, on my side."[51]

In accordance with these self-imposed restrictions Burns, in the prefaces to two manuscript collections of his poems which he made

---

[48] To Lady Cunningham. Letters, 379.
[49] To John Geddes, 3rd Feb. 1789; Letters, 308.
[50] Letters, 299. Similarly to Moore, 4th Jan. 1789, and to Lady Cunningham, 22nd Jan. 1789. Letters, 294 and 298.
[51] Letters, 379.

at that time—one for Riddell,[52] the other for Mrs. Stewart of
Stair[53]—definitely stated his desire that nothing from them should
be published, as they consisted almost entirely of pieces that owed
their existence to a passing mood—"bagatelles," written, as he put
it, "simply *pour passer le temps*." And yet both collections contain "Tam o' Shanter"! He repeated this request with regard to
the Glenriddell MS., when after his friend's death in 1794 there
was a danger of the MS. falling into the hands of an unauthorised
person.

> "You know," he wrote to a female relative of Riddell, "that at the
> wish of my late friend I made a collection of all my trifles in verse
> which I had written.—They are many of them local, some of them
> puerile and silly, and all of them unfit for the public eye."

And as his fame was at stake, he asked that the manuscript be
destroyed or returned to him. It was given to Riddell, he said, as
a pledge of friendship: therein lay the whole value of its contents.[54]

If we examine the positive side of his production more closely,
we recognize, mainly in connection with the theoretical discussions
on which we have just touched, the tender shoots of new schemes.
His search for a poetic subject of greater dimensions and more
manifold possibilities than had been offered him by any of the
material he had hitherto handled, is in keeping with the high
conception he had of his art.

> "I muse & rhyme, morning, noon & night," he wrote in January
> 1789 to Lady Cunningham, "and have a hundred different Poetic plans,
> pastoral, georgic, dramatic, &c., floating in the regions of fancy, some-
> where between Purpose and resolve."[55]

Since the autumn of 1788 his letters occasionally contain fragments
of satirical poetry in the style of Pope; one such fragment of forty-

---

[52] The famous Glenriddell MSS., in two volumes, the first of which contains
poems, the second a selection of letters. Contents given in Ch. W., iii, 453-459; cf.
also H. A. Bright, "Some Account of the Glenriddell MSS. of Burns' Poems";
Liverpool, 1874. Until 1913 the volumes were in the Library of the Liverpool
Athenæum. Then they were sold, and fortunately came into the possession of
that eminent collector and authority of Burns, John Gribbel, Wyncote, Pennsylvania,
U.S.A. Col. Gribbel generously gave the volumes back to Scotland. They are
now and for all time, we hope, in the Scottish National Library, Edinburgh, where
as a national possession they may be considered safe from grasping speculators!

[53] The so-called Afton MS., now in the Burns Museum at Alloway. Contents
quoted by Ch. W., iii, 459-460. For exact description, see J. M'Vie, "Burns and
Stair," ch. xiv (pp. 88-97). The MS. was presented by B. to Mrs. Stewart.

[54] Letters, 624.

[55] Letters, 298.

five lines, which was sent to Mrs. Dunlop on 29th October of that
year, bears the title: "The Poet's Progress. An Embryotic Poem
in the Womb of Futurity." He might, he wrote, one day use it as
an instrument of vengeance. The poem was laid aside, provided
three years later with introductory and closing lines, and in this
form sent to Robert Graham of Fintry.[56] It is one of the many
efforts in which Burns, partly from personal ambition and partly
in obedience to narrow minds such as that of the well-meaning
John Moore, strove to emulate the poets of the Augustan age, in a
domain rendered inaccessible to him by Nature.

At this time he also repeatedly mentions his intention of writing
a play.[57] In the first letter referring to this idea—written to
Graham, on 10th September 1788[58]—he defined the sphere in which
the scene was to be laid as "rural." That the subject was intended
to be Scottish, in contrast to the much-acted pieces by O'Keefe,
Mrs. Inchbald, and others, may be seen from the letter of December 1789 to Lady Cunningham;[59] and judging from an order for
books sent to Peter Hill on 2nd March 1790, it is almost certain
that the comical element was to play a considerable part in it.
Furthermore, Currie quotes an account given by John Ramsay of
Ochtertyre of a conversation the latter had with Burns that same
year, i.e., in 1790. In the course of this conversation, according to
Ramsay, the plan of the drama was alluded to, and Burns mentioned as its subject an episode from the life of Robert the Bruce:
once, after Bruce had been defeated on the Cairn, the heel of his
boot had become loosened and a helpful shoemaker named Robert
MacQuechan had, with the best of intentions, driven his awl nine
inches into the King's heel. The drama was to bear the title of
"Rob MacQuechan's Elshon."[60] What dramatic possibilities may
have been latent in this material we cannot judge from the scrappy
data at our disposal concerning it. Burns may also have been
spurred on by the fact that there was in Dumfries a good theatrical
company with whose manager, George S. Sutherland, he was on
friendly terms. The poet wrote a prologue for the New Year's

[56] H. H., i, 271-274; note, 427-431.
[57] See J. De Lancey Ferguson, "Burns and the Drama," *Scots Magazine*, 1934.
[58] Letters, 269.
[59] Letters, 379.
[60] Ch. W., iii, 199-200.

performance of 1790,[61] a second prologue being spoken by Mrs.
Sutherland on her benefit night, on 3rd March, 1790. In this second
prologue there is an unmistakable reflection of its author's dramatic
project: he appeals to the audience to value home-grown goods in
preference to the wares imported from London, and asks:

> "Is there no daring Bard will rise and tell
> How glorious Wallace stood, how hapless fell?
> Where are the Muses fled that could produce
> A drama worthy o' the name o' Bruce?
> How here, even here, he first unsheath'd the sword
> 'Gainst mighty England and her guilty lord,
> And after monie a bloody, deathless doing,
> Wrench'd his dear country from the jaws of Ruin!
> O, for a Shakespeare, or an Otway scene
> To paint the lovely, hapless Scottish Queen!"[62]

The themes of Wallace, Bruce, and Mary Stuart seemed to him
equally worthy of treatment by the longed-for Scottish dramatist.
It was not given to him himself, however, to answer his own
request and to carry out his plans, or to advance along the road on
which John Home, who is likewise mentioned in the Prologue, had
embarked with considerable success three years before Burns's
birth with his "Douglas" tragedy. Not a line of the projected
work was executed, so that we have no reliable basis on which to
build any speculation as to whether Burns did or did not possess
the necessary faculty for dramatic creation. Least of all are we
justified in lamenting, with Sir Walter Scott, that his constant
activity as a lyric poet "diverted him from his grand plan of
dramatic composition."[63] That his lyrical work was the natural
expression of his inspired hours, we know; whether, however, the
desire for dramatic work would have been accompanied by the
necessary inspiration, or how far premeditated schemes could,
under particularly favourable circumstances, have reached maturity,
we may only conjecture, but we cannot state with any degree of
certainty.

A considerable amount of occasional poetry, similar to that
with which we have already become familiar in the foregoing

[61] H. H., ii, 146-147.

[62] H. H., ii, 147-149. Burns wrote "A Lament of Mary Queen of Scots" in
June 1790. Text in H. H., i, 268-270 (note 425-427).

[63] See Scott's review of Cromek's "Reliques of Robert Burns" in the *Quarterly
Review* for Feb. 1809.

pages, bridges the gulf between what was planned and what was accomplished. Besides the pieces called forth by ecclesiastical and political causes, we have poetical epistles in the well-known form, as those to *James Tennant of Glenconner* (1789),[64] *Dr. Blacklock,*[65] (21st October 1789); and the New Year's Day poem to *Mrs. Dunlop,* written in the same year.[66] In addition to these, there are several elegies, such as that on *Captain Matthew Henderson* (who died in 1788),[67] which Burns finished with great care in the summer of 1790 from various rough drafts; on *Miss Burnet of Monboddo* (who died in 1790), written in January, 1791;[68] and on his noble patron, the *Earl of Glencairn* (who died on 30th January 1791),[69] for whom Burns wore mourning and in memory of whom he named his fourth son James Glencairn. The last-named poem is a fine, sincere piece of work, though not quite free from the influence of literary models. Let us complete the list by mentioning the "Ode to Mrs. Oswald of Auchencruive," a tactless, biting, and witty poem written in 1789;[70] the sentimental lines "On Seeing a Fellow Wound a Hare with a Shot," April 1789;[71] and the "Address to the Shade of Thomson,"[72] written at the request of the Earl of Buchan for a superfluous ceremony of crowning a bust of the Poet of the Seasons, arranged by the Earl in the summer of 1791. It is impossible and to some extent also unnecessary to devote to these and other works of a similar nature more than a passing glance.

With the publishing of the third volume of Johnson's "Scots Musical Museum" we come to an event of much higher rank. The preface, whose every sentence reveals the authorship of Burns, is dated 2nd February, 1790. The volume contains forty hitherto unpublished songs by Burns, among them "My Heart's ·in the Highlands" (No. 259), "John Anderson my Jo" (No. 260), "Ca' the Yowes to the Knowes" (No. 264) and the elegy to Mary: "Thou

---

[64] H. H., ii, 124-126.
[65] *Ibid.,* ii, 128, 131.
[66] *Ibid.,* ii, 64-66; Dunlop Corr., 133-134.
[67] *Ibid.,* i, 262-268.
[68] *Ibid.,* ii, 224-225.
[69] *Ibid.,* i, 274-277.
[70] *Ibid.,* i, 260-261.
[71] *Ibid.,* i, 287-289.
[72] *Ibid.,* i, 288-289.

Ling'ring Star, with Less'ning Ray" (No. 279), besides a number
of others whose lines unmistakably reveal Burns's sure, revising
hand. "Auld Lang Syne," also written during this period, in
December 1788, was not published until after the poet's death.[73]
The demands which the publishing of the "Musical Museum"
imposed upon Burns must have been constantly present in his
mind. They form a kind of permanent literary background and
explain his uninterrupted and intense lyrical activity better than
can be done by trying to connect each poem with the influence of
a definite incident in his life. That an external stimulus frequently lent wings to his imagination and fire to his pen cannot and
must not be doubted, but we must not forget that in the forming of
his individual lyrics the impulse came not so much from the
anecdote (frequently of such doubtful origin at that) as from the
great and passionately conceived idea: the rebirth of Scottish
Song; the furnishing of the nation's treasury of songs with texts
worthy of it and able to stand the test of time. With this important
qualification in our minds, we may be permitted to speak of Burns's
lyrical poetry as "occasional." Where the autobiographical element
is unmistakable, it carries us back to his milieu, to that homely
atmosphere from the consciousness of which we must never allow
ourselves to be entirely separated, even in the presence of the poet's
most inspired utterances. Thus his longing for the absent Jean
during the first months of his life at Ellisland, while his house was
being built, produced "Of a' the Airts the Wind can blaw"[74] and
"O were I on Parnassus' Hill";[75] after he had moved into his
house and farm with his young wife, and all the good spirits of
happy Providence hovered round him, he sang, proud of his
happiness and his independence, the sturdy "I Hae a Wife o' My
Ain."[76] Later, friends came to see him: Allan Masterton, the
Edinburgh schoolmaster and talented musician, visited him when in
the district in the autumn of 1789. William Nicol, who was always
glad of an excuse for drinking, was in the neighbourhood at the
same time, at Moffat, where he was spending the autumn holidays.
Burns and Masterton were not long in paying him a visit. They

---

[73] *Ibid.*, iii, 147-149 (note 407-410); Dunlop Corr., pp. 123-124; Letters, 290.
[74] H. H., iii, 56.
[75] *Ibid.*, iii, 59-60.
[76] *Ibid.*, iii, 109-110.

are said to have met half-way, in the vicinity of Craigieburn, where a mighty carousal took place. "We had such a joyous meeting," declared Burns, "that Mr. Masterton and I agreed, each in our own way, that we should celebrate the business." The result was the incomparable drinking-song, "Willie Brewed a Peck o' Maut," for which Masterton wrote the music, the text and the melody, in James C. Dick's opinion, being equally inspired.[77] The circumstances surrounding the celebrated lament on Mary, to which Burns in a letter dated 8th November 1789, to Mrs. Dunlop, gave the short title of *Song*,[78] are less clear. They are obscured by a veil of sentimental anecdotes, and it is possible that we are here faced with a case in which it was not so much a specific event which inspired the song, as the purely literary necessity of finding a suitable text for a serious air; meditating on this air, the poet perhaps remembered a deceased sweetheart named Mary, and wrote the song in memory of her.

On the other hand, we have Burns's own account to fall back upon in dealing with another famous drinking-song, the ballad of "The Whistle."[79] The poet spent many a happy hour under the hospitable roof of his neighbour, Robert Riddell, the owner of Friars' Carse, in the company of jovial cronies of his host's social standing, who were always glad to welcome the inspired and brilliantly eloquent peasant-poet as one of their equals. Burns cherished a grateful memory of these carefree gatherings, the pleasant atmosphere of which used to inspire him to high achievement. The fact that intellectual interests of the most varied kind did not fare too badly over the noble Bordeaux which was consumed in large quantities on such occasions proves, if such testimony were needed, what sort of man the host was. Riddell, born in 1757, bore the rank of Captain, as an officer of an infantry regiment stationed in Ireland. By inclination, however, he was more of a student than a soldier, and in point of fact devoted his time chiefly to studying the antiquities of the Nith valley, and, within a wider radius, of Dumfriesshire. He became a member of the Edinburgh and London Societies of Antiquaries, and towards

---

[77] *Ibid.*, iii, 80-81; 359-360; Dick, "Songs," 440-441.

[78] H. H., iii, 71-72, 355-356; Letters, 371.

[79] *Mus.*, 314; the anecdote on p. vi, after the Index.—H. H., i, 304-308, note, 452-456.

the end of his short life received the degree of LL.D. from the
University of Edinburgh. He pursued his studies from his com-
fortable country seat, with the leisure of the aristocratic dilettante,
happy in his marriage and in stimulating intercourse with numerous
friends of similar tastes. As poet he tried his hand rather unsuccess-
fully in a ballad imitation, "The Bedesman of Nithsyde." On the
other hand, his versions of popular ballads, which he left behind him
as part of his collection of Scottish antiquities—a collection com-
prising at least eleven folio volumes—form an important contribution to the study of genuine popular literature. The ballads were
in Scott's hands for a time and provided him with valuable
material for his "Minstrelsy of the Scottish Border."[80] That
Riddell's musical ability was above the average is shown by two
books of Scottish dance-tunes, partly his own composition, partly
of popular origin, which were engraved and published by Johnson
in 1787 and 1794, as well as the tunes which he wrote for some of
Burns's songs in the "Musical Museum."[81] His love of country,
of the art of poetry, of music and the social joys, made him a man
after Burns's own heart, and all these qualities were combined
when, on 16th October 1789, the famous contest was held for the
possession of an old whistle to which was attached an interesting
and lively story or legend. A Dane of gigantic stature and incomparable powers in the service of Bacchus had, according to the
tradition recorded by Burns, come to Scotland in the train of
James VI's wife, Princess Anne of Denmark, and had brought
with him this whistle, which he used to offer at the beginning
of his orgies as a prize, saying that it should belong to the man
who was last able to blow it. For a long time the Dane was
undefeated, but finally Sir Robert Lawrie of Maxwelton succeeded,
after three days' and nights' continuous drinking of claret, in
putting him under the table and "in blowing on the whistle his
requiem shrill." The trophy was afterwards lost to a member
of the house of Riddell, and thus came into the possession of the
laird of Friars' Carse. Once more a challenge was issued, and

---

80 For further details see "Dictionary of National Biography."   F. Miller
discusses the ballad—MS. in *Archiv*, vol. 128, 79-86.

81 "New Music for the Piano-Forte or Harpsichord . . . consisting of a Collection
of Reels, Minuets, Hornpipes, Marches and two Songs in the old Scotch taste, with
variations, &c." and "A Collection of Scotch, Galwegian—and Border Tunes for
the Violin and Piano-Forte, with a Bass, &c." It must be noted, however, that
experts set little value on most of Riddell's compositions.

was taken up by two of the victorious Sir Robert Lawrie's descen-
dants, both of whom were, by the way, related to the Riddells. One
was at this time member of Parliament for Dumfriesshire and
likewise bore the name of Sir Robert Lawrie; the other was a
highly esteemed lawyer and landowner, Alexander Fergusson of
Craigdarroch. The contest was held according to the rules of
traditional usage before a court of arbitration, and apparently
also in the presence of Burns, who had already accompanied the
preparations for the wager with outbursts of brilliant humour.[82]
The result, according to the testimony of the original witnesses
taken by John MacMurdo as judge, was: "Won by Craigdarroch—
he drank upwds. of 5 Bottles of Claret." Burns's ballad followed
on the heels of the affair, if it did not actually coincide with it,
and has, in its boisterous, racy stanzas, left to posterity a faithful
record of the uproarious, ludicrous scene. Glenriddell was first to
surrender. The poet excuses him, for—he was an elder of the
Kirk:

"A high Ruling Elder to wallow in wine!
He left the foul business to folks less divine!"

Then the member of parliament fell out, the sun rose, and the
poet got up "like a prophet in drink" to carry out the crowning
of the one who was left: the lawyer, in whose house the historic
whistle is preserved to this day. Burns was justly proud of his
poem and sent numerous copies of it to his acquaintances. He even
sent one to the Duke of Queensberry, with the remark that it
was his best ballad.[83] It appeared from November 1791 in a
number of newspapers, and then in the fourth volume of the
"Musical Museum," with an effective tune written for it by Riddell.

At some period during the year 1789—we are not quite certain
as to the exact date—this convivial circle was enriched by a person
of extraordinary charm, whose individuality suited the habits
and interests of the members so wonderfully that one would have
thought that it had been created for them. We refer to the antiquarian, Captain Francis Grose. Born at Guildford, Middlesex, in
1731, Grose had received a good education, and had developed his
talent for drawing at the Royal Academy. After that, however,
he had become an officer, and had for some time held the position

---

[82] Cf. his letter to Riddell on the day of the event, Letters, 365.
[83] Letters, 471.

of captain, adjutant, and paymaster in the Surrey Militia. In the
carrying out of his duties it is said that he kept note neither of
income nor expenditure, but regarded his left and right trouser
pockets as the two sides of his ledger. Under these circumstances
he soon found that his budget balanced very unfavourably for him,
and this caused him to put away his uniform and turn the fruits
of his scientific and artistic education to account in the domain of
antiquarian research. He wrote an imposing number of books,
which were often permeated with delightful humour, and acquired
a certain reputation through his chief work, the "Antiquities of
England and Wales," which occupied him from 1773 to 1787. The
success of this book encouraged him to continue his research, and
brought him next to Scotland, where he was permitted to make
the house of his fellow-soldier and fellow-antiquary, Robert Riddell,
his headquarters. He was all the more welcome as he was preceded by the reputation of being a radiantly good-natured, original,
highly entertaining person—a man who knew how to bear his
tremendous corpulence and the jests concerning it with the best of
humour; who could handle crayon, chalk, or pen; and who could
always produce a robust thirst or a good story:

> "But wad ye see him in his glee—
> For meikle glee and fun has he—
> Then set him down, and twa or three
>   Guid fellows wi' him;
> And port, O port! shine thou a wee,
>   And then ye'll see him!"

When Burns, who is the author of this stanza,[84] first mentioned
the antiquary in a letter of introduction to Mrs. Dunlop, in which
he gave her a character-sketch of the good fellow,[85] Grose had
already published (in April 1789) the first volume of his "Antiquities
of Scotland" and, starting from Friars' Carse, had visited Annan-
dale, Nithsdale, and Galloway. He was now about to set out for
Ayrshire on a similar expedition. Burns, who had formed a warm
friendship with him, was at this point his most fitting and best-
informed adviser. "I have to the best of my recollection of the old
buildings, &c., in the County, given him an Itinerary through Ayr-

---

[84] "On the Late Captain Grose's Peregrinations thro' Scotland." H. H., i,
289-292; see also "On Captain Grose," H. H., ii, 62-64, and an epigram on him,
ibid., 247.
[85] 17th July 1789; Letters, 352.

shire," he wrote to Mrs. Dunlop. The thought of Ayrshire brought back all his reverent love for his native place, and in musing on the "old buildings" the first to enter his mind was one that stood close to the cottage where he was born: the deserted church whose ruins rose above his father's grave. He asked Grose to include a picture of it in his work, and added to his request a suggestion about the many stories of ghosts and witches which were current in connection with the old church. In Grose's case that sort of thing fell on fertile ground, and he promised to do his best, provided that Burns contributed one of those witch stories as an accompanying text.[86] The bargain was struck. The picture of Alloway Kirk appeared in the second volume of the "Antiquities of Scotland" (April, 1791). The text which accompanied it on pages 199-201 was "Tam o' Shanter."[87]

Written probably in one happy effort in November 1790,[88] this great piece has cast an eternal halo round the white farmhouse and the path that leads along the farmyard wall, beneath high ash-trees, down to the river. Burns chose as his metre the eight-syllabled lines rhyming in pairs which had already been successfully used for similar purposes in Scottish literature, notably in Ramsay's "Fables and Tales," the language, rhyme, and narrative style of which have influenced Burns's in minor technical details.[89] Burns himself, in an undated letter to Grose, gives a masterly account of the popular tradition on which his poem is based.[90] The second of the three stories known to him was its immediate source. It runs as follows:

> "On a market day in the town of Ayr, a farmer from Carrick, and consequently whose way lay by the very gate of Aloway kirk-yard, in order to cross the river Doon at the old bridge, which is about two or three hundred yards farther on than the said gate, had been detained by his business till by the time he reached Aloway it was the wizard hour, between night and morning. Though he was terrified with a blaze streaming from the kirk, yet as it is a well-known fact, that to turn back on these occasions is running by far the greatest risk of mischief, he prudently advanced on his road. When he had reached the gate of the kirk-yard, he was surprised and entertained,

---

[86] Gilbert Burns to Currie, Ch. W., iii, 210-211.
[87] H. H., i, 278-287 with notes on pp. 433-441.
[88] See Dunlop Corr., 289-290; 292-293; Letters, 427.
[89] For other forerunners see H. H., i, 319.
[90] Letters, 401.

through the ribs and arches of an old gothic window which still faces
the highway, to see a dance of witches merrily footing it round their
old sooty blackguard master, who was keeping them all alive with the
power of his bagpipe. The farmer stopping his horse to observe them
a little, could plainly descry the faces of many old women of his
acquaintance and neighbourhood. How the gentleman was dressed,
tradition does not say; but the ladies were all in their smocks; and one
of them happening unluckily to have a smock which was considerably
too short to answer all the purpose of that piece of dress, our farmer
was so tickled that he involuntarily burst out, with a loud laugh, 'Weel
luppen' (well-leaped), 'Maggy wi' the short sark!' and recollecting himself, instantly spurred his horse to the top of his speed. I need not
mention the universally known fact, that no diabolical power can
pursue you beyond the middle of a running stream. Lucky it was
for the poor farmer that the river Doon was so near, for notwithstanding the speed of his horse, which was a good one, against he reached
the middle of the arch of the bridge, and consequently the middle
of the stream, the pursuing, vengeful hags were so close at his heels,
that one of them actually sprung to seize him: but it was too late;
nothing was on her side of the stream but the horse's tail, which
immediately gave way to her infernal grip, as if blasted by a stroke of
lightning; but the farmer was beyond her reach.—However, the
unsightly, tail-less condition of the vigorous steed was to the last hours
of the noble creature's life, an awful warning to the Carrick farmers,
not to stay too late in Ayr markets."

Burns incorporated in this version of the legend a few motifs from
the first of the stories referred to by him: the wild and stormy
night, so suitable for devilish cantrips; the fact that the farmer's
courage was fortified above the ordinary by the strong drink of
which he had partaken liberally; and the odious ingredients of the
cauldron which he saw hanging from the roof of the church,
simmering over a fire.[91]

The poet hit upon the happy thought of turning the vague hero
of popular tradition into a sharply defined personality, by giving
him a name and individual characteristics. This proved so effective
that people have tried to find prototypes not only for Tam o'
Shanter himself, but also for his scolding wife, for Souter Johnny,
the smith, the miller, and Kirkton Jean, the assumption being that
only now, after so many years, had Burns been inspired to revive
the memories of the months he had spent in Kirkoswald and to
give them life and form. It will be hard to corroborate this claim.
In many points the poem itself may have suggested the anecdotes

---

[91] Ritter, "Quellenstudien," 217, note.   In the poem, of course, the ingredients
lie upon "the holy table."

connected with its origin. In inventing men and incidents which were supposed to correspond to those in the poem, people were only obeying an irresistible urge to have something real and tangible as a background, but in no case are these "realities" truer or more life-like than the creatures of the poet's imagination. At the same time, there are in the poem unmistakable reminiscences of the poet's native landscape. The inn in the High Street of Ayr, where the two men, Tam and Souter Johnny, used to meet, is still preserved, in a comparatively unchanged form, as one of the "sights" of the town. Here they would sit drinking, comfortably ensconced by the merrily crackling fire, heedless of the storm outside, laughing, to the applause of the host and hostess of the inn, at the warnings of the anxious, scolding wife, and feeling gloriously happy and victorious "o'er a' the ills o' life." Then Tam would take the road from Ayr to Alloway—the road that Burns had traversed countless times in his boyhood. As Tam rode homeward, the stormy night would waken in his memory the evil events which had taken place in that very neighbourhood. At last he would reach the old ruin where the witches used to dance. It would be gleaming under the towering, groaning trees with a ghostly radiance. Then he would come to the old Brig o' Doon (where he was rescued in the poem), its high arch spanning the angry, brawling waters of the river. All that was for Burns familiar ground. Welded together by the swiftly moving plot, the scenes rise up with vivid clearness before the mental eye of the reader or listener. In the development of the action Burns followed his prose sketch very closely, except that the central scene, the dance round the devil, who is playing the bagpipes, is filled out with a number of details which the inquisitive Tam, as he peers in through a paneless window, beholds with horror and yet with mirth, until his rash cry of admiration plunges everything in sudden darkness. Away dash horse and rider, behind them sweep the witches, with terrible, menacing howls and screeches, led by Nannie, for whom the offending ejaculation had been intended— one last spring—the mare's tail is left in the hands of the wicked pursuer, and Tam is safe! Each smallest detail of the scene is vividly described, the language and the ideas being cunningly interwoven so as to form a perfect unity, in a series of striking pictures and images; while, by making technically brilliant use of observations and interjections the narrator reveals his own eager participation in the drama, and by this artificial expedient increases the effect of the individual episodes. Each figure, be it of earth or of Hell, is alive; no one would dare to question the diablerie of Auld Nick: the uncanny scene in the old Kirk at Alloway is as real as the anger of the lonely Kate, seated by her fireside, "nursing her wrath to keep it warm"—it is as real as Souter Johnny and the "glorious" Tam themselves. But above all the horrors of Hell there rises radiantly triumphant the incomparable humour of the poet, who in "Tam o' Shanter" has created a work in honour of his native place that for power of inspiration and perfection of execution is worthy to stand beside the best tales in the literature of the world. Burns with justifiable pride described "Tam o' Shanter" as his greatest poetic achievement and his favourite poem.[92]

As early as 12th March, 1791, a discerning and learned critic, Alexander Fraser Tytler, while under the strong impression which the poem had made upon him, wrote to Burns:

> "Go on—write more tales in the same style—you will eclipse Prior and La Fontaine; for, with equal wit, equal power of numbers and equal naïveté of expression, you have a bolder and more vigorous imagination."

Burns replied:

> "Your approbation, Sir, has given me such additional spirits to per-severe in this species of poetic composition, that I am already revolving two or three stories in my fancy."[93]

A vein of gold had been struck, and with fruitless regret one reflects on the value of the treasures which Burns might have dug from it. In addition to the satirical pictures of Scottish country life, and the wealth of lyric poetry in which the joys and sorrows of the people are successfully portrayed, we might possibly have had a third great literary feat—the adaptation and remodelling of the folk-legends and popular tales, which, handled in the style of "Tam o' Shanter," would have been unique. As it is, we are left with one single work, which is great not only in what it has accomplished, but also in the expectations of further achievement which it offers—and leaves unfulfilled.

---

[92] Letters, 443.
[93] Ch. W., iii, 255-257; Letters, 445.

With the year 1791, Burns's sojourn at Ellisland drew to a close. The poet does not seem to have been painfully conscious of the radical change which was taking place in his life, or to have had any sentimental regrets about definitely leaving the country and the plough. The fact is that he was acting in accordance with conclusions he had formed and decisions he had reached a long time before. His landlord, Patrick Miller, made all the fewer difficulties as he found himself in the position of being able to sell Ellisland advantageously. The harvest for once was a good one, and brought prices which exceeded Burns's expectations; and the general satisfaction found vent in a scene of wild exuberance, with fighting in the open and tremendous drunkenness in the house, all of which Burns as spectator has described with unconcealed enjoyment in a letter of 1st September 1791.[94] In November his live stock and implements were publicly auctioned, likewise with satisfactory results, and a few months later he was able to tell Mrs. Dunlop that he had got rid of the farm, the further cultivation of which had threatened to ruin him, with little, if any, loss.[95] Dumfries was well known to him; the continuation of his service with the Board of Excise offered him the prospect of imminent promotion and official recognition, with a consequent increase in salary; his old friends were still within reach; the animated, busy town, of which he was a burgess, promised new and valuable contacts and intellectual and social stimuli in abundance, so that the giving up of the idyllic but unprofitable existence by the Nith seemed of only secondary importance in comparison with the hoped-for gain in external security and inward peace. Burns moved with his family to Dumfries in November 1791, and settled at first in a small house in the upper storey of a building in a street then known as the Wee Vennel. Only a few steps away the Nith, coming from Ellisland, flows under an old bridge towards the Solway and its journey's end.

---

[94] To Thomas Sloan, Letters, 466.
[95] Letters, 491.

Chapter IX

BURNS AS A SONG-WRITER

WE must here interrupt the continuity of our narrative in order to consider Burns's work as a song-writer in its totality. Hitherto, instead of showing how his songs were connected with the various phases of his career, we have limited ourselves to a few more or less brief remarks concerning them, in order to give the subject the benefit of a comprehensive investigation. To do this, we must go back to his first poetic efforts, and anticipate matters by discussing the greatest part of his literary output in Dumfries.

The aimlessness of his existence, which he deplores in his auto-biographical letter to Dr. Moore as the great misfortune of his life, seems merely to have been a supplementary aspect of his temperament, which on the artistic side found expression in a pronounced gift for writing lyric poetry, resulting in a higher degree of unity between his life and his creative genius. In both we recognize the inward urge of his nature, which was ever receptive of new impressions (perhaps at times it yielded too much to them), and was better suited to noting the endless changes in life's passing show, than to working out slowly maturing, well-considered plans. Keats on one occasion calls the poet "the most unpoetical of anything in existence, because he has no identity. He is continually in for and filling some other body"—while he himself sinks his individuality in his creations.[1] This adaptability of the highest poetic faculty is one of the basic elements of Burns's lyrical art. Even in the case of the almost supernaturally ethereal Keats, however, the poet's personality asserts its rights unhesitatingly; while the personality of Burns reveals itself with the shattering force of a titanic self-confidence. When we come to consider Burns's song-writing as a whole, we must also qualify our statement that in his writing of poetry he followed no regular plan, though this is strictly true of his individual poems and even of his purest lyrics. Through-

---

[1] Letter to Woodhouse, 27th Oct. 1818. Complete Works (ed. Buxton Forman), iv, 173.

out his life Burns placed his poetic skill in ever greater measure and with an ever growing sense of confidence at the service of that one, great, national idea, to which he clung with passionate fervour: viz., the wish to leave to posterity, in an ideal and permanent form, a complete collection of the songs of Scotland, purified of alien elements and dross, as something new and yet permeated to the marrow with the spirit and strength of preceding generations. He wished to create a new folk-song for Scotland, to put into the mouths of his fellow-countrymen words suited to the great stock of old tunes which they sang and to which they danced, so that they might be brought closer together by their songs—so that in their hours of joy and sorrow, of meditation or patriotic fervour, they might not lack a fitting, liberating vehicle of expression. That was the medium with which he, as a true poet of the people, wished to provide them. He desired, by the magic of his art, to give an imperishable form to the sentiments common to all. It would be impossible to imagine a better interpreter. His roots sprang from the innermost core of the Scottish people. In his own life he had had to face the storm and stress of every passion. His heart overflowed with sympathy for the oppressed and with wrath against the oppressor; it suffered with the afflicted, rejoiced with the happy, and burned with the brave and the patriotic. He was gifted with the power of judging impartially both high and low, and, after the manner of the greatest poets, of raising the particular to the typical. If, then, his rich endowments were joined to what was best in traditional literature, it was possible that poet and people might become one, and that those rare conditions which form the basis of the older folk-songs and the so-called genuine folk-ballads might be created—that is, the boundary-line between the one who made the song and the many who sang it might disappear. The magnitude of this idea of Burns's is tremendous and unique, and the manner of its execution of inexhaustible interest.

Burns wrote or revived at least three hundred and fifty songs. These fall, according to their chronological order and their purpose, into three groups, the second and third of which have a certain degree of unity, in spite of essential differences, in so far as they were both composed from the angle of the great national work of song-collecting. The first group appeared spasmodically in Ayrshire, between 1773 and the end of 1786; the second began in the spring of 1787 with Burns's friendship with James Johnson, the Edinburgh publisher and engraver, and comprised Burns's contributions to the latter's compilation, "The Scots Musical Museum"; the third was the result of his connection with a rival venture, the "Select Collection of Original Scottish Airs," whose publisher, George Thomson, had in September 1792 approached Burns, as the greatest contemporary Scottish poet, with the request for his collaboration. From that moment onward, Burns helped Thomson as well as Johnson by word and deed, though under very different conditions, until Death took the pen from his hand.

The smallness of the number of lyrical poems which Burns wrote while resident in Ayrshire is striking and gives food for thought. The country, where the folk-song must have been alive in some form or other, proved far less productive than the town. The "Poems, Chiefly in the Scottish Dialect," published in 1786, contained not more than three songs, to which seven were added in the first Edinburgh Edition (1787), and two in the second (1793). The explanation of this insignificant total doubtless lies in the fact that the majority of the "Poems" were not lyrical but descriptive and satirical in character. Apart from that, however, these years cannot, as far as we can see, be considered to have been strong in lyrical production, even if we include the cantata, "The Jolly Beggars." We are all the more struck by the instinctive sureness with which, after a few immature efforts, he produced masterpieces such as "It was upon a Lammas Night,"[2] "John Barleycorn,"[3] "Green grow the Rashes, O,"[4] and "Mary Morison."[5] These songs also clearly reveal his attitude to his sources. His method of dealing with the old Scottish songs and airs was already fixed, as was his judgment of them, in the main. He had become familiar with them, and had long studied them with the liveliest interest, in several collections of texts and airs such as Allan Ramsay's "Tea-Table Miscellany," "The Lark" of 1765, Robert Bremner's "Scots Songs," street ballads, and the living tradition and production around him.

"The Collection of Songs[6] was my vade mecum," he says in his

---

[2] H. H., i, 189-181.
[3] *Ibid.*, 243-246.
[4] *Ibid.*, 251-252.
[5] *Ibid.*, iii, 286-287.
[6] "The Lark."

autobiographical letter. "I pored over them, driving my cart or walk-ing to labor, song by song, verse by verse; carefully noting the true tender or sublime from affectation and fustian.—I am convinced I owe much to this for my critic-craft such as it is."[7]

Thus, in addition to his creative power and artistic intention, he had already a marked—and, to a certain extent, developed—urge to get a thorough insight into the traditional poetry and music of his country, and rationally to select the elements in it capable of development. Viewed from this standpoint, Burns's entries in his Mossgiel Common-place Book for September 1785 are of the greatest interest. He has been struck by the metrical irregularity of Scottish folk-songs compared with anglicised song-writing, but at the same time he has noted the fact that, thanks to this very irregularity, the Scots songs "glide in most melodiously with the respective tunes to which they are set." To illustrate his remark, he quotes the example of "the fine old song, 'The Mill Mill O.'" If, he says, the text of this song is read as simple prose, it cannot, as far as exactness of metre is concerned, compare with the words set to the same tune in Bremner's collection; but let both versions be *sung,* and—"how flat and spiritless will the last appear, how trite, and lamely methodical, compared with the wild-warbling cadence, the heart-moving melody of the first!"[8] He then generalizes and states that he has found this irregularity in the many poems and fragments which he hears sung daily by his com-peers, the common people. The thought occurs to him that it might be possible for a Scottish poet with a nice, judicious ear to compose texts for many of the most popular melodies, without regarding the technicalities of rhyme. With inward emotion and the proud consciousness of being one of their number, he mentions the name-less, "glorious old Bards," the poets of those fragments full of noble sublimity and heart-melting tenderness, "which show them to be the work of a masterly hand." He then gives a poem of his

---

[7] Letters, 125.

[8] Ch. W., i, 140 ff. The old text of "The Mill Mill O'" may be found in Herd's MSS. (my edition, p. 115), and in the "Merry Muses" (1911 ed., p. 84). The text given in Bremner (pp. 30 and 31)—"To Fanny fair could I impart"—is taken from Ramsay's *Tea-Table Miscellany* (1760 ed., pp. 388-389); *ibid.,* pp. 76-77, under the title of "The Mill Mill O'," a less refined version, which retains traces of the original text and influenced Burns, as far as the contents are concerned, when he wrote his lyrical ballad, "When Wild War's Deadly Blast" to this tune for Thomson (H. H., iii, 212-214). See Letters 554 and 567 (To Thomson, April and June, 1793).

own, "Montgomerie's Peggy,"[9] to the tune of "Gala Water," in
which he has imitated an old Scottish piece, "McMillan's Peggy,"
unfortunately now lost.   The rhythm, varied by means of putting
several unaccented syllables between the stressed ones, and the
intentional assonance of the rhymes, show us, perhaps a little too
deliberately, the characteristic traits of his models.   Continuing,
Burns, referring to another song "well known among the country
ingle-sides," praises the excellent unison existing between the air
and the text, and goes on to say :

> "By the way, these old Scottish airs are so nobly sentimental that
> when one would compose to them: to *south* the tune, as our
> Scotch phrase is, over & over, is the readiest way to catch the inspira-
> tion and raise the Bard into that glorious enthusiasm so strongly
> characteristic of our old Scotch Poetry."[10]

This whole passage of the Common-place Book is extremely instructive.   It shows in what spirit Burns approached the writing of
songs, how for him the song always, and under all circumstances,
meant unity of words and melody; and, indeed, there is no doubt
that he even at that time recognized the air as the starting point
for new texts.   The texts of the folk-songs which were still sung had
for long been in a fragmentary condition.   Burns saw the artistic
value of these fragments, and was convinced that they could be
completed, as far as the sense at least was concerned: indeed, he
himself had successfully attempted this art of restoration in several
cases.   Street ballads and professional poetry he found useful as
sources, but they, too, needed revising.   His attitude to the Anglo-
Scottish song, that is, the union of Scottish airs with mediocre
English lyrics, was a negative one.   He felt it was in bad style,
and was anxious to replace it by more genuine strains.

Taken as a whole, these ideas and sentiments clearly reveal the
future reformer of the Scottish folk-song.   It may even be asserted
that the guiding principles set down in the Common-place Book
of 1785 continued for the most part to set the standard for his later
years, when his lyrical power was fully developed.   Before this
glowing enthusiasm for the sublime cause could be transformed into
beneficial acts of universal greatness, however, he needed certain
stimuli which were lacking in the rural environment of Mauchline.

---

[9] H. H., iv, 3; see also Ritter's "Quellenstudien," 13-15.
[10] Ch. W., i, 142.

These he found in Edinburgh, the centre of Scotland's literary life, and they exercised a strong and decisive influence upon him.

The day on which William Dunbar, Colonel of the "Crochallan Fencibles," introduced Burns to James Johnson was of decisive importance for the poet's whole future literary life. We know little either of Johnson's personality or of his life, beyond the fact that he was an unassuming man of imperfect education. He belonged to the silent ones of the earth, to those who wield no definite influence on the life of the world, and yet seek to benefit their fellows by faithful and devoted service, at the same time without criticism or envy, letting stronger natures take the precedence. That is exactly the rôle which Johnson played in the history of the Scottish folk-song. Born in 1753 or 1754, he served his apprenticeship, to all appearances, with James Read, the music-publisher, setting up for himself as an engraver of music about the beginning of the 'seventies. From that time onward, numerous pieces of music, especially the endless series of dance tunes, bear his signature. He is credited, in particular, with having reduced the cost of printing music by introducing pewter plates in place of copper, which had hitherto been used. He may deserve that honour as far as Scotland is concerned, but the process had long been known in England. Johnson died on 25th February 1811, so poor that his widow shortly afterwards found herself in the most destitute circumstances and had to apply to the Poor Law authorities for assistance.[11] During the years of his friendship with him, Burns esteemed him as an efficient and honourable collaborator with whom it was easy to work, but although he probably also allowed him occasionally—if only for the sake of good form—to decide whether his (Burns's) contributions should be accepted or not, he never really discussed matters with him as he did later with Thomson. A business letter from Johnson to Burns,[12] written during the year 1794, gives a vivid picture of his shy, rather repressed, yet always tactful nature. It also shows that Johnson never quite mastered the difficulties of spelling.

This man, who was in no way outstanding, but who pursued

---

[11] See Glen, "Early Scottish Melodies," 256-257. Title pages for the dances printed by Johnson, in the "Glen Collection of Scottish Dance Music," i, pp xviii-xx, and ii, pp. xix-xx.

[12] Ch. W., iv, 88-89.

his calling with zeal and a certain enthusiasm, decided, after
issuing a number of useful but more or less ephemeral publications,
to embark on a more ambitious venture, the first volume of which
was entitled: "The Scots Musical Museum, humbly dedicated to
the Catch Club, &c., Vol. 1. Price 6s. Edinburgh. Sold and subscriptions taken in by and for the publisher, N. Stewart, R.
Bremner, Corri and Sutherland, R. Ross, Edinburgh, and all the
music sellers in London."[13] The preface is dated 22nd May 1787,
and is addressed to the "true lovers of Caledonian music and
song." It states that this new collection will be cheaper and more
complete than any of its predecessors, which were, moreover, so
large and unwieldly that they could not fulfil their purpose as
"pocket-companions," this being no small disadvantage, especially
to the admirers of social music. The "Museum," the preface goes
on to say, is intended to do away with this and other evils. It
rejoices in the patronage of "a number of gentlemen of indubitable
taste, who have been pleased to encourage, assist and adorn the
whole literary part of the performance." Each volume is to contain
a hundred songs, the musical arrangement of which is in the hands
of one of "the most skilful masters." Johnson himself is responsible for only the mechanical part of the undertaking and is devoting
the greatest possible care to it. We learn that the original intention
was to include a considerable number of the tenderest and most
melodious English and Irish songs,[14] but that this plan was rejected
because of decided opposition on the part of the subscribers, and
had therefore been postponed for the time: a remarkable demon-
stration of Scottish patriotism in things artistic! Johnson finally
requests that any unpublished songs with the music "in the true-
caledonian style" be submitted to him: if they are approved by
the appointed judges, they will be preserved in "the present reposi-
tory of our national music and lyric poetry."

Among the staff of patrons and helpers referred to by Johnson
in this modest, quiet, impersonal preface, let us look first at the
musical collaborator, so happily chosen, for special mention. This
was Stephen Clarke, music teacher and organist in the Episcopalian

---

13 After the appearance of the 6th volume (1803) the title was altered. From
that time the publication was dedicated to the "Society of Antiquaries of Scotland."
See the bibliographical note in Dick's "Songs of Robert Burns," p. xxxvi.

14 Johnson's prospectus of Feb. 1787, in Glen's "Early Scottish Melodies," p. 16.

Chapel in the Cowgate, and in truth one of the "most skilful masters." Burns was on friendly terms with him and called him, in a letter to Skinner, "the first musician in Edinburgh."[15] As a collaborator in the "Museum," his special merit consisted in the fact that he chose the best available versions of the tunes to be incorporated in the work, and kept them in their natural form, deliberately avoiding every excess in the harmonizing of the airs and in the accompaniments. He wished the melodies to produce their effect through their own beauty and not through superimposed flourishes or pompous introductions and finals. By strict adherence to this principle, Clarke has in the "Musical Museum" produced a masterpiece of artistic restraint, which may serve as a model for the treatment of folk-songs. In addition, he was musical adviser to Burns as well as to Johnson, and helped the former to write down newly found melodies; and he composed, among other things, the music to Burns's martial song, "Does Haughty Gaul Invasion Threat." He died in August 1797, and was replaced on the "Museum" by his less talented son William.[16]

Among the "gentlemen of indubitable taste" who were in charge of the textual part of the work, we recognize James Beattie and Thomas Blacklock, along with whom Burns also mentions the historian William Tytler of Woodhouselee (1711-92), a personal friend of Allan Ramsay and the author of a much-quoted "Dissertation on the Scottish Music" (1779),[17] written with more imagination and love than knowledge of the subject. The result of their united efforts lies before us in the first volume of the "Musical Museum," whose contents reveal only too clearly the evils from which Burns freed the Scottish folk-song. The compilers of the "Museum" had still a wealth of material at their disposal, and strove to the best of their ability to make their publication contrast favourably with the numerous collections already in existence. They succeeded as far as the tunes were concerned. In spite of a few imitations in the Scottish style and several interpolations of English origin, these bear witness to Stephen Clarke's expert judgment and thorough knowledge. At the same time, we must remember that Clarke had a considerable number of excellent models at his

---

15 Letters, 147.

16 See D. F. Harris, "Saint Cecilia's Hall," Edinburgh, 1899, 100-106.

17 Letters, 147 (to Skinner) and 145 (to Hoy).

disposal, such as, for instance, Thomson's "Orpheus Caledonius" and Oswald's "Caledonian Pocket Companion." In skilful use of these and similar collections there was as yet neither progress nor gain. The main difficulty lay in the getting up of the textual part: with what words should the airs, which were folk-music in the widest sense of the term, be provided?—airs whose simplicity, pathos, noble melancholy, and strange wild rhythm appealed to every Scot as something absolutely national, rousing the most fervent patriotic feelings in his breast? What quality must the texts possess in order to preserve and, if possible, to strengthen—at all events, not to destroy—these emotions? The solving of this problem, which has perhaps never before or since been set in such a pronounced form, was a task in the highest degree worthy of a genius. There is not the slightest doubt that the editors of the first volume of the "Museum" failed to grasp its full significance, in spite of their sincere devotion to the sacred cause. The old tunes are redolent of the open country and reflect, as it were, the clear, spacious firmament. They seem to reverberate from knowe to knowe. The majority of the texts which accompanied them in the "Museum" and elsewhere had, on the other hand, been written by the elegant poets of the seventeenth and eighteenth centuries, who had frequently let themselves be guided by considerations of decorum. They had made the folk-songs suitable for the drawing-room, and, in so doing, had sacrificed many an invaluable old stanza. Thus, songs of the heath, the glen, and the mountain had become diversions of the tea-table, hybrids without any real vitality of their own. The first volume of the "Museum" belongs to this category, and is neither better nor worse than the average. Its hundred items include a few good old pieces, such as four verses of the ballad, "The Lass of Loch Royan": "O open the door, Lord Gregory" (No. 5);[18] "Saw ye Johnnie cummin, quo' she" (No. 9, first printed in Bremner's "Thirty Scots Songs," 1757, pp. 6-7); "When I think on this warld's pelf" (No. 33, same collection as the foregoing, pp. 2-3); and "My ain kind Deary, O" (No. 49, tune from Oswald's "Caledonian Pocket Companion," Book VIII, p. 20, text adapted by Robert Fergusson from an older version). By far the greatest number of the texts—some seven-eighths—have simply

---

[18] See Child's "Ballads," No. 76, version J.

been taken from Allan Ramsay's "Tea-table Miscellany," while the remainder come from song-books of a similar nature, or consist of isolated contributions by various poets and poetasters, to enumerate whom would be superfluous here. This predilection for Allan Ramsay is in itself neither strange nor objectionable. The "Tea-table Miscellany" by no means lacks a strong element of popular poetry. But for this copious collection, which, as the "Museum" shows, was of predominating influence right up to the last quarter of the century, many valuable fragments of old folk-poetry would have been lost to us, for Ramsay's method was similar to that of Burns, in that he was fond of collecting old song-titles, half stanzas, refrains, and fragments of greater compass, which he arranged to suit the needs of his public, and which in many cases may be easily detached from their context. In spite of that, however, the artificial element remained markedly in evidence, replacing the untrammelled spirit of the folk-song, to which it was unsuited, by something false, tedious, and mediocre, for which there could be no future, however popular it might be in its day. Therein lay the danger to the "Scots Musical Museum": the texts in the first volume suffered from the questionable tradition of the "correct poetry" of the "Tea-table Miscellany," which was un-Scottish and, therefore, contrasted unnaturally with the national airs. An example will illustrate the point. Under No. 41 in the "Museum" appears the old tune "I Wish my Love were in a Mire," which probably dates from the seventeenth century. Of the old text nothing has been preserved but the title.[19] The "Museum," however, prints two poems along with the melody, the first, a translation by Ambrose Philips from the Greek of Sappho, being taken from the "Orpheus Caledonius":

> "Blest as th' immortal gods is he,
> The Youth who fondly sits by thee,
> And hears and sees thee all the while,
> Softly speak and sweetly smile," &c.

For those who did not care for these words, the following poem from the first volume of the "Tea-table Miscellany" is given, to the same tune:

---

[19] See the air in Dick's "Songs of Burns," 91, and *cf*. Burns's "Glenriddell Notes," with notes on the song.

To Chloe[20]

"O Lovely maid, how dear's thy pow'r.
At once I love, at once adore:
With wonder are my thoughts possest,
While softest love inspires my breast.
This tender look, these eyes of mine,
Confess their am'rous master thine;
These eyes with *Strephon's* passion play;
First make me love, and then betray.

"Yes, Charming Victor, I am thine,
Poor as it is, this heart of mine
Was never in another's pow'r,
Was never pierc'd by love before.
In thee I've treasur'd up my joy,
Thou can'st give bliss, or bliss destroy:
And thus I've bound myself to love,
While bliss or misery can move.

"O should I ne'er possess thy charms,
Ne'er meet my comfort in thy arms,[21]
Were hopes of dear enjoyment gone,
Still would I love, love thee alone.
But, like some discontented shade,
That wanders where its body's laid,
Mournful I'd roam with hollow glare,
For ever exil'd from my fair."[22]

Concerning a similar poem in the first volume of the "Museum" (No. 27) Burns later made the pungent remark: "to sing such a beautiful air to such damned verses is downright sodomy of Common Sense!"[23] The fact that he himself was not always able to resist the influence of this artificial style did not alter the aversion which he felt for it in moments when his critical sense was unblurred. David Laing, referring to the first volume of the "Museum" in the preface to his edition of Stenhouse's "Illustrations," is fully justified when he writes that without Burns's intervention the work would probably never have got beyond the two volumes originally planned, and would certainly never have attained the lasting renown which it enjoys. In spite of its advantages, and in spite or because of the "indisputable taste" of its patrons it would have perished in mediocrity.

[20] No title in the *Mus.*
[21] *Mus.*; my arms.
[22] The signature L. which the poem bears in Ramsay's publication has not yet been identified.
[23] Glenriddell Notes, 10.

When Burns became acquainted with Johnson, which was probably not before February 1787, the printing of the first volume of the "Museum" was already too far advanced for him to exercise any decisive influence on it. Of Burns's songs it contains only "Green grow the rashes, O" (No. 77), "Young Peggy blooms our boniest lass" (as second text to "Loch Eroch Side," No. 78),[24] written in Allan Ramsay's weakest style and far away from the spirit of genuine folk-poetry; and an adaptation, with one additional stanza, of "Bonie Dundee": "O Whar did ye get that hauver-meal bannock?" (No. 99).[25] After the publication of the Edinburgh Edition of his poems, however, his head and his hand were free, and he applied himself to Johnson's work with all the burning fervour of enthusiasm which the great national undertaking roused in him. The result of his collaboration may be briefly summed up thus: in place of Ramsay and his imitators, whose amiable but outworn art dominated the first volume of the "Museum," we have from now onward the powerful vigour of Burns's genius. He struck off the fetters of conventionality. The freshness of a great personality made itself felt, and drove into the background the purely literary element taken over from preceding generations. The philandering with English "correct poetry" ceased, and, supported by the whole treasury of Scottish melodies, carefully supplemented by new collections, by the most suitable songs of contemporary native poets, and by the still existent texts and fragments of old traditional lyrics, which found in Burns a congenial restorer and adapter animated by a very real understanding of the people, there rose up the imposing structure of a comprehensive collection of Scottish song. Nothing can more clearly illustrate the sudden change in the management than a comparison of the hesitating tone of that first preface signed by Johnson and the introduction of the second volume of the "Museum," which is anonymous but betrays its author at the first glance. We quote it in full:

"In the first Volume of this work, two or three Airs not of Scots

---

[24] H. H., iii, 1.

[25] H. H., iii, 3-4. No. 98, "The Joyful Widower," is also attributed to Burns in some editions. H. H., iv, 55-56, put it among the *Improbables*. See Ritter, *Archiv*, 103, 153-154, where verses 2 and 3 are traced back to Camden's "Remaines." Glen found the complete poem in a collection which was also known to Burns: "The Scots Nightingale; or Edinburgh Vocal Miscellany," 2nd ed.; Edinburgh, 1779. See Glen's "Early Scottish Melodies," p. 90. Accordingly it should be omitted from the list of Burns's works.

composition have been inadvertently inserted; which, whatever excellence they may have, was improper, as the Collection is meant to be solely the music of our own Country.—The Songs contained in this Volume, both music and poetry, are all of them the work of Scotsmen. —Wherever the old words could be recovered, they have been preserved; both as generally suiting better the genius of the tunes, and to preserve the productions of those earlier Sons of the Scottish Muses, some of whose names deserved a better fate than has befallen them— 'Buried midst the wreck of things which were.'[26] Of our more modern Songs, the Editor has inserted the Authors' names as far as he could ascertain them; and as that was neglected in the first Volume, it is annexed here.—If he have made any mistakes in this affair, which he possibly may, he shall be very grateful at being set right.

"Ignorance and Prejudice may perhaps affect to sneer at the simplicity of the poetry or music of some of these pieces; but their having been for ages the favourites of Nature's Judges—the Common People, was to the Editor a sufficient test of their merit.

"Materials for the third Volume are in great forwardness."

It is at once evident from Burns's correspondence that immediately he took up the work he became its driving force and inspiration, although as a matter of fact we have only a few letters written to Johnson himself during the first period of their collaboration. Personal contact took the place of correspondence. Burns's first letter, dated 4th May 1787, contains little more than the flattering assurance that Burns had found Johnson's company pleasant and his sentiments congenial.[27] Immediately afterwards Burns set out on his trips to the south-west Borders and the Highlands, journeys which he himself regarded as pilgrimages to the classical ground of Scottish song. After his return to Edinburgh, he spoke of his travels as "perfectly inspiring," and as late as 26th January 1793 he wrote to Thomson:

"I am such an enthusiast, that in the course of my several peregrinations through Scotland, I made a pilgrimage to the individual spot from which the song took its rise—Lochaber & the braes of Ballenden excepted, so far as the locality, either from the title of the air, or the tenor of the Song, could be ascertained, I have paid my devotion at the particular shrine of every Scots Muse."[28]

If a letter to Johnson, dated 25th May 1788, immediately before Burns's removal to Ellisland, contains no reference to the

---

[26] Quotation from Blair's "Grave," i. 30.
[27] Letters, 104.
[28] *Ibid.*, 535.

"Museum,"[29] another letter, written on 15th November of the same year, is brimful of creative zeal and proud confidence regarding the future of the work:

> "If you have got any tunes, or any thing to correct, please send them by return of the Carrier.— . . . I can easily see, my dear Friend, that you will very probably have four Volumes.—Perhaps you may not find your account, *lucratively,* in this business; but you are a Patriot for the Music of your Country; and I am certain, Posterity will look on themselves as highly indebted to your Publick spirit.—Be not in a hurry; let us go on correctly; and your name shall be immortal. . . . I am preparing a flaming Preface for your third Volume.—I see every day, new Musical Publications, advertised; but what are they? Gaudy, hunted butterflies of a day, & then vanish for ever: but your Work will outlive the momentary neglects of idle Fashion, & defy the teeth of Time."[30]

Other letters show him busy working for Johnson, soliciting and collecting contributions. Thus we find him writing to the Duke of Gordon's librarian, James Hoy, requesting the Duke's words to "Cauld Kail in Aberdeen,"[31] with which he had become acquainted on the occasion of his visit to Gordon Castle; to John Skinner, author of "Tullochgorum" and other favourite popular songs,[32] and a man whom Burns esteemed very highly; and to James Candlish in Glasgow, with the confession: "I have collected, begg'd, borrow'd and stolen all the songs I could meet with."[33] As early as August 1787 he had sent several texts to William Tytler with the remark that they were still to be found among the peasantry of the West, that is, in Ayrshire, among them being a version of the ballad of "Young Hynhorn"; "I had once a great many of such fragments," he wrote, "and some of these here entire; but as I had no idea that any body cared for them, I have forgotten them."[34] Despite this fact, his letters belonging to this period contain a striking increase in the number of quotations from folk-songs and allusions to dance tunes.[35] Enthusiasm and

---

[29] *Ibid.,* 242.

[30] *Ibid.,* 288.

[31] 20th Oct., 1787. The song appeared as No. 162 in the *Mus.* Letters, 145.

[32] Letters, 147, 203.

[33] Letters, 193; Ch. W., ii, 294-296. The date of these letters is given by Ch. W. as Feb. 1788. I consider this too late. Scott Douglas places them in Nov. 1787.

[34] Letters, 126.

[35] *E.g.,* to Ainslie, 23rd Aug. 1787; to Miss Chalmers, 21st Nov. 1787, and 1st Dec. 1787; to Clarinda, 7th Mar. 1788. Letters, 130, 152, 155, 218, and others.

the actual work of collecting had probably jogged his memory
and recalled to him many a piece which he had thought lost.

The effect of Burns's activity on the "Scots Musical Museum"
can be seen at a glance in the number of contributions which he
handed over for insertion in the various volumes and which in the
following estimate is placed if anything at too low a figure. The
second volume (March 1788) contained thirty-six songs, either
original pieces by Burns or amplifications of old fragments which
he had rendered suitable for publication.   In the third, fourth
and fifth volumes (February 1790; August 1792; April 1797), about
half the contents in each volume originated from Burns.   The fifth
volume did not appear till after his death, but it is quite clear from
the manuscript material preserved in the British Museum[36] that its
contents had to all intents and purposes been compiled by Burns.
It was six years before Johnson was able to publish the sixth and
final volume: the last hundred songs appeared in June 1803.
Even this volume contains, according to the index, twenty-six
hitherto unused songs by Burns.   It is to be noted at this point
that Burns at no time either received or desired any kind of
remuneration for his great achievement.   He would not have
accepted any, even if Johnson had been a rich man.   For him the
patriotic cause was high above worldly reward.   Nay more:
during his lifetime very few of his contributions were signed with
his name, so that even to-day it is possible to pick out one or
other of the songs in the "Museum" and ascribe it, in part at least,
to Burns.   As far as he was concerned it was sufficient reward to
be included in the company of the many nameless poets whose
oblivion he has lamented as an undeserved fate; he was content
faithfully to guard and augment their art, which was addressed
to their native land and its people, and with which he felt himself
intimately associated in spirit.   In the preface to the fifth volume
of the "Museum" Johnson could well say that that collection was
indebted to his great deceased collaborator for "almost all of these
excellent pieces which it contained," and refer with pride to a
deeply affecting letter addressed to him by the poet shortly before
the latter's death and containing the prophetic sentences:

"Your Work is a great one; & though, now that it is near finished,

---

[36] In the so-called Hastie Collection (Brit. Mus. ms. Add. 22307). *Cf.* also the
list of 94 songs for the 3rd vol. of the *Mus.* in Dick's "Songs of R.B."

> I see if we were to begin again, two or three things that might be mended, yet I will venture to prophesy, that to future ages your Publication will be the text-book & standard of Scotish Song and Music."[37]

But enthusiasm and genius alone were not sufficient to bring the venture to this high goal. It is essential that we should realize clearly that Burns did not only study the old Scottish songs as an enthusiastic artist, but that he rapidly became so absorbed in them that his technical knowledge, combined with extraordinarily favourable personal factors, is in itself sufficient to merit our attention. In the letters quoted we have already pointed out this attitude towards the scientific side of his work, and it may be said without exaggeration that Burns, regarded purely as a connoisseur of Scottish popular songs, can take his place beside the best authorities of his time—in fact, he is perhaps superior to them. This part of his work has hitherto not received the attention it deserves. Burns himself was not a little proud of the extent and accuracy of his knowledge, and, animated by this feeling, asked in his very first letter to Thomson for a list of the airs to be included in Thomson's "Collection," with the first line of the verses intended for them:

> "I say, the first line of the verses, because if they are verses that have appeared in any of our Collections of songs, I know them & can have recourse to them."[38]

His determination to deal with Scottish Song on a large scale made it necessary for him to review what had already been published.

To do this, he had to deal with three kinds of collections: (1) those containing instrumental music alone; (2) text-books without music; and (3) song-books which, like the "Scots Musical Museum," combined the texts with the melodies. Referring to the comprehensive bibliographies by Sir John Stainer,[39] Glen[40] and Dick,[41] we may here quote the titles of a few works from each of the three categories, with special regard to those which have been proved to have been in Burns's possession. Purely instrumental music he

---

[37] Letters, 696. A facsimile of this letter is in Stenhouse's "Illustrations," ed. 1853.

[38] Letters, 507.

[39] "Catalogue of English Song Books" (Private impression), London, 1891.

[40] "Early Scottish Melodies," pp. xi-xvi; "Glen Collection of Scottish Dance Music," 1, pp. xviii-xx; 11, pp. xix-xx, with reproductions of title-pages and important biographical notes.

[41] "Songs of Burns," pp. xxviii-xliii.

found in James Oswald's "Caledonian Pocket Companion,"[42] a collection of small oblong volumes in duodecimo, published in the years 1743-59 in twelve parts, and described in the sub-title as "a favourite collection of Scotch Tunes, with variations for the German Flute, or Violin." It contains about 560 tunes, partly Oswald's own compositions, and not all of equal value, but on the whole, according to Glen, it is a meritorious compilation, deserving our respect, for it gave refuge to many an old tune which would other-wise have fallen into oblivion. The airs are provided with titles which we may in many cases assume to be the first lines of the old texts to which they belonged. Both airs and titles made a strong impression on Burns, and furnished him with many ideas. As he thought on these old tunes and fragmentary lines, the memory of some experience in his own life or in the life of some one known to him would suggest a new song to him, and he would gradually evolve and complete the new text. Here are a few of these titles from the first and second volumes of the "Companion":[43] "When she cam ben she bobed" (i, 14), "To dauntin me" (i, 16), "The last Time I came o'er the Moor" (i, 60), "Over the Hills and far away" (ii, 23), "We're a' kissed sleeping" (ii, 114), and "Beware of the Ripples" (ii, 138). Burns's own copy of the "Caledonian Pocket Companion," which he is said to have presented to Nathaniel Gow (1763-1831), the popular violin virtuoso and composer of dance music, contains numerous pencil notes in Burns's hand which prove how thoroughly the poet studied the melodies and their structure.[44] To this category also belong the numerous collections of Reels and Strathspeys, judging by which the dance-loving Scottish people in town and country must have been insatiable in their demands for such music: Glen enumerates no less than fifty such collections between the years 1752-1800. The following are only a few of those which Burns has mentioned[45] and which in all probability he also possessed, especially as most of them had been engraved by Johnson: Angus Cumming's "Collection of Strathspeys or Old

---

[42] See article on Burns's own copy of this in *Scots Magazine*, August 1933 (Davidson Cook).

[43] *Cf.* Ritter 'Neue Quellenfunde zu Robert Burns," Halle, 1903. Appendix.

[44] Dick, pp. xli-xlii; specimen of one of Burns's marginal notes, *ibid.*, p. 411 (to No. 177). See Letters 111, and note 42, above.

[45] Numerous such references in the Hastie Collection.

Highland Reels," Edinburgh, 1780;[46] Neil Gow's "Collection of Strathspey Reels," Edinburgh, 1784; Neil Gow (1727-1807) was the more famous father of the Nathaniel Gow just mentioned;[47] John Bowie's "Collection of Strathspey Reels & Country Dances," Edinburgh, 1789; and similar works by James Aird, Malcolm Macdonald, William MacGibbon, Riddell and many others, to enumerate whom would take up too much space. The line of demarcation between dance-tunes and song-tunes cannot be sharply defined. In many cases the song-tune had become a dance-tune after the words had been lost; but as such it has frequently preserved, in the manner indicated, a few traces of the old text or its chorus as a title.

Among the song-books without music Allan Ramsay's "Tea-table Miscellany" reigned supreme. The first volume of this work had appeared in 1724, the second in 1724 or 1725, the third in 1727, and the fourth in 1740. Up to the year 1792 it had been reprinted eighteen times. We have already dealt with the merits and dangerous disadvantages of this, for its time, epoch-making collection. Its influence can be clearly traced in Johnson's "Museum," and it was one of the chief tasks of Burns, who had been intimately acquainted with the "Miscellany" from his youth, to criticize this influence and at certain important points to overcome it. In spite of its shortcomings, however, the "Miscellany" is assured of a place of honour in Scottish literature. In compiling it, Ramsay had undoubtedly been animated by the same great idea carried into effect by Burns, and had tried to create a popular song-book, based on whatever old texts were still available and on the work of gifted contemporary poets—a song-book which would satisfy every class of society. His "Miscellany" fulfilled this purpose for many years, but at the same time it brought about an unhealthy dependence upon the typical drawing-room poetry of the eighteenth century, the smooth insipidity of which was first exposed and denounced by Burns's original and, in the true sense of the word, fundamental force. The advance from Ramsay to Burns, who both took their material from the same source, was the decisive event in the history of the Scottish folk-song. Along with the "Tea-Table Miscellany" we may mention a few other collections which have escaped

---

[46] See letter to A. Cunningham, 11th Mar. 1791. Letters, 441.

[47] Burns knew him personally; cf. the description of his meeting with him in the diary of the Highland tour, under date 31st Aug., 1787. Ch. W., ii, 160.

oblivion partly because they were known to Burns and used by him in his studies, the great mass of this material being still far from having been properly sifted. Our order is chronological, and the place of publication, unless otherwise stated, Edinburgh. James Watson's "Choice Collection of Comic and Serious Scots Poems" (in three parts: 1706, 1709, 1711)[48] grew out of the widely spread interest in old Scottish poetry. The lyrical element plays a slight rôle in it, but it heads the list of a number of publications of an antiquarian nature, which testify to the growing sympathy with the works of the earlier school of national poetry, the best known and in many ways also the most abused product of which was Ramsay's "Evergreen" (1724). The following are typical of the song-books in the true sense of the word: "The Charmer," printed for the bookseller, J. Yair, first in 1749, then in two volumes in 1752, and in subsequent editions; "The Blackbird," 1764, third impression 1771; "The Lark," 1765, the book which Burns called his constant "vade mecum,"[49] "The Scots Nightingale," second impression 1779;[50] and "St. Cecilia," published by Charles Wilson, 1779. A further group owes its existence to the stimulus which Percy's "Reliques of Ancient English Poetry" had given to the study of poetry. David Herd's "Ancient and Modern Scots Songs, Heroic Ballads, &c." fall into this category. This collection had appeared anonymously in 1769, then, substantially enlarged and enriched, in 1776. We shall have more to say about Herd and his services to the Scottish folk-song. Partly as a result of utilizing Herd's rich material, John Pinkerton published—likewise anonymously—his "Scottish Tragic Ballads," London, 1781, and his "Select Scotch Ballads," London, 1783, which, besides ballads, also contain numerous songs. On the whole, Pinkerton's texts are notoriously unreliable.

Comprehensive collections of the third kind, containing both words and music, were less frequently published, and when they were, suffered badly, as Johnson saw, from the disadvantage of being too cumbersome. This was true, for instance, of William

---

[48] New impression, Glasgow, 1869.

[49] Described on the title-page as "volume one." A second volume was never published. The collection is extremely rare, and has nothing to do with "The Lark," which was published in London in 1740 and 1742, and with which it is often confused. See my essay in *Archiv*, vol. 143 (1922), pp. 176-183.

[50] Mentioned by Burns in a letter to Johnson, 1795. Letters, 684.

Thomson's popular "Orpheus Caledonius," London, 1725 and 1733; Robert Bremner's "Thirty Scots Songs," first and second series, 1757, the texts in both editions being taken chiefly from Allan Ramsay; and William Napier's "Selection of the most favourite Scots Songs," 1790, second series, 1792; third series, 1794. The likewise widely used "Musical Miscellany," Perth, 1786, which appeared in 1788 in a second edition in Edinburgh and London under the title of "Calliope: or the Musical Miscellany," was handier in size. We conclude this list, which is by no means exhaustive, with the distinguished work (published anonymously) of Joseph Ritson: "Scottish Songs," in two volumes, London, 1794. Even to-day Ritson's introductory essay on the history of the Scottish song is indispensable to students. It contains a flattering reference to Burns, although even here Ritson had to pacify his philological conscience by expressing his sharp disapproval of the poet's editorial technique.[51] This collection, as well as Ritson's three-volume "Collection of English Songs," London, 1783, was sent to Burns in the autumn of 1794, and roused his keenest interest.[52]

Needless to say, this mass of literature did not remain a dead-letter as far as Burns was concerned, but merely supported the living tradition which he incorporated in himself, and which he met with in the most varied forms wherever he went. We have seen that he had already, in his Ayrshire home, learned to know and appreciate the "glorious fragments" from olden times. Among these fragments there was many a coarse-grained piece whose contents rendered it unsuitable for public recitation in the cultured society of ladies, but which was not less popular on that account with the convivial song-loving male sex, whether they belonged to the Bachelors' Club in Tarbolton or to the gentlemen's clubs in Edinburgh. Besides, in a great number of cases these humorously scurrilous songs formed the oldest available texts to many famous airs (although this does not mean that they invariably consist of the original words). That Burns knew a great number of such songs, that he found pleasure in their joyous sexuality, and that he wrote similar songs himself, is beyond doubt. They appealed to him as a man and as a student of the folk-song. He collected them

---

[51] Pp. lxxiv-lxxv, with note 69.
[52] Thomson to Burns, 14th and 27th Oct. 1794, and the latter's answer, 19th Oct. and Nov. 1794. Ch. W., iv, 146, 160-161; Letters, 644, 646.

in Edinburgh for the "Crochallan Fencibles," probably in response to the express demand for such wares, beginning in the winter of 1786, before he met James Johnson.   Some poems point back to the Mauchline period, others were added as the years went on.   To Burns as a student of popular poetry nothing could be unimportant, no matter how obnoxious it might be, and it is from the dregs of this very type of song that he frequently got the inspiration for the purest and most sublime of his own lyrics.   At the same time he was acutely conscious of the boundary-line between his circle of boisterous cronies and the general public, and this feeling caused him to show these literary gleanings to a few intimate friends only. After his death the MS. containing them disappeared from among his papers and was published in 1800, very much against Burns's intention, under the title of "The Merry Muses of Caledonia." Only one copy of this first impression seems to have been preserved, but, on the other hand, there is no lack of venal reproductions, in which the original contents appear disgustingly interspersed with lascivious cabaret stuff, with which Burns's name must in no way be associated.   A new edition of "The Merry Muses" of 1800 was issued in 1911 by Duncan M'Naught for the Burns Federation, so that it is comparatively easy for the present-day student of the Scottish folk-song to have access to this important material.   It is to be hoped that it will in future be kept free from impure and inferior elements.[53]

Some of the texts in the "Merry Muses" correspond in the main to poems and fragments, the preservation of which we owe to David Herd's activity as a collector. These were first published in the "Ancient and Modern Scottish Songs, Heroic Ballads, &c.," the collection already singled out for special mention in the group of song-books without melodies, and are to be found in the second edition published in Edinburgh in 1776 by John Wotherspoon. There is no trace of them in the first edition of 1769.   It is quite possible that Burns got his knowledge of these fragments, as they reappear in the "Merry Muses," from the texts printed in Herd's collection.   The form given by Burns differs slightly from that which we find in Herd, but we cannot go far wrong in assuming

---

[53] See my essay on "The Merry Muses of Caledonia" and the questions connected therewith in *Archiv*, vol. 129, 363-374, and vol. 130, 57-72. See also *B. Chr.*, 1st series, vol. iii (1894), p. 24 ff., and vol 20 (1911), p. 105 ff., articles by D. M'Naught.

that Burns may have altered the songs when he first took a note of them. We must, however, also take into account the possibility that it was the living tradition and not only the book that influenced Burns, or at least strengthened and enriched the impression already in his mind. Herd was living in Edinburgh at the same time as Burns, but the modest office-clerk moved and had his being far from the brilliant sunshine that fell upon the path of his great contemporary, although we must bear in mind that Herd obviously had a considerable knowledge of literary affairs and was recognized as an authority by not a few prominent antiquaries, as can be seen from his correspondence. The paths of Burns and Herd must have crossed, if not in the drawing-rooms of the social leaders, then possibly in such cosy and tempting "howffs" as John Dowie's in Libberton's Wynd, which has long since disappeared. The dark and narrow rooms of this tavern, famous as much on account of its jovial host as of its excellent food and drink, had of yore resounded to the exuberant mirth of Robert Fergusson. Since then it had become the favourite haunt of a small circle of antiquaries such as George Paton and James Cummyng. David Herd himself seems to have spent a considerable portion of his leisure there: one of his letters names "John Dowie's" as the place where he happens to be at the moment of writing, another fixes it as a suitable rendezvous, and several anecdotes associate him with it. Burns used to frequent this same tavern, when he wished to descend from the heights of society and, in stimulating conversation with men like William Nicol and Allan Masterton, enjoy the liberties of the lower spheres of Edinburgh life. Until it was pulled down in 1834, Dowie's tavern was one of the "sights" of the city and was shown to the poet's admirers as "Burns's Tavern." The small room where these meetings were held was also kept intact. It bore the uncanny but characteristic name of "the coffin."

Here, then, Burns and Herd would sit wall to wall, perhaps back to back: Herd, the man whose interest in ballads and songs had made him break through the bounds of decorum à la Ramsay, and collect and publish precious fragments of rapidly vanishing folk-songs in exactly the form he could lay hands on them; and Burns, the author of incomparable new poems, who appreciated the full value of these very fragments, discerning all their latent possibilities, and who was busy developing from the ideas they gave

him new life both for them and for his own poetry. And yet
there is no proof that the two ever met—in fact, it seems as
though Burns did not even know that Herd was the collector of
"Ancient and Modern Scottish Songs," in referring to which he
always uses the name of the publisher, Wotherspoon or Wither-
spoon. This may have been due to the shy, retiring nature of
Herd, who later never thought of entering Scott's hospitable house
but on the twofold condition that his friend, Archibald Constable,
the book-seller, should be present, and that Scott's womenfolk
should be absent—a misogynous trait that Burns, presumably,
would have found hard to understand!

Meanwhile, Herd possessed a manuscript which was quite
unique in its way and of extraordinary importance to Burns. It
had formed the groundwork of the second edition of Herd's ballads
and songs, and still contained a large number of unpublished
pieces, mostly of a fragmentary character. This manuscript collection had gradually been built up by Herd since 1769 and has
played an important part in the history of the Scottish folk-song.
As far back as 1774, George Paton had sent it to Thomas Percy, and
it was hoped for a time that the celebrated editor of the "Reliques"
would himself undertake the revision of the "fragmentary antiquities" which it contained, and lend them the consecration of his
own artistic touch: a blessing, by the way, which is but lightly
esteemed by modern critics. Nothing came of it, however. A
year later Percy sent back the manuscript—untouched. Later,
thanks to George Chalmers, it came into the hands of Ritson, who
recognized the value of its contents; Scott took valuable matter
from it for his "Minstrelsy of the Scottish Border," likewise
Jamieson for his "Popular Ballads and Songs"; and even after
that it has again and again, right up to the twentieth century,
rendered important services to students interested in ballads and
songs. It is certain that Burns also had access to it. The second
volume of the "Musical Museum" and its successors contain quite
a number of song-texts built up by Burns on Herd's fragments,
and not exclusively on those published in the printed collection.
Burns has often added only a few touches, perhaps a verse or two,
while at other times he has only borrowed a hint from the Herd
manuscript, but there is never any doubt as to his source, and his
association with it casts a halo round the unpretentious but good

and important work of the worthy David Herd. The period during
which Burns made the contents of the Herd manuscript his own
marks the zenith of its history. Who let Burns have access to it is,
if we exclude Herd himself, a question to which no definite answer
can be given. Perhaps Stephen Clarke, who like Herd was a
Knight of the "Cape," was the person responsible.[54]

We must also consider as part of the living tradition the
popular recitals of Scottish songs which were frequently given
not only in private circles but also in the Edinburgh concerts, held
chiefly in St. Cecilia's Hall. Italians won special fame at these
concerts. The great Sienese singer, G. F. Tenducci, for instance,
is said to have rendered Scottish songs with a profound understanding of the words and the music. No less popular was the
Milanese singer, Pietro Urbani, who had carried on work in Edinburgh since 1784 as a music teacher and singer, and had made
such a thorough study of Scottish vocal music that he was actually
able to publish six volumes of Scottish songs between the years
1792-1804. Urbani's settings were distinguished by the rich
harmonies of the accompaniment and by elaborate opening and
closing symphonies, and competed for public favour with the contemporary publication of Thomson, who rather uncompliment-
arily dubbed his rival's work "water-gruel music." Urbani was
one of the practical musicians whose personal acquaintance Burns
made while living in Dumfries. He met the Italian in the summer
of 1793 at Lord Selkirk's. Although on one occasion he called
him a "narrow, contracted creature," he was delighted with his
prowess as a singer and set store by his judgment of Scottish airs.[55]

To James C. Dick must be given the credit for having in his
two volumes on Burns's lyric poetry[56] emphasized Burns's musical
abilities, the importance of his work as a collector of popular music,
and the place which should be accorded to it in judging his song-
writing as a whole. Dick calls Burns an apostle of Scottish folk-
music. None of his contemporaries knew it better than Burns,
he says, and he supplements the title of his book "The Songs of
Robert Burns" by adding significantly: "A Study in Tone-Poetry."

---

[54] See introduction to my edition of the "Songs from David Herd's Manuscripts,"
Edinburgh, 1904.

[55] Letters, 578 (Aug. 1793).

[56] "Songs of R. B." London, 1903, and "Notes on Scottish Song by R. B."
London, &c., 1908.

Dick's comprehensive investigations have shown very clearly
that any study of Burns's songs which is based solely on the words
must always remain incomplete. It is only when we take the
music into account at the same time that we acquire a full understanding of what he accomplished for Scottish song. No song
by Burns should ever be printed without the air belonging to it,
for in his eyes words and music formed an indissoluble unity
which we destroy if we study the one without the other. He who
would really know folk-songs must hear them sung. Thus we are
not surprised to find Burns devoting as much careful thought to
the critical survey and collecting of the tunes as to the treatment of
the texts themselves, the only difference being that the creative
element naturally played a smaller part in the case of the former;
for even in his earliest lyrical efforts Burns started out from the
tune, and in his dealings with Johnson and Thomson he did not
write poems for which airs had to be composed, but provided existing melodies with suitable words. At the same time, we learn from
an entry made in his first Common-place Book in the year 1784
that he once tried his hand at writing a folk-tune: he set about
composing an air in the old Scottish style, he says, but owing to
lack of technical skill, did not succeed in writing it down. The
tune consisted of three parts, so that the three-stanza'd text (which
he kept) "just went through the whole air."[57] He gave up the
attempt after this isolated experiment, clearly recognizing his own
limitations.

There can be no doubt that Burns was out of sympathy with
the high-class, polyphonic concert style of music, although he had
the opportunity of hearing much that was good in Edinburgh,
including Handel's "Messiah." This does not necessarily mean
that he was less musical than the majority of concert-goers, either
then or now. He quite openly discussed this matter; for instance,
he wrote to Thomson in September 1793:

> "You know that my pretensions to musical taste, are merely a few
> of Nature's instincts, untaught & untutored by Art.—For this reason,
> many musical compositions, particularly where much of the merit lies
> in Counterpoint, however they may transport & ravish the ears of you,
> Connoisseurs, affect my simple lug no otherwise than merely as
> melodious Din.—On the other hand, by way of amends, I am
> delighted with many little melodies, which the learned Musician

---

[57] "O, raging Fortune's withering blast," H. H., iv, 7.

despises as silly & insipid.—I do not know whether the old air, 'Hey tutti taitie,' may rank among this number; but well I know that, with Fraser's Hautboy, it has often filled my eyes with tears."[58]

It was to this air that Burns wrote his battle-song before Bannockburn: "Scots, wha hae wi' Wallace bled."[59]

Burns was intimately acquainted with these "little airs," the tunes which the people sang and to which they danced. He was master of them in every sense of the word. They had been in his blood from the days of his childhood, and he loved them and guarded them jealously, trying to keep them uncorrupted. He knew, says Dick, several hundred different tunes, and not superficially at that, but thoroughly, even to the details of their structure and their rhythm, so that he was in the position of being able to put his finger on the most trivial discrepancies in the various versions which passed through his hands, and to justify his point of view.[60] We have seen how, just as he studied the texts of the folk-songs, he also increased his knowledge of the airs by careful, thorough scrutiny of the rich, printed material at his disposal. Not content with that, he endeavoured to note down unpublished airs from the lips of the people, and, according to Stenhouse's calculations, actually succeeded not only in preserving from oblivion about forty tunes, but, by providing them with new words, based where possible on old fragments, in giving them a new lease of life. To illustrate this point, it will be sufficient to mention the beautiful tune of "Ca' the yowes to the knowes," concerning which Burns wrote to Thomson in September, 1794, that he had heard it excellently sung about seven years previously by a clergyman named Clunzie, and had made Clarke take it down for Johnson's "Museum."[61]

Mention of Clarke, whom we already know as the musical adviser of Burns and Johnson, raises the question as to whether Burns's technical education in music was extensive enough for him to be able to write down a tune after hearing it. We know that he could not do it in his youth. Later on he may, by constant practice, have acquired a certain degree of skill. In any case,

---

[58] Letters, 582; similarly 637 (to the same). See below, p. 299-300.

[59] H. H., iii, 251-252.

[60] "Songs of B.," p. ix.

[61] *Mus.*, No. 264; Letters, 636.

we cannot dismiss his reiterated statement, "I took down the tune,"
&c., without more ado. It is, however, admissible to suggest that
Burns, assisted by his keen, reliable memory, perhaps also by
scrappy notes, "took down" the tunes in the sense that he stamped
them on his mind, and whenever he got an opportunity asked an
expert to help him to write them down in full. In this he was
by no means entirely dependent upon Stephen Clarke, who was
mostly engaged in his professional work in Edinburgh. He can
never have lacked musical support in Dumfries, and even at Ellisland he was always sure of the collaboration of his neighbour,
Robert Riddell of Friars' Carse, a man with whom he had much
in common. In a letter of uncertain date written from Ellisland
to Johnson we see how Burns sought help of another kind from
his friends. In it Burns mentions a collection of Highland airs
which Johnson had given him in Edinburgh, and which he hopes
to be able to utilize for the "Museum":

> "I have had an able Fiddler two days already on it," he writes,
> "& I expect him every day for another review of it.—I have got one
> most beautiful air out of it, that sings to the measure of Lochaber.—
> I shall try to give it my very best words."[62]

Judging by this, the answer to our question is that Burns was a
past-master as far as his knowledge of Scottish melodies was concerned, but when it came to noting them down was obliged in
most cases to fall back upon expert help.[63]

We may gather from a number of authentic reports with what
care he set about uniting the words and the airs. Josiah Walker
tells how one day in October 1787, during the Edinburgh period,
when Burns was busy with the preparations for the "Museum,"
he met the poet at the house of his friend William Cruickshank,
whose daughter Janet was, despite her great youth, an accomplished
pianist and singer. Burns was seated beside the harpsichord,
eagerly listening to Janet singing his verses, which he brought into
satisfactory harmony with the music by trying the effect over and
over again. "In this occupation," says Walker, "he was so totally
absorbed, that it was difficult to draw his attention from it for a

---

[62] Letters, 258.

[63] Mrs. Carswell has published a musical notation of Burns's in her book (facing
p. 416). We cannot, however, deduce much from this, not even the fact that the
notes were written by the poet himself.

moment."[64]   At Ellisland his Jean, whose natural gift of songs he often took pleasure in praising, could render him a similar service. He thought it no trouble, either, to ride up the Nith occasionally to Closeburn to visit Christina or Kirsty Flint, a mason's wife well known as a good singer and judge of Scottish folk-songs and ballads. Burns would listen from an arm-chair beside the fire while Kirsty in a high, strong voice sang the songs he had just written; and he would interrupt her the moment he noticed a discord between words and music, and put the matter right at once. Kirsty Flint, we are told, had such an extensive knowledge of old Scottish airs that she was often able to suggest to the poet a tune better suited to the song she was singing than that to which he had set it.[65]

No further proof is needed to illustrate the fact that Burns in every case considered he had reached his goal only when he had succeeded in fusing words and music into a perfect unity. Behind his achievements, as behind most masterpieces, there lay a tremendous amount of careful work, which did not neglect even what seemed most trivial. This applied not only to the words, but also to the airs, which, as we have seen, in many cases inspired the words, for Burns was musical in the highest sense of the term, in so far as these airs both stimulated his poetic imagination and kept it within the bounds of their own particular mood. A thorough understanding of them was part of his creative technique, the peculiar nature of which he has described in an important letter to Thomson (September 1793):

> "Untill I am compleat master of a tune, in my own singing, (such as it is) I never can compose for it.—My way is: I consider the poetic Sentiment, correspondent to my idea of the musical expression; then chuse my theme; begin one Stanza; when that is composed, which is generally the most difficult part of the business, I walk out, sit down now & then, look out for objects in Nature around me that are in unison or harmony with the cogitations of my fancy & workings of my bosom; humming every now & then the air with the verses I have framed: when I feel my Muse beginning to jade, I retire to the solitary fireside of my study, & there commit my effusions to paper; swinging, at intervals, on the hind-legs of my elbow-chair, by way of calling forth my own critical strictures, as my pen goes on.—
>
> "Seriously, this, at home, is almost invariably my way.—"[66]

---

[64] Ch. W., ii, 198-199.
[65] Ch. W., iii, 162-163.
[66] Letters, 586.

In September 1792, when Burns's genius was at its zenith, he was, for the second time, called upon to take part in the work of making a great collection of Scottish songs, and he enthusiastically embarked upon this second undertaking, without in any way prejudicing his connection with Johnson. The prime mover in this new enterprise was a certain George Thomson, at that time principal clerk to the Board of Trustees for Manufacturers in Scotland, in his leisure hours an amateur violinist and singer. He was a popular, modest, unassuming man of pronounced bad taste and unbounded devotion to the cause of music. His portrait by Raeburn shows us a man with mild, calm features—rather a weak face despite the powerful glasses which cover the large, gleaming eyes. His life was a very long one. Born on 4th March 1757, he entered the above-named office in his twenty-third year, and remained at his post for fifty-nine years, gradually reaching the point where he had amassed a considerable amount of capital. He married, had two sons and six daughters (one of whom became Charles Dickens's mother-in-law), travelled little and that little unwillingly, for something always drove him back to the familiar surroundings of Edinburgh. He died on 18th February 1851 in his ninety-fourth year, after an externally completely uneventful life.

His biographer Hadden justly remarks that from 1792 onward the story of Thomson's life is identical with the history of his song-collections: he lived in them and for them, and all else was but a shadow.[67] This inner life brought him, through correspondence, into touch with the leading poets and composers of his time, but in spite of all his efforts, it accomplished nothing and was a disappointment both to himself and to posterity. He has won a certain immortality through his connection with poets such as Scott, Byron, Moore, and Campbell, and with great and small continental composers like Pleyel, Kozeluch, Haydn, Beethoven, Weber, and Hummel, whom he got one after the other, in return for hardly-earned money, to place their art at the service of his collections of Scottish, Irish, and Welsh songs. Above all he owes his fame to his association with Burns, which led to one of the most remarkable literary correspondences of its time.

[67] J. Cuthbert Hadden: "George Thomson, The Friend of Burns, His Life and Correspondence." London 1898.

This correspondence took its origin in the organisation of his Collection of Scottish Songs. He was an ardent supporter of the Edinburgh St. Cecilia concerts. He played in the orchestra, sang in the choir at performances of Handel's oratorios, and had a passion for Pleyel and for Haydn's "incomparable fantasies." At the same time he found constant pleasure, like many of his compatriots, in studying the old Scottish folk-music, and it was through song-recitals in St. Cecilia's Hall that he came under the influence which turned the enthusiastic listener into the assiduous editor: he there heard Scottish songs sung in a style of surpassing excellence, he tells Robert Chambers, and, curiously, by two Italians at that—the great Tenducci and Signora Domenica Corri. It was while under the influence of this ardent enjoyment that he "conceived the idea of collecting all our best melodies and songs and of obtaining accompaniments to them worthy of their merit."[68]

Of his collaborators, who were also to contribute financially to the project, only one is known—the talented and reckless Andrew Erskine, brother of the sixth Earl of Kelly; but this partnership was soon dissolved in tragic fashion: in September 1793, Erskine, who was up to his ears in gambling debts, was taken from the Firth of Forth, drowned, with his pockets full of stones. William Tytler of Woodhouselee, who died in 1792, and James Beattie also seem to have been among Thomson's counsellors, but they were of no practical use to the venture, the whole responsibility for which soon rested upon Thomson's own shoulders.

After he had succeeded in securing Burns's help, Thomson gave himself up to the rosiest hopes concerning the future prospects of his collection. He thought that this collaboration could not fail to produce the supreme collection of Scottish songs, which would be looked upon as a model for all time. He was so optimistic that he even refused to admit any doubts as to the probable material profits: "A loser I cannot be," he wrote to Burns on 1st July 1793. "The superior excellence of the work will create a general demand for it as soon as it is properly known."[69] He did not guess upon what a thorny path he had embarked.

The first part of Thomson's "Select Collection of Original Scottish Airs for the voice, &c.," which contains twenty-five songs,

68 Hadden, 20.
69 Ch. W., iii, 431.

appeared in June 1793. The first volume was ready in August 1798, that is, two years after Burns's death. The second volume followed in 1799, the third in 1802, and the fourth in 1805. Then there was a longer interval, the fifth volume not being published in complete form until 1826. A sixth volume brought the collection, which contained in all 315 songs, many of them with double texts, to a conclusion. In the intervals Thomson brought out another collection of selected Welsh songs in three volumes (1809-14), and a similar one of Irish songs in two volumes (1814-16), rounding up his venture by publishing in 1822 selections from the three works in six volumes octavo. The publications were in every case excellently got up, the volumes being distinguished by large, easily read print and a number of fine engravings by recognized masters, in addition to the opening and closing symphonies by the great continental musicians, headed by Haydn and Beethoven, with whom Thomson had carried on a long-drawn and at times very unedifying correspondence. These great musicians were all well versed in practical matters, and Thomson often had great difficulty in raising the gold ducats for which they were constantly clamouring. With the poets—Burns excepted—he fared no better, only in this case the difficulties were mostly of another kind: his collaborators were incapable of practising an art which Burns handled with the obvious ease of a highly developed natural talent—the art, namely, of writing suitable words to prescribed airs. When the handsome folio and quarto volumes were finally published, after infinite difficulty, the public held aloof from them. The Scottish collection, helped along at first by Burns's name, had a slight sale, as had the relatively cheap and well-stocked octavo edition of 1822, but in neither case can one talk of real success. The Welsh and Irish collections turned out to be complete failures. After many disappointments, Thomson at last parted with his life-work, stock, plates, and copyright—work to which, in addition to his unceasing labour, he had sacrificed £2000 in ready cash—for £150, and the buyer, an Edinburgh music-seller named George Wood, had a bad bargain at that. The causes leading up to this melancholy conclusion are obvious and are attributable to no one but Thomson himself: the people did not recognize the dear old tunes under the burden of the continental accompaniments which were hard to play, and for the high artistic value of which they had no understanding. The texts, especially in the later editions, must also have had an unfamiliar sound. The public's unerring instinct sensed Thomson's grave faults in style, and instead of being willing to rejoice in something fresh and natural, it drew back with hostile shyness and a certain cruelty towards the well-meaning man, from the ornately decorated edifice into which he wished to invite it.

This all happened years after the period with which we are dealing, but the same destructive forces were already at work when Thomson collaborated with Burns, a period of his literary activity to which Thomson may well have looked back with longing in later days.

Burns wrote or touched up for the first four volumes of the "Scottish Airs" 114 songs in all, of which some sixty were there printed for the first time. He lived, as we have said, to see the appearance in June 1793 of the first part only. The correspondence about the songs, which was eagerly carried on from both sides, extends, with a few trifling interruptions, from September 1792 till just before Burns's death, when a desperate appeal for help, addressed to Thomson by the dying poet, brought it to a heart-rending conclusion.[70] When we remember that Burns, apart from attending to the duties of his calling, was at the same time also working steadily for Johnson's "Museum," the first impression we get is of a tremendous intellectual achievement. Whether we are passionate admirers of the poet's habits or not, we cannot escape that impression. "Not many days passed during his stay in Dumfries," wrote James Gray, who had been rector of Dumfries Academy since 1794, and had taught Burns's son Robert, "in which he did not compose some piece of poetry, or some song, destined to delight the imagination, and soften the heart for ages to come."[71] When we look closer into the matter, we are again struck by the earnest fervour and selfless idealism with which Burns devoted himself to this new task. Right at the beginning,. in his very first letter to Thomson, he firmly refused any remuneration for his services, saying that people might think his songs either *above* or

---

[70] Thomson had all the letters and songs which Burns had sent him carefully bound in folio, and, as long as he lived, treasured the volume, as was fitting, as a precious possession. After his death it passed into the hands of the Earl of Dalhousie. It is now in the Morgan Library, New York. J. De Lancey Ferguson has collated the originals carefully for his edition of the "Letters." Earlier impressions are unreliable and incomplete.

[71] Ch. W., iv, 526-527.

below price, but in the honest enthusiasm with which he embarked upon the venture, to talk of money, wages, fee, hire, &c., seemed to be "downright sodomy of soul." And when Thomson, notwithstanding this attitude, sent him a five-pound note, after the publication of the first part of the *Airs,* Burns wrote in reply that he would not return it, as that might savour of affectation, but

> "as to any more traffic of that Dr. & Cr. kind, I swear, by that HONOUR which crowns the upright Statue of ROBT. BURNS's INTEGRITY!—On the least motion of it, I will indignantly spurn the by-past transaction, & from that moment commence entire Stranger to you!—BURNS's character for Generosity of Sentiment, Independence of Mind, will, I trust, long outlive any of his wants which the cold, unfeeling, dirty Ore can supply: at least, I shall take care that such a Character he shall deserve.—"[72]

In themselves, Burns's letters to Thomson are of inexhaustible interest. They contain his theoretical commentary to the song practice of his last four years, and sum up his results, experiences, and convictions as a song-writer. His detailed analyses of Thomson's lists in the letters of September 1793,[73] 19th October 1794,[74] and November 1794,[75] deserve special mention. The rich material included in these notes to the songs has been fully utilized in the more modern editions of Burns's poetry and in the research work connected with it. The strongly personal element in the letters affords us welcome glimpses into his workroom. We see the songs being made, as it were. A good example of this is to be found in the letter dated 19th August, 1793.[76] Burns here describes how he had gone out on the evening of 18th August with the first volume of Johnson's "Museum" in his hand. Stumbling by chance on the air "Allan Water" (No. 43) he considers the text from Ramsay's "Tea-Table Miscellany" ("What numbers shall the Muse repeat," by Crawford) unworthy of it, and as the air was on Thomson's list, he sits down under an old thorn and meditates upon it. While so doing, he remembers that in the "Tea-Table Miscellany," under the title "Allan Water," there occur the additional words: "or, My

---

[72] Letters, 569.
[73] Letters, 586.
[74] Letters, 644.
[75] Letters, 646. The letter to Johnson, autumn 1795, Letters, 684, must also be mentioned in this connection.
[76] Letters, 577.

Love Annie's very Bonie," probably a line of the original song.[77] Although there was so little to go upon, he grasped at the idea contained in this line, and in his new poem tried to put it back into what he presumed to have been its original place, the last line of the first verse:

> "By Allan stream I chanc'd to rove,
> While Phebus sank beyond Benledi;
> The winds were whispering thro' the grove,
> The yellow corn was waving ready;
> I listen'd to a lover's sang,
> An' thought on youthfu' pleasures monie,
> And ay the wild-wood echoes rang:—
> 'O, my love Annie's very bonie!' " &c.[78]

"Bravo!" said Burns, "it is a good song." "Bravissimo!" replied Thomson, "it is an excellent song."[79] The reader of to-day will agree with this opinion neither in its positive nor in its superlative form, though he will admit that Burns's song is a great improvement on Crawford's intolerable piece, with its Amyntor, Damon, and Cupid.

The simplicity of the popular style, which he failed to achieve in this case, was one of the postulates upon which Burns constantly insisted in his dealings with Thomson.

> "Of pathos, Sentiment & Point," he wrote, "you are a compleat judge; but there is a quality more necessary than either, in a Song, & which is the very essence of a Ballad, I mean Simplicity";

and this last feature he felt Thomson was a little apt to underestimate. In the same letter he mentions airs which he has picked up mostly from the singing of country lasses, and which he still has by him in MS. He thinks them delightful, but supposes that the very quality that endeared them to him would displease "the learned lugs" of his collaborator.

> "I call them Simple; you would pronounce them Silly."[80]

Accordingly he demands that tradition be respected and the versions kept as near the original as possible. He himself, he says, only alters where he thinks he can amend.[81] In the interests of the cause, he feels justified in leaving out verses, especially if

---

77 Cf. H. H., iii, 462.
78 H. H., iii, 231-232.
79 Ch. W., iv, 28.
80 April 1793; Letters, 554; similarly Letters, 559 and 637.
81 Letters, 507: his first letter to Thomson.

they are improper, and it can be done without spoiling the whole;
but he considers that there should be no interference with the
works of dead poets: reverence should make *them* sacred. From
this point of view, he disapproves of the remodelled version
of one of Ramsay's songs submitted to him by Thomson, although
he admits that the revised version is better than the original; and
he remarks *à propos* of this that the amender should have followed
the example of the Highlander who repaired his gun by giving it
a new stock, a new lock, and a new barrel![82] He expresses his
views still more strongly with regard to the airs, warning Thomson
against Pleyel, a collaborator of whom Thomson thought very
highly; he should not be allowed to alter one iota of the original
Scots airs:

> "Let our National Music preserve its native features.—They are,
> I own, frequently wild, & unreduceable to the modern rules; but on
> that very eccentricity, perhaps, depends a great part of their effect."[83]

As for himself, he requests that he should be permitted to use
the dialect with which he is familiar, or that he should at least be
allowed to introduce a sprinkling of it into his contributions. He
is fully conscious of the fact that his best work is rooted in the
tradition and the soil of his native land, and that, if he is to be
sincere, he must write as one of the people. He also realizes that
the spirit of folk-poetry is lost as soon as foreign idioms interpose
themselves between the idea and the expression of it. "These
English Songs gravel me to death," we find him writing to
Thomson, who was incapable of grasping the absolute logic of
Burns's method and line of thought, and again and again made
the poet relinquish the point of view which his instinct forced
upon him.

> "I have not that command of the language that I have of my
> native tongue. In fact, I think my ideas are more barren in English
> than in Scotish."[84]

If we put all those opinions together, it is not difficult to form
an idea of the character which Burns wished to stamp upon
Thomson's collection, about the future of which he, like the editor,
was rather optimistic. In spirit it should not and could not be
other than Johnson's "Museum": in both cases the contents were

---

[82] Letters, 554.
[83] *Ibid.*, 559.
[84] Letters, 644 (ii, p. 268).

to be distinguished by the noble simplicity of the texts based on ballad fragments and songs of the past, and the best old melodies in uncorrupted versions. In addition to this, Thomson's collection was to be beautifully got up, and, in contrast to the "Museum," where completeness was aimed at, its contents were to be carefully selected and revised, with a view to publishing only the very best, and thus illuminating only the highest peaks in the mass of literary material which the collaborators had at their disposal. It was hoped in this way to produce a song-collection of unsurpassable merit, a collection which might serve the past as a reverent memorial, the present as a proud emblem of its own strength, and the future as an inspiring and fortifying symbol of national manners and customs.

That these lofty expectations were in no wise fulfilled has already been stated. Individual songs in Thomson's versions have survived, but the collection as a whole has not. In addition to its many inherent weaknesses, it has repeatedly been asserted that Burns's contributions were uninspired, and from that it has been concluded that the poet's creative power had declined during his last years. It was said that dissipation and misfortune had broken his mental faculties. Now, though it cannot be denied that a large number of the songs composed by Burns for Thomson were, compared with his contributions to the "Museum," lacking in freshness and often mediocre, sometimes even trivial, it is going too far to make them the criterion of the poet's capabilities. Such a statement is contradicted by a number of songs in his best style, the irresistible verve and dazzling humour of which by no means suggest a falling-off in his literary powers. Till the end of his life, when the call came, he was ready. Thus, to take only a very few examples, the following songs were composed for Thomson's "Scottish Airs": "Auld Rob Morris," the second version of "Duncan Gray," "Last May a Braw Wooer," "Scots wha hae," "Logan Water," "Is there for honest poverty," and "O, let me in this ae night." The war-song, "Does haughty Gaul invasion threat,"[85] also belongs to this period (1795), and even when Burns was dying he succeeded in writing one of the most passionate of his numerous love-songs: "O, wert thou in the cauld blast."[86] With these facts

---

[85] H. H., iii, 195-196.
[86] *Ibid.*, iv, 43.

in mind, we may talk of an occasional suspension but never of a cessation of inspiration in Burns. The greater part of the blame doubtless lies on the side of Thomson, whose philistine taste not only failed to understand Burns's deep-rooted genius, but did not cease obstinately and emphatically to combat it. He had in view— and who can reproach him for it?—the financial success of his venture and for that reason did not wish to spoil its prospects either with the ladies or with his countrymen south of the Tweed. He, therefore, wanted his texts to be decorous, polished, and as free as possible from dialect.

> "One thing only I beg," he writes to Burns, "which is, that however gay and sportive the Muse may be, she will always be decent. Let her not write what beauty would blush to speak, nor wound that charming delicacy which forms the most precious dowry of our daughters."[87]
>
> "Let me tell you that you are too fastidious in your ideas of Songs & Ballads,"

was the poet's reply. While admitting that there were grounds for criticism, he went on to say: "but who shall mend the matter? —Who shall rise up & say, 'Go to, I will make a better?' "[87a] Unfortunately, he did not always offer the necessary resistance to Thomson, who knew how to manage him, although he sometimes defended his convictions sharply, energetically, and confidently. In any case, he would probably not have gained much by it, for Thomson did not hesitate, if he thought fit, to alter the texts entrusted to his care, and transform them to suit *his* taste, but not that of posterity.

It is impossible to give even an approximate idea here of the great variety of songs written or renovated by Burns; it is also obviously undesirable to spoil the charm and glamour of the poetic form by describing them in prose. Words, meaning, and music must act as a unity and be conceived as such. J. C. Dick, on one occasion, draws a pretty comparison between Schubert and Burns: it was said of Schubert that, had he lived, he would have set the whole German language to music; similarly, one might say of Burns that, had he lived, he would have written words for the whole of Scottish music.[88] Not only for Scottish music, one might

---

[87] Ch. W., iii, 353.

[87a] Letters, 511.

[88] "Songs of R.B.," p. 370.

add, but for all that affected the heart of the Scot: character, manners, and customs; for, when we analyse his lyrical poetry, his tendency to add descriptive elements to the purely lyrical ones is obvious. It is not without justification that he puts himself on a par with David Allen, the "Scottish Hogarth": "I will say it, that I look on Mr. Allen & Mr. Burns to be the only genuine & real Painters of Scotish Costume in the world," he once wrote to Thomson,[89] and when we consider this statement, we must assuredly not think exclusively of those poems in the Kilmarnock Edition which are descriptive in the strictest sense of the word, but also of songs such as "Duncan Gray," "Last May a braw wooer," "Tam Glen,"[90] "O, leeze me on my spinning-wheel,"[91] and, even if it is not up to the standard of the foregoing, of "When wild war's deadly blast was blawn."[92] He sings of the joy and sorrow of love, of courtship, acceptance, refusal, and hope, with an inexhaustible wealth of expression, from the point of view of the lover and of his lass, both in monologue and dialogue, and enlivens this kind of poetry by such varying themes as the value— or absence—of the dowry; the wealth or poverty of the wooer; admonition, disapproval on the part of the parents; defiance on the part of the lovers, and secret meetings. Descriptions of con-jugal life easily give rise to light-hearted humour: the husband's hopes are disappointed, the gentle girl whom he has loved so tenderly revealing herself after the wedding as an ill-natured shrew, or the generous lover has turned out to be a miserly, suspicious lord and master. Sometimes blows help to make matters more tolerable, but in other cases the unhappy partner must wait till Death releases him or her. Yet this group also includes the best song ever written on the happiness of married life, "John Anderson my Jo,"[93] which glorifies the life-long devotion of a husband and wife to each other:

> "John Anderson my jo, John,
> We clamb the hill thegither,
> And monie a cantie day, John,
> We've had wi' ane anither;

---

[89] Letters, 647 (ii, 278-79).
[90] H. H., iii, 84-85.
[91] Ibid., iii, 114-115.
[92] Ibid., iii, 212-214.
[93] H. H., iii, 63.

> Now we maun totter down, John,
> And hand in hand we'll go,
> And sleep thegither at the foot,
> John Anderson my jo."

As regards the songs of friendship, we need only remind the reader of "Auld Lang Syne";[94] while we would again indicate "Willie brew'd a peck o' maut"[95] as the crown of Burns's bacchanalian songs. Longing for the Highlands has found world-famous expression in "My heart's in the Highlands."[96] In addition to the hunter, the tinker, the tailor, the miller, the soldier and, last but not least, the exciseman, all have songs connected with their trades; "gangrel bodies" of the most varied description are brought together in the "Jolly Beggars"; and freemasons' songs celebrate the order in whose midst Burns, animated with the truest feelings of brotherly love, at every period of his life enjoyed hours of carefree pleasure and social intercourse. We possess revised versions of old songs and ballads, contributions to the great garland of Jacobite poetry written in memory of the glorious, sinful, deluded—and yet, to their people, unforgettable—royal Stuart race. Such a song is "The Bonie Lass of Albanie."[97] Burns also wrote songs in imitation of street ballads, or rendered specimens of such poetry suitable for higher artistic spheres by abridging them. Vigorous, thoughtful poems re-echo his simple but lofty philosophy, his burning patriotism and his belief in the dignity of human nature, an idea to which the American and French Revolutions gave a tremendous fillip, and which reaches its climax in "Is there for honest poverty," sent to Thomson on New Year's Day, 1795. In this song Burns exultantly and defiantly expresses the sentiments of the great social movements of the age, strengthened by the force of his own passionate convictions. His own personality he keeps in the background, except when it acts as the interpreter of certain trends of thought, although it is true that in several early poems he portrays his spiritual and material distress and his poverty while under the effects of these experiences. Thus "The gloomy night is gathering fast,"[98] written while he was contemplating emigration

---

94 H. H., iii, 147-149.
95 H. H., iii, 80-81.
96 H. H., iii, 62-63.
97 H. H., iv, 22-23.
98 H. H., i, 255-256.

to the West Indies, expresses his sorrow at the prospect of leaving his native land; while "There was a lad"[99] is a dashing and prophetic description of himself. There are, however, no poems containing subtle analyses of the poet's mind, poems dealing, let us say, in an abstract manner with his passive moods of absorption in nature. His work contains no nature poems as such, and, except in a few almost negligible instances, no examples of that ascent to the metaphysical, of that advance from the concrete impression to the symbol, which we find in Goethe's "Über allen Gipfeln ist Ruh." Lastly, there is no trace of the romantic-visionary element which distinguishes, say, Coleridge's "Kubla Khan." Burns's lyric poetry is, rather, markedly unromantic. It avoids the mystic twilight, it builds no new world in the blue wonderland of Fancy, but clings to the clear realism of its chief sources: the Scottish popular and traditional songs. It is only when we realize fully his far-reaching dependence upon these sources that we grasp the full scope of his achievement as a lyric poet. He mastered and completed what generations had prepared for him. His expert knowledge of these old forms, however, does not detract from his mastery as a poet. He had the luck to find a still living tradition, with whose purest forms he was in close contact because of his peasant origin; he had the noble mind to recognize the national importance of this tradition, the inspired patience to study its technical peculiarities down to its smallest details, and the great genius to preserve and at the same time to rejuvenate what had come down to him, to save the old tunes from extinction and at the same time to sing a new song; and in all that he did, to retain his own individuality.

Burns did not live to see the end either of Johnson's "Museum" or of Thomson's "Scottish Airs"; consequently he was not able to put the finishing touches to his contributions in either of the two works. Above all, he was not privileged to write down the historical notes and anecdotes which he had intended to add to the airs and the songs. Only fragments of such a commentary have been preserved, in his letters and in an interleaved copy of the "Scots Musical Museum," which he prepared for Robert Riddell,

---

[99] H. H., iv, 13-14.

probably in the year 1793.[100] In October 1793 he got Johnson to order a second copy of the same kind from Hill,[101] and in November 1794 he informed Thomson that he had begun to note down his anecdotes for his (Thomson's) work, and promised them to him soon in the form of a letter, as he considered that most suited to their unsystematic character. His only fear was that the matter would grow too large in his hands.[102]

Burns himself was quite aware that the collections were of unequal value, and realized that much of their contents might be improved. Already in the Preface to the fourth volume of the "Museum" we find the sentence: "All our songs cannot have equal merit." In September 1794 he wrote to Thomson, after he had already referred several times to the unusual difficulties of writing words to airs which were often exceedingly complicated in their rhythm:

> "It is too much, at least for *my* humble rustic Muse to expect that every effort of hers must have merit: still, I think that it is better to have mediocre verses to a favorite air than none at all.—On this principle I have all along proceeded in the Scots Musical Museum."[103]

He did not, however, mean the matter to rest there. It is evident from two letters to Thomson that Burns even in the last weeks of his life was planning to revise the work done by him for Johnson and Thomson. In May 1796 he wrote:

> "When your Publication is finished, I intend publishing a Collection, on a cheap plan, of all the songs I have written for you, the 'Museum,' &c.—at least of all the songs of which I wish to be called the Author.—I do not propose this so much in the way of emolument, as to do justice to my Muse, lest I should be blamed for trash I never saw, or be defrauded by other claimants of what is justly my own."[104]

He accordingly asked for the manuscripts of his songs, or at least for copies of them, as

> "I have taken a fancy to review them all, & possibly may mend some of them; . . . I had rather be the author of five well-written songs than of ten otherwise."[105]

---

[100] The original copy was sold to America in 1903. It now forms one of the treasures of the Gribbel Collection. Before it left England, James C. Dick managed to make an exact transcription of it, and this was published after his death as "Notes on Scottish Songs." H. Frowde, 1908. No other edition is reliable.

[101] Letters, 513.

[102] Letters, 646.

[103] Letters, 637.

[104] Letters, 695.

[105] Letters, 694.

It is easy to imagine, from the material at our disposal, to what great and impressive heights such a volume would have risen, once it had cast off the shackles of the unessential, the ephemeral, and the insignificant. Even without this last revision, Burns's output of songs is an achievement with which no other nation has anything to compare. The complete treasury of Scottish songs had passed through his mind and been stamped by his personality with a new national spirit, so that it has been given the fullest measure of immortality conceivable for any human creation. The immense difficulty of this work of recasting, the tremendous amount of labour involved in carrying it through, may not be evident to the casual observer at the first glance. Very often one comes across the phrase that during the last ten years of his life Burns wrote nothing of importance, apart from "Tam o' Shanter"—"only songs." Such critics should consider the greatness of the plan he had in his mind. They are also mistaken in their estimate of the individual lyric, and should remember what Burns wrote as far back as the year 1787:

> "Those who think that composing a Scotch song is a trifling business, let them try!"[106]

---

[106] To James Hoy, 6th Nov. 1787; Letters, 149. Similarly, to J. Skinner, 25th Oct. 1787; Letters, 147.

Chapter X

DUMFRIES. THE END

1791-1796

MANY of Burns's biographers have felt it necessary to pass quickly over the last phase of his life, with apologetic euphemisms. This was Heron's attitude as far back as 1797, and it was that taken up by Currie, Walker, Irving, and, to a certain extent, Carlyle. Lockhart endeavoured to arrive at a more unbiassed appreciation, whilst W. S. Henley, again, begins the sketchy last part of his essay on Burns in the old strain: "I purpose to deal with the Dumfries period with all possible brevity. The story is a story of decadence." He then goes on to say:

> "We can see for ourselves that the Burns of the Kilmarnock Volume and the good things of the *Museum* had ceased to be some time before the end; there is evidence that some time before the end he was neither a sober companion nor a self-respecting husband. And the reflection is not to be put by, that he left the world at the right moment for himself and for his fame."[1]

This is a cruel and, in our opinion, unjust judgment which cannot stand the test of an unprejudiced examination of the facts, such as it is incumbent upon us to make here.

We know the exuberance of Burns's temperament and the brutality of his peasant nature which often manifested itself during his life, but which we have little right either to excuse or blame, since the poet himself frequently sat in judgment on these foibles and often condemned them in prose and verse. We expect to see the poet guilty of many a lapse and involved in many a conflict in Dumfries, and, as a matter of fact, the reality does not differ greatly from that of the Ayrshire and Edinburgh periods. We can scarcely call this a decline. It is rather a deepening of the natural channels of his temperament, chiefly as a result of his sympathy with that outstanding event: the French Revolution and its effects on England and Scotland. To attempt in the case of an impulsive

---

[1] H. H., iv, 334, 336-337.

man like Burns, whose actions were so often swayed by passing
emotions, to count how many love-affairs he had or how often he
indulged too freely in the pleasures of the tavern, is a pitiful and
futile undertaking, and has, moreover, been notoriously overdone
in the present case. Maria Riddell, that clever woman who had
certainly no reason to comment flatteringly on Burns's self-control,
wrote, within a fortnight of his death, in a character-sketch that
appeared in the *Dumfries Weekly Journal*:

> "I will not . . . undertake to be the apologist of the irregularities
> even of a man of genius, though I believe it is as certainly understood
> that genius never *was* free of irregularities, as that their absolution may
> in great measure be justly claimed, since it is evident that the world
> must have continued very stationary in its intellectual acquirements,
> had it never given birth to any but men of plain sense. . . . It is only
> on the gem we are disturbed to see the dust; the pebble may be soiled,
> and we do not regard it."[2]

Apart from this, the questions we have to answer are: Were
Burns's mental faculties during this last period unable to cope with
contemporary problems? Was his poetic power growing so feeble
that, given the necessary incentive, it could no longer be expected
to produce anything new or great? It is only if the answer to these
questions is in the affirmative that we dare speak of decadence and
mental deterioration. A further question is that concerning the
physiological causes which led to his sudden and premature death.
It is the doctor and not the moralist who must answer this. Sir
James Crichton-Browne has done this in a justly esteemed little
book, in which he has embodied the fruits of his courageous
investigations.[3]

Burns's reasons for renouncing agriculture, giving up the lease
of Ellisland, and settling in Dumfries, have been discussed in an
earlier chapter. It has also been shown that this change did not
mean a violent, painful break for him, but was the result of a
gradual transition under auspices which he had every reason to
believe favourable both with regard to his pocket and to his art.
As late as the spring of 1795, in a very lucid and well-phrased letter
to the liberal M.P. for Kirkcudbright, Patrick Heron, a man bound
to him by ties of gratitude, he summed up his claims upon life in
the short sentence: "A life of literary leisure, with a decent com-

---

[2] See the essay in Ch. W., iv, 520-525. A proof-sheet, the only copy known to
exist, is in the Burns Museum, Alloway. (Catalogue, 134B.)
[3] "Burns from a New Point of View," London (1937).

petence, is the summit of my wishes."[4] It was with this hope in his
mind that he had planned and carried out his removal from Ellisland to Dumfries.

As a place of residence, Dumfries, the "Queen of the South,"
may be called worthy of the poet. From the Observatory the eye
roams with pleasure over Maxwelltown to the hills which enclose
the town protectively in a wide semi-circle, terminating in the
characteristic mass of Criffel to the South-west away towards the
Solway. The view extends over the winding course of the Nith,
which passes through rich pasture-land, its waters overhung by
mighty, immemorial trees, then flows clear and calm round Dumfries, and, finally, spreads out into a tidal river near its estuary.
Beyond the Nith stand stately houses surrounded by fine parks;
the town itself lies spread out before us, the red sandstone of its
buildings giving it a strong yet warm and festive appearance. Its
streets and squares are bright and roomy, and its public buildings
bear witness to its former prosperity and to careful tending. The
chief historical associations are those connected with Lady
Devorgilla, who built the old bridge (c. 1280) and Sweetheart
Abbey (Dulce Cor), where she buried the heart of her husband,
John Balliol, and was herself laid to rest; and with the rivalry
between Pretenders to the Scottish crown, which led to the slaying
of John of Badenoch by Robert the Bruce and his followers. The
beautiful ruins of Lincluden Abbey at the spot where the Cluden
meets the Nith recall more peaceful pictures of mediæval life: the
idyllic monastic existence of the canons would but seldom be disturbed by contemporary upheavals or by an occasional fugitive.
Downstream, however, defiant strongholds such as Caerlaverock
Castle, the keep of the Maxwells on the Solway, tell of the wild
Border feuds of the sixteenth century and of the Anglo-Scottish
passages-at-arms in the time of Elizabeth and Mary Stuart. The
broad Solway itself often witnessed bold landings and adventurous flights. The memory of the distress of the religious wars
of the seventeenth century, of Claverhouse's dragoons and the
sufferings and faith of the Covenanters, has been perpetuated in
Dumfries in the graves in the old churchyard of St. Michael's
beside which there now rises the granite pyramid of a Martyrs'
Monument.

----

[4] Letters, 660.

The traditions of this richly peopled past were carried on in the industrious, energetic life of the cheerful Border town, the enterprising spirit and bright healthy atmosphere of which made it appeal to strangers as a desirable place of abode. The opinion which Smollett, in an oft-quoted passage from "Humphry Clinker" (1771), makes young Melford write, is well-known:

> "Dumfries," he says, "is a very elegant trading town near the borders of England, where we found plenty of good provision and excellent wine, at very reasonable prices, and the accommodation as good in all respects as in any part of South Britain. If I was confined to Scotland for life, I would choose Dumfries as the place of my residence."

At that time, indeed, many well-to-do families had already settled in the town and its vicinity, attracted by the sporting pleasures it offered, by its healthy climate, and by its excellent educational facilities. We have many vivid and delightful descriptions[5] of the happy and animated bustle which prevailed in Dumfries on gala days, during the Race Week of the Dumfriesshire and Galloway Club, for instance, in which our old Edinburgh friends, the "Caledonian Hunt," used to take part, or at the shooting competition held by the corporations for the silver gun presented by James VI and competed for annually on the King's birthday. The waves of life ran high during these festivities. The town swarmed with hairdressers, wigmakers, valets, and stable-boys. Carriages rattled to and fro. The forenoons were devoted to sport, the evenings and nights to the joys of the play and the table, to cards and dancing. The high-spirited members of the one sex, as one writer tells us, were naturally attracted by the gay and beautiful members of the other, and the result was a display of beauty and elegance such as few country towns in Scotland or England could have produced on similar occasions.

Such was the stimulating and congenial environment which Burns entered shortly before the beginning of the winter of 1791-92, not as the bachelor and literary victor of his Edinburgh days, but as a married man with a wife and a steadily increasing family, and as an exciseman in the lowest grade of the service, with a salary of £75, rising to £90, and whatever extra emoluments he might earn, these being subject to considerable fluctuation in those bad

---

[5] *Cf.* John Mayne's "Siller Gun," and W. Dickie, "Dumfries and Round About," 1910, p. 39.

times. At first, as we already know, he lived very simply near the
quay, then, from Whitsunday 1793 till his death, in what was for a
man in his circumstances an almost pretentious house, where he
and his family were sole tenants, situated not far from the theatre,
his favourite tavern, and St. Michael's Church.[6] His landlord was
in both cases a highly respected citizen, John Hamilton, who went
out of his way to be friendly to Burns and felt hurt when the latter
let some time elapse without taking advantage of the hospitality
so generously offered him. Burns excused himself, pleading
shyness, which proceeded, he said, "from the abashing consciousness of my obscure station in the ranks of life."[7] Nothing could
more clearly show the contrast between his life in Dumfries and his
life in Edinburgh, but it is unfair to conclude from that that
Burns had degenerated morally and was for that reason slighted
and avoided by many people. The truth is that he stood more
firmly and securely on his feet in his self-chosen office and under
the restraint of his self-imposed duties, than he did in the flattering
but, for him, unhealthy atmosphere of the Edinburgh aristocracy
and the literary world of that city. We can also gather from a
great deal of evidence (some of which has been interpreted, with
gross unfairness, to his disadvantage) that to the end of his life he
remained "the observed of all observers," the most famous man in
the town whose free burgess he was, and in whose interests he
took an expert and beneficial part, as witness the founding of the
library (1792) and the opening up of new sources of revenue.[8]
He was appreciated and exploited as the most entertaining of social
assets, the most fascinating and eloquent of speakers, and the
sharpest and boldest of critics of public and private affairs—a man
to whose table people flocked when, after a day's service conscien-
tiously performed, he appeared in the little back room of the
Globe Tavern in the High Street. This dark, narrow, comfort-
able room, by the way, is still in a good state of preservation and
is one of the most inviting corners in the whole county. When
Burns was present, one must have felt as if the force of his words
would rend its walls and ceilings asunder. That these sittings,

---

[6] The house is now a museum, under the auspices of the Dumfries and Galloway
Infirmary as trustees.

[7] Letters, 655.

[8] Letter to Provost David Staig: 534 (of uncertain date).

which were often prolonged into the morning, were for Burns accompanied by perils which were all the more fatal the more fragile his health became, cannot be denied. The same is true of the results of the invitations which took him to the houses of the neighbouring landed gentry. On 2nd January 1793, fully realizing the gravity of the great contemporary evil and its serious dangers for himself, he wrote to Mrs. Dunlop:

> "You must not think, as you seem to insinuate, that in my way of life I want exercise.—Of that I have enough; but occasional hard drinking is the devil to me.—Against this I have again & again bent my resolution, & have greatly succeeded.—Taverns, I have totally abandoned: it is the private parties in the family way, among the hard drinking gentlemen of this country, that does me the mischief—but even this, I have more than half given over."[9]

In spite of these laudable resolutions, it was a drinking bout of this kind that led in the following year to one of the most painful and humiliating episodes in the poet's life. The ties of warm friendship which had bound Burns to his former neighbour at Ellisland, Robert Riddell of Friar's Carse, extended to the family of his younger brother Walter, who had taken an estate in 1791 a few miles South-west of Dumfries, naming it Woodley Park in honour of his wife, Maria Woodley. This widely travelled, cultured, and charming woman made Burns free of her house, where she treated him with the social camaraderie of an equal. Burns for his part had been able in 1792 to do her the important service of inducing his old friend Smellie to publish her "Voyages to the Madeira and Leeward Caribbean Isles" for her, and had at the same time introduced her to that Edinburgh worthy and admirer of the fair sex.[10] Until late in December 1793 Burns's relations with Maria Riddell were both pleasant and stimulating, and were of course flavoured with that spirit of philandering without which it is impossible to imagine Burns's associations with any woman.[11] Then, on the occasion of a dinner-party at Woodley Park, there was an unedifying eruption. It seems that under the influence of the liquor they had consumed the gentlemen carried out a playful raid (modelled on

---

[9] Dunlop Corr., 376; Letters, 529.

[10] See R. Kerr's "Memoirs of the Life of Smellie," ii, 352-399; Letters, 492. The title-page mentions Peter Hill and T. Cadell as publishers, but of course Smellie backed them.

[11] J. De L. Ferguson, "R. B. and Maria Riddell." Mod. Phil. xxviii (1931), 169-184.

the rape of the Sabine women) on the ladies assembled in the
drawing-room, and that in the course of this foolish jest Burns had
the ill-luck to lay his hands in unseemly fashion on his hostess. The
awakening from this drunken folly was terrible. Next day Burns
sent the insulted lady a desperate letter "from the regions of Hell,
amid the horrors of the damned," begging her to forgive him, but
at the same time, as he was fully justified in doing, absolving himself from part of the blame:

> "To the men of the company," he wrote, "I will make no apology.
> —Your husband, who insisted on my drinking more than I chose, has
> no right to blame me; and the other gentlemen were partakers of my
> guilt."[12]

The letter was unsuccessful, and in place of the mutual attraction
there was now, in the easily understandable revulsion of feeling,
an equally mutual and violent bitterness. Unfortunately, the
incident also caused an estrangement between Burns and his distinguished friend Robert Riddell. The latter died in April 1794,
without having been reconciled to the poet: a grievous epilogue to
long years of friendship which had been rich in common interests.
It was only in March 1795 that Maria Riddell relented, and Burns
died reconciled to her, comforted by a last intimate meeting at
Brow. After this, she rendered unforgettable services of love to the
poet's memory and fame.

It is easy to imagine how this incident and others like it were
exaggerated by Burns's enemies in Dumfries, for there were many
who envied and disliked him. After all, to generalize from one
particular episode has ever been one of gossip's typical methods
of warfare. It does not mean that we are extolling Burns's obvious
failings if we do not criticize them, but, keeping the most essential
part of his development in view, prove that in a threefold sense
he kept his feet on solid ground, right up to the end: (1) in his
care of his family; (2) in the carrying out of his work, on which
his personal future depended; and (3) in the fulfilment of his poetic
mission, on which rests his national fame. With the last of these
points we are not at present concerned. For the first two we have

---

[12] Letters, 608. Ms. not traced.—The letter was owned by Maria Riddell, who,
to all appearances, was also the addressee. Cf. her letter to J. Currie, July 1800,
reprinted in B. Chr., 32 (1923), p. 78. If Walter Riddell was still absent from
England, it is difficult to reconcile this fact with the passage quoted above. There
remains the possibility that the text of the original may have been tampered with,
before its publication by Currie. As it is, we must wait for further elucidations.

at our disposal, along with other evidence, two quite indisputable accounts already used by Lockhart, one of which has since been authenticated in every detail by the discovery of further documents. The first is the letter of James Gray, Rector of Dumfries Academy, and concerns Burns's domestic life. The second is Alexander Findlater's letter, dealing with the poet's work in an official capacity. Both letters were addressed in the year 1814 to Alexander Peterkin, who was endeavouring to rend the veil of unctuous moral censure which seemed to have descended upon Burns's memory.[13]

Gray emphasizes the care which Burns devoted to the education of his children, and tells how he often came upon him initiating his son Robert into the beauties of the English poets from Shakespeare to Gray, or sharpening the boy's appetite for deeds of heroism, as they are recorded in the works of the English historians. Gray explicitly lays stress upon the fact that till the day of Burns's death he saw no sign of deterioration in his mental faculties. "To the last day of his life, his judgment, his memory, his imagination were fresh and vigorous as when he composed the 'Cotter's Saturday Night.'" Findlater, who with Mitchell was Burns's superior in the Excise, lays stress on the fact that the poet was most painstakingly thorough in the discharge of his duties, and that he was jealously watchful of his reputation as a conscientious official. The documents given by Sinton throw conclusive light upon the measure of strength and labour which the Excise service demanded in those days. Even in February 1795, as we see from the schedules of service kept personally by Burns,[14] he was busy from five in the morning until seven at night. After that he had to attend to his book-keeping and the writing-up of his reports. The accomplishing of these tasks, as Gray and Findlater unanimously agree, relegates to the kingdom of fables and malicious exaggeration the legend of Burns as the habitual drunkard, who was capable of carrying out his duties only when under the influence of alcohol. The closing stages of his life might not be calm or immaculate, but they were logical and marked by the old power up till the moment when the fatal malady that lay dormant within him declared its presence and laid low his body, but not his indefatigable spirit.

---

[13] Both reproduced by Ch. W., iv, 525-532.
[14] Facsimile by Sinton, p. 45.

There is much which we must pass over in silence, such as the many and varied honours which were conferred on him (he was a freeman of six royal burghs before he died)[15] and the short journeys and excursions which he made from Dumfries. We have not even time to discuss more fully friends and political associates like John Syme (1755-1831), to whom we owe several interesting but not always reliable items of information about Burns; and Dr. William Maxwell, who had lived in Dumfries since 1794, and of whom it was said that he was one of those who had dipped their handkerchiefs in the blood of the beheaded King of Paris. It was Maxwell who attended Burns during his last illness. No more can we speak of the poet's last and innocent affection for the unfortunate Jean Lorimer, the "Lassie wi' the Lintwhite Locks," and the heroine of numerous other songs in Thomson's collection,[16] for our attention is claimed by a group of outstandingly important events which belong to world history, and which by their far-reaching, dynamic effects upon Burns's life have left their distinctive mark upon the Dumfries period.

The French Revolution, in whose storms there still persisted some of the forces of the American War of Independence, had also thrown its sparks upon British ground, with the result that an outcry for decisive measures both in home affairs and in foreign politics could no longer be suppressed. Long-sought reforms, such as greater freedom and legislative authority for the middle and lower classes, a fairer and more wholesome apportioning of the franchise, and revision of the municipal constitution, seemed to brook no further delay. The country was seething with unrest. The differences between the two great political parties were becoming more and more acute. The revolutionary events in France had brought about a far-reaching quarrel within the Whig party itself, causing a decisive split between Burke's adherents and those of Fox. The moderate Liberals took their creed from Burke's prophetic "Reflections on the Revolution in France" (November 1790), while the text-book of the Radicals was Thomas Paine's inflammatory reply "The Rights of Man" (1791, 1792), of which hundreds of thousands of copies were sold. The one side clamoured

---

[15] See above, p. 160, note 21. He was also a member of that most select body, the Royal Company of Scottish Archers.

[16] See James Adams, "Burns' Chloris, A Reminiscence"; Glasgow, 1893.

for war against the destroyers of the organic law and order of the
State, the other advocated friendship with the harbingers of liberty
and the common brotherhood of the whole human race, an
attitude which was not exclusively influenced by politics, but by a
definite belief in the imminent fulfilment of sentimental and
romantic dreams. The excitement in the radical division of the
liberal camp led at the beginning of the 'nineties to the founding
in England of a number of clubs of more or less revolutionary
tendencies, in which many eminent Scotsmen held prominent posi-
tions.[17] The conflagration soon spread to Scotland herself, where
the postponement of what were regarded as urgently necessary
municipal reforms, with a strong democratic bias in the local governing bodies, had accumulated a heap of highly combustible material.

The movement began in the spring of 1792 with demonstra-
tions against the Secretary of State, Henry Dundas, who was closely
allied with Pitt and was justly regarded as the most determined and
the most influential opponent of the Scottish reform movement.
This was followed in the summer of the same year by the founding
in Edinburgh of a society known as "The Associated Friends of
the People," which grew rapidly, split up into local branches, and,
filled with Paine's ideas, created focuses of ill-feeling and resistance
throughout the whole country. "There were few men of better
rank and education who were not affected in some degree with the
plausibility of the accusations brought against our excellent Constitution," wrote the Rev. Thomas Somerville in his Memoirs.[18]
The South-west, Glasgow, Kilmarnock, and Paisley, that is, Burns's
own native district, seem to have been particularly restless, while
in Dumfries the conservative element was in the ascendant at the
moment. As the year 1792 advanced, it brought storms and bad
crops, thus adding social distress to the political difficulties. It also
brought the fall of the monarchy and the Reign of Terror in France,
and with these events the fulfilment of Burke's prophecies. Horror
at this caricature of freedom, with a resultant revulsion in the
mood of the English people, was the consequence: the state-sup-
porting elements were able, amid the applause of a considerable
number of the population, to pass measures for the suppression of

---

[17] For what follows, cf. W. L. Mathieson, "The Awakening of Scotland.'
Glasgow, 1910.
[18] Quoted by Mathieson, l.c., p. 122.

the reformers and the friends of the Revolution, and began to put
them into effect in the first months of the year 1793, while the
impression created by the execution of Louis XVI was still fresh
in the public mind. Scotland now witnessed a number of political
law-suits which, taken in conjunction with similar reprisals in England and Ireland, left no doubt as to the Government's state of
mind. Thomas Muir, who in December 1792 had played a leading
part in the "Convention of the Delegates of the Associated Friends
of the People," was condemned by a biassed court to fourteen years'
deportation, without any pretence at convincing proof, for seditious
conduct; the Rev. Thomas Fyshe Palmer was sentenced to seven
years' deportation for a similar offence; while William Skirving,
secretary of the Edinburgh Reform Club, and two delegates, Joseph
Gerald and Maurice Margarot, who had been sent to Scotland by
the London Corresponding Society, were each condemned to fourteen years' deportation. The Reform Club, in growing bitterness,
increased its hostile activities, and the word was given for armed
resistance against the Government. "Get weapons and use them"
was the message printed in a broadsheet of the Edinburgh Corresponding Society, and soon rumours of carefully planned armed
risings in different parts of the Kingdom came to the knowledge
of the parliamentary committees appointed to look into the movement. In 1794 the Habeas Corpus Act was repealed and did not
come into force again until 1801. This was followed in 1795 by
special edicts to deal with seditious intrigues and rebellious meetings. In 1799 the democratic clubs in England, Scotland, and
Ireland were put down by law, and trade-unions were forbidden, the
Government showing that it was in earnest by trying a number of
persons for high treason.

> "Englishmen had now to learn that they must hold their tongues,
> and that to express an opinion that the Constitution was not perfect,
> or that there was corruption in the Government or Parliament, might,
> probably would, be twisted into treason or seditious libel by the judges
> on the bench and by Crown lawyers scavenging in the reports of spies
> and *agents provocateurs*."[19]

Influenced by the French Revolution and the Napoleonic wars
which had sprung from it, the Government had succeeded for a
time in suppressing, but not in stamping out, the reform move-

---

[19] C. G. Robertson, "England under the Hanoverians"; London, 1911, 364.

ment, which was ready to blaze up again at any moment. The above-mentioned injustices, festering in the minds of the people, made the situation worse, and demanded radical treatment. This was gradually accorded them in the nineteenth century, after no less violent and dangerous conflicts in the internal politics of the country.

It is desirable that we should have in our minds a clear picture of this agitated historical background, before dealing with Burns's attitude to those fundamental problems. On the one hand, we have a dissatisfied section of the people, encouraged by the French Revolution and the American War of Independence, clamouring for reform; on the other hand, an utterly unsympathetic Government, shrinking from no violence in its efforts to protect the Constitution entrusted to its care. If we remember these circumstances, we no longer see Burns as an isolated, reckless hothead, but as a man in whose behaviour was reflected a strong contemporary movement, to represent which we can conceive no one better suited by nature than our poet. That he was a born democrat needs no further proof here. His origin, his practical experience, his pride, his self-confidence, his keen intellect, and his sympathetic heart all bound him fast to the Opposition. Just as in his introspective moods he passed sentence upon himself, so from the time when he began to think for himself he did not shrink from judging conditions around him according to his standards of freedom and justice, and his faith in a happiness which would be accessible to all humanity. As his thoughts gained in power and in range, and rose above the personal distress of himself and his family to the needs of the community, his questioning became more and more insistent and clear-sighted:

> "If I'm design'd yon lordling's slave—
>   By Nature's law design'd—
> Why was an independent wish
>   E'er planted in my mind?
> If not, why am I subject to
>   His cruelty, or scorn?
> Or why has Man the will and pow'r
>   To make his fellow mourn?"

We find these and many similar ideas in a poem in the Kilmarnock Edition.[20]

---

[20] "Man Was Made to Mourn," st. ix, H. H., i, 133.

We have already referred to Burns's letter to the editor of the *Edinburgh Evening Courant* and the similar one to Mrs. Dunlop, both written during the Ellisland period. On 4th March 1789, after a visit to the capital, he wrote to the same faithful friend, telling her that the bustle of Edinburgh filled him with disgust:

> "When I must sculk into a corner, lest the rattling equipage of some gaping blockhead, contemptible puppy, or detestable scoundrel should mangle me in the mire, I am tempted to exclaim—What merits these Wretches had, or what demerit have I had, in some state of Pre-existence, that they are ushered into this scene of being with the sceptre of rule and the key of riches in their puny fists, and I am kicked into the world, the sport of their folly, or the victim of their pride?"[21]

Thus Burns in the year in which the Bastille fell! When the revolution actually broke out, it seemed an unexpected and magnificent answer to the poet's harsh questions and to the problems of humanity, in which he took such an absorbing interest. The spring-time of the nations was at the door! What joy for its prophets to throw open the door and let it in—to be the harbingers of liberty for the oppressed, equality for the struggling, and brotherhood for all mankind! The moment seemed to have come when Burns's personality and abundant creative gifts might burst through their local bounds and flow into the main stream of a movement that was coursing through the whole of Europe; when his voice might resound as powerfully as those of the great party leaders in France and England, in his capacity of speaker, singer, and herald of a newer, nobler, purer epoch in the history of the world.

If Burns cherished any such dreams, they must soon have been followed by a disillusioning awakening. He was not independent enough to face the consequences which would inevitably have resulted from publicly opposing those in power. He lived in an essentially conservative town, served George III's Government as an excise official, and was the sole support of a numerous and rapidly increasing family, whose welfare he considered as a sacred pledge entrusted to his keeping. That he fully realized his responsibilities is shown by a letter to Mrs. Dunlop (6th December 1792):

> "A few years ago, I could have lain down in the dust, careless, as the book of Job elegantly says, 'careless of the voice of the morning'; & now, not a few & these most helpless, individuals, would, on losing me & my exertions, lose both their 'Staff & Shield.'"

---

[21] Dunlop Corr., 151; Letters, 319.

He adds a favourite quotation from Thomson's drama "Edward and Eleanora":

> "The valiant, *in himself,* what can he suffer?
> Or what does he regard his single woes?
> But when, alas, he multiplies himself
> To dearer selves, to the loved tender Fair,
> To those whose bliss, whose beings hang upon him,
> To helpless children! then, O then! he feels
> The point of misery festering in his heart,
> And weakly weeps his fortune like a coward."

And in the last part of the letter he reports:

> "We, in this country, here have many alarms of the Reform, or rather the Republican spirit, of your part of the kingdom.—Indeed, we are a good deal in commotion ourselves, & in our Theatre here, 'God save the King' has met with some groans & hisses, while Ca ira has been repeatedly called for.—For me, I am a *Placeman,* you know, a very humble one indeed, Heaven knows, but still so much so as to gag me from joining in the cry.—What my private sentiments are, you will find out without an Interpreter."[22]

Small wonder that in the conflict between duty and inward sympathy, discretion and regard for the opportune did not always keep the upper hand. He would not have been the full-blooded fighter we know if the suppressed flame had not flared up now and then.

Before Burns had been settled in Dumfries more than a few months, he is said to have taken part in an incident which is characteristic alike of the atmosphere of the times and of Burns's ability to "control his personal feelings." According to Lockhart, a smuggler-brig, the "Rosamond" of Plymouth, was sighted in the Solway Firth on 27th February 1792, and was seized a few days later by customs officers, among whom was Burns, aided by the military, the vessel being put up to auction, with all her arms and stores, in Dumfries on 19th April: "upon which occasion," Lockhart goes on, "Burns . . . thought fit to purchase four carronades, by way of trophy." There would have been nothing reprehensible about that, but Burns is said to have gone further, and to have sent these guns to the French Convention in Paris, accompanying the gift with a letter expressing his admiration for their activity. Guns and letter, however, were seized by the customs at Dover and did not reach their destination. The anecdote, for

---

[22] Dunlop Corr., 367-369; Letters, 524.

whose authenticity Lockhart cites the diary of one of the excisemen who took part in the affair—probably John Lewars—has often been repeated, and no less often been doubted both as a whole and in part. F. B. Snyder goes furthest in scepticism, and would like to see the "Rosamond" affair absolutely deleted from any account of Burns's life.[23] We are not justified in taking such a summary step, however, for there have recently come to light certain documents relating to the episode, one of them containing official notes in Burns's own handwriting.[24] The first part of the report, concerning the stranding, watching, disarming, and auctioning of the ship, is based in all essentials upon reliable evidence, although Lockhart's manner of telling the story gives it an obtrusively theatrical air. Leaving out that aspect, Burns seems to have carried out his official duties with prudence, courage, and energy, under difficult circumstances. As for the second part, the buying of the carronades, the sending of them with a letter to the French Convention, and their subsequent confiscation at Dover, documentary evidence has hitherto not come to light. In this respect we must wait for further discoveries, and till then reserve our judgment. It is certain, however, that Burns's superiors neither then nor later saw fit to take any steps in this matter, as would have been inevitable if Burns had thus shown his sympathy with the political programme of a hostile power.

As the year went on, however, and the political situation grew more and more tense, threatening clouds gathered over his head. It was obvious that he belonged to the extreme left wing of the reform party. He was known to be on intimate terms with men like Syme and Maxwell and to be a subscriber to the democratic *Edinburgh Gazeteer*, to the proprietor of which he had addressed a compromising letter,[25] while he had published a spirited poem in praise of Fox and his adherents in its columns: "Here's a Health to them that's Awa," containing the provocative lines:

---

[23] "Life of Burns," pp. 396-97. But see his recent article in *Publ. Mod. Lang. Ass.* L. (1935), 510-521, with the necessary corrections and retractions.

[24] See H. W. Meikle, "Burns and the Capture of the Rosamond"; *B. Chr.* (1934), pp. 43-52. The documents come partly from the library of Sir W. Scott, who was interested in the affair.

[25] Letters, 515.

"Here's freedom to them that wad read,
  Here's freedom to them that would write!
There's nane ever fear'd that the truth should be heard
  But they whom the truth would indite!"[26]

People probably also talked of rash toasts proposed by Burns while under the influence of drink, although these were generally given in the intimate circle of friends whose opinions were similar to his own. In the end some anonymous scoundrel—probably a professional informer, whose name it would be a satisfaction to publish —denounced Burns to the Board of Excise as an enemy of the existing Government. It is easy to understand from the nervous tension prevalent in every governing body at that time that Burns's position was in grave and instant danger. Voices were raised requesting his immediate dismissal without previous investigation of the facts, a step which was within the power of the Board of Excise, but which was prevented undoubtedly through the influence of the faithful Robert Graham of Fintry. Instead of this, Burns's immediate superior, a collector of Excise named Mitchell, was ordered to enquire into the poet's political views. It was while Mitchell, who was one of his well-wishers, was carrying out this duty that Burns received the first intimation of the proceedings which had been instituted against him. He was "surprised, confounded and distracted." In a flash he saw what would happen to himself and his family if he were dismissed: they would be faced with shame, distress, and lack of the most elementary necessities of life as a result of base, groundless slander, as he wrote on 31st December 1792[27] to Graham, while still smarting under the impression of the first news of the disaster. In these agitated lines he declared that, next to God, he was devoutly attached to the revolution principles of 1688. Graham did his best to calm him down. In response, he received an elaborate letter[28] in which Burns endeavoured to refute the charges brought against him, repeating his belief in the creed of the British Constitution as expressed in a hurriedly formulated sentence of his previous letter, but adding a qualifying clause, which, under the prevailing circumstances, bears striking testimony to his manly courage and sincerity:

---

[26] H. H., iv, 35-36.
[27] Letters, 528.
[28] Letters, 530 (of Jan. 5, 1793).

"At the same time, I think, & you know what High and distinguished Characters have for some time thought so, that we have
a good deal deviated from the original principles of that Constitution;
particularly, that an alarming System of Corruption has pervaded the
connection between the Executive Power and the House of Commons."

Graham laid this letter in the original before the Board of Directors,
who did not feel inclined to let those critical remarks from a subordinate pass uncensured, even though that subordinate happened
to be Robert Burns. They sent the General Supervisor of Excise,
William Corbet, who, by the way, was a friend of Mrs. Dunlop and
no stranger to Burns himself, to Dumfries, to enquire on the spot,
with the assistance of Mitchell and Findlater, into Burns's political
conduct, and expressly charged him at least to impress upon
Exciseman Burns that his business was to act and not to think, and
that whatever his opinions about men and measures might be, it
behoved him to be silent and to obey. Unquestionably the Board
of Excise was justified in taking this view. What Burns as a man
and a poet felt about it is another matter.

While the enquiry conducted by Corbet in Dumfries was developing along lines that soon allowed Burns to breathe more freely
and to recover his good humour, although he was not wholly
exonerated, the report had spread abroad that he had actually been
dismissed from the Excise on account of his political opinions. In
March, Mrs. Dunlop wrote asking anxiously and sympathetically
for news,[29] while William Nicol sent him a letter bubbling over
with frivolity and whimsical wit:

"What concerns it thee whether the lousy Dumfriesian fiddlers play
'ça ira' or 'God save the King'? Suppose you *had* an aversion to the
King, you could not, as a gentleman, wish God to use him worse than
He has done. The infliction of idiocy is no sign of Friendship or
Love."

Holding up the Vicar of Bray as a shining example of how it is
possible to live in harmony with the times, Nicol proceeded to give
Burns good advice, to which the latter replied in a similar strain.[30]
The liberal Earl of Mar, John Francis Erskine, having heard the
same rumour, set about opening a subscription for the poet, first
applying for information to Robert Riddell, who in turn told Burns
of the project, and read him part of Erskine's letter. Burns's answer

---

[29] Dunlop Corr., p. 379.
[30] Ch. W., iii, 394-396; Letters, 537.

to the Earl, written on 13th April 1793, is one of his greatest and proudest letters.[31] He himself' thought it important enough to be included in the selection of his letters which he prepared for Riddell. It contains at the same time the poet's reply to the embargo on thought and speech laid down by his superiors. After expressing his deepest gratitude to the Earl for his intended kindness, he rectifies the erroneous report of his dismissal, and repeats, with somewhat stronger emphasis on his criticisms, the contents of his second letter to Graham of Fintry. The last part of the letter is purely personal: in spite of his poverty and lowly rank in life, Burns claims the right of every free-born Briton to independent utterance of opinion for himself and his three sons, to whom he wishes to bequeath it unimpaired, as befits men. He continues:

> "Does any man tell me, that my feeble efforts can be of no service; & that it does not belong to my humble station to meddle with the concerns of a People?—I tell him, that it is on such individuals as I, that for the hand of support & the eye of intelligence, a Nation has to rest.—The uninformed mob may swell a Nation's bulk; & the titled, tinsel Courtly throng may be its feathered ornament, but the number of those who are elevated enough in life, to reason & reflect; & yet low enough to keep clear of the venal contagion of a Court; these are a Nation's strength."

We cannot fail to notice that these sentences foreshadow a powerful song, to be quoted later. In conclusion, Burns begs the Earl to commit this letter to the flames. He has, he says, drawn himself in it *as he is*:

> "but should any of the people in whose hands is the very bread he eats, get the least knowledge of the picture, it would ruin the poor Bard for ever."

In spite of the prudence displayed in this request, in spite of the decree of silence and the warning with which Corbet had very indulgently brought his enquiry to an end, and in spite of his promise to Graham to keep his lips sealed in future, Burns could not in the long run conceal his sympathy with the reform movement. In April 1793 he gave the toast "On the Commemoration of Rodney's Victory,"[32] and improvised the stanzas against "General Dumouriez";[33] in June 1794 he composed the "Ode for

---

[31] Letters, 558.

[32] H. H., ii, 170-171.

[33] ii, 228-229.

General Washington's Birthday,"[34] and the song which was originally permeated with similar thoughts on freedom, "As I stood by yon roofless Tower,"[35] written on seeing Lincluden Abbey. He thought fit to provide a copy of De Lolme's "Constitution of England," which he presented to the Dumfries Library, with an ambiguous inscription, and while intoxicated, proposed the toast: "May our success in the present war be equal to the justice of our cause!" In the last two cases at least he felt obliged to try to put matters right: he covered the inscription by pasting two pages together in the book,[36] and the morning after he had given the toast, when he was able to appreciate clearly what he had done, he wrote an excited and not altogether sincere letter, begging the recipient to intercede for him and avert the threatened evil consequences.[37] That he was never again censured by his superiors, in spite of occasional lapses, and that his promotion would have followed at the first opportunity, has been irrefutably proved by Sinton by means of documentary evidence.[38] As it was, he held the temporary post of inspector towards the end of April, and would in the ordinary course of events have been advanced to that position in August 1797, and at the same time transferred to Dunblane, near Stirling, a place which he knew well. His political sins were, as he himself rightly felt, forgiven him.[39] Also, he had not committed them without considerable inward gain. It seems as though the crisis brought about by his conflict with the authorities had also supplied the high pressure necessary for the purification of his restlessly effervescent political beliefs, causing him to give form not only to the international and universally humane ideas of the revolution period, and to the thoughts contained in the more or less casual poems cited above, but also to his equally sincere love of his country and of his people. This combination of patriotic and universal sentiments called forth the three hymns which seem to us the noblest fruits of his life-long

---

[34] ii, 171-173.

[35] iii, 144-146. Song and Ode, according to a theory in Ch. W., iv, 124, and Dunlop Corr., p. 406, are supposed to form a unity. "The Tree of Liberty," H. H., iv, 58-62, is considered by the editors of the Centenary Edition as not genuine. There is, however, no proof for this assumption.

[36] The copy is now in the Burns House, Dumfries. Text in Letters, 589.

[37] Letters, 631 (with facsimile).

[38] pp. 55-56.

[39] Letters, 649.

struggle for freedom and justice. They should always be considered together, as being the purest reflection of his participation
in the most stirring event during the Dumfries period.

Taking them in chronological order, "Robert Bruce's Address
to his Army before Bannockburn," to the tune "Hey, tuttie taitie,"
comes first. Burns sent this song to Thomson at the beginning of
September 1793, with an uncommonly interesting letter. The air
was again the starting-point. Burns tells how he had often heard
it played by Fraser on his hautboy, and been moved to tears by it.
There was a tradition that this stirring tune had inspired Bruce
and his followers as they advanced towards the English at Bannockburn. One evening, as Burns was out walking and thinking of this
air and the legend attached to it, he got the idea of writing a poem
in which the Scottish hero was to give his troops an inspiring
address on liberty and independence. But, the poet adds in a
postscript, it was only when he accidentally recollected "that
glorious struggle for Freedom, associated with the glowing ideas
of some other struggles of the same nature, *not quite so ancient*,"
that his "rhyming mania" came upon him.[40] Thus it was really
the memory of the French Revolution and the success of the
Republic against the first Coalition that gave Bannockburn its
decisive importance in Burns's eyes, whilst the battle-cries against
usurpers and tyrants, in the last stanza, are based on lines familiar to
Burns since his childhood (they are taken from the popular adaptation of the old Wallace epic by William Hamilton of Gilbertfield[41])
and seem to glorify purely patriotic sentiments.

The second poem in this group, "Is there for Honest Poverty,"[42]
was sent to Thomson in January 1795, not as a contribution to the
"Airs," but "merely by way of 'vive la bagatelle.'" The piece,
Burns wrote, was indeed not poetry at all, since it would not fit in
with Aiken's definition of the lyric, which says that a song must

---

[40] Letters, 582 and 584.—We possess three versions of the text: a first sketch,
in which the revolutionary views are more clearly revealed than in the later versions
(a facsimile is given by H. H., iii, 474); see also Ch. W., iv, 537; the version now
recognized as the standard one in Thomson's "Scottish Airs," iii, 1801, H. H., iii,
251-252; and the insipid version based on the air "Lewie Gordon," "Scotish Airs,"
ii, 1799. According to Syme (Ch. W., iv, 17 and 20), the song was written during
the last days of July; but his account smacks of the invented anecdote. For the
whole matter, see notes, H. H., iii, 474-478, and Dick, 448-451.

[41] Book vi, chap. ii, 91-92.

[42] H. H., iii, 271-273.

turn exclusively on love and wine, but it "will be allowed . . . to
be two or three pretty good *prose* thoughts, inverted into rhyme."[43]
Actually, it incorporates the poet's confession of faith; it is his
creed which he preached all his life, upholding honest manhood
and human dignity against the conceit and arrogance of unjustifiable
class prejudices, and for which he had now, thanks to the inspiring
influence of Paine's ideas, found an adequate form and a liberating,
rousing vehicle of expression. The famous refrain with its defiant
"for a' that an' a' that" is traditional popular song-property and
had already rendered Burns yeoman service in the "Jolly Beggars."
Here, however, it does not merely indicate the contrast between two
in themselves rather trifling alternative events or situations, but
the antagonism between two epochs, between the present age with
its unequal distribution of wealth, the riches often belonging to
worthless wretches, and the confidently expected future era, when
the elect will be in power and the free and the just will be united
in one great brotherhood—the era that will dawn when all revolutions and reactionary periods are past, "for a' that an' a' that!"

In the end Burns and his friends got an opportunity to demon-
strate their patriotism by action, and in this way to prove their
reconciliation with the Government authorities they had so often
defied. Since the Coalition had started on its unhappy course,
France had no longer appeared a state whose dearly bought rights
were in peril, but a powerful enemy of Britain, bent on conquest.
The British army, badly organized and badly led, was spread out
over the various battle-areas on the Continent. To protect the
shores of the Motherland, corps of volunteers were raised by the
Ministry of War. Two such companies were formed in Dumfries
by an order issued on 24th March 1795, under the command of an
old, experienced campaigner, Colonel Arent Schuyler de Peyster
(1736-1822). Burns, Syme, Maxwell, and many others at once
enlisted. The Colonel and Burns were soon on a friendly footing,[44]
and the poet wrote a song in honour of his company: "Does
Haughty Gaul Invasion Threat?"[45] Set to a lively air by Clarke,
it was immediately after its composition circulated throughout

---

[43] Letters, 651.

[44] *B. Chr.*, 1930, pp. 104-115.

[45] H. H., iii, 195-196, facsimile of a ms. 440; Dunlop Corr., 419; Letters, 683;
Johnson's "Museum," vi, No. 546, under the title of "The Dumfries Volunteers."

Scotland by means of broadsheets and the newspapers,[46] and was everywhere received with enthusiasm. In this song the poet exhorts his fellow-countrymen to forget internal strife in face of the external enemy. It is possible, he says, that there are faults in "the kettle o' the Kirk an' State," but no foreign tinker must be allowed to touch the vessel which their forefathers bought with their blood; the whole nation must collaborate in putting it to rights and in contributing to the general safety and common good of the community :

> "The wretch that would a tyrant own,
>   And the wretch, his true-sworn brother,
> Who would set the mob above the throne,
>   May they be damn'd together!
> Who will not sing, *God save the king,*
>   Shall hang as high's the steeple;
> But while we sing *God save the king,*
>   We'll ne'er forget the People !"

The difficult problem of combining democratic opinions with stirring patriotism has here found an artistic solution, in which Burns has conceded nothing, yet which was calculated to make people forget many an indiscretion committed in the heat of party warfare.

After considering these eminent individual productions, we are now ready to cast a comprehensive glance at Burns's literary activity during the Dumfries period. A few lines will suffice. A new edition of the "Poems," this time in two volumes, which Creech had planned as far back as 1790,[47] had been in process of preparation since 1792. Burns promised to furnish some fifty pages of new material for this edition, and undertook to revise the first Edinburgh Edition thoroughly. In spite of this notable task—"Tam o' Shanter" was among the new texts—Burns kept to the contract he had made with Creech in 1787, and desired to be recompensed for his labour in the most modest way—viz., by a few books, the choice of which he left to his friends and literary advisers, Mackenzie, Stewart, and Tytler, with, in addition, as many free copies of the new edition as he might want for presents.[48] The volumes were published for Cadell and Creech on 18th February

---

[46] See letter to Johnson, who supervised the printing; Letters, 692.
[47] See letter to Peter Hill, Letters, 475; also H. H., i, 314-315.
[48] Letters, 502.

1793, as "The Second Edition Considerably Enlarged." By the beginning of 1794 it was necessary to issue a new impression, the last to appear during Burns's life-time. Unauthorized editions continued to appear and testify to the insatiable demand of the public for Burns's poems. The additions to the new edition consist of poems composed during his various tours and while he was resident at Ellisland, and, as far as they affect our present survey, have been discussed in the previous chapters of this book.[49]

A number of occasional poems of very unequal value, composed in Dumfries, may be mentioned in passing. They include two prologues for Miss Fontenelle, which were recited in November 1792 and December 1793 in the newly opened theatre in Dumfries, an institution in which Burns from the beginning took a keen interest.[50] His friendship with Mrs. Maria Riddell and his subsequent fall from grace are reflected in lines such as the "Impromptu on Mrs. Riddell's Birthday" (4th November 1793),[51] the "Monody on a Lady famed for her Caprice,"[52] the "Epistle from Esopus to Maria,"[53] and several excessively sharp, revengeful epigrams.[54] On the death of his friend Riddell of Glenriddell (20th April 1794) he composed a sonnet expressing his grief at this event.[55] Politics are represented by a group of four ballads dealing with incidents during the election of Patrick Heron of Kerroughtrie (1795-96)[56] and by the scathing and brilliant satire "The Dean of the Faculty,"[57] in praise of Henry Erskine, who had been defeated by the all-powerful Robert Dundas in the election held by the Edinburgh advocates in January, 1796, to choose a Dean of the Faculty. Up to the very end Burns's interest in public affairs never flagged; he maintained his right to give vent to his own convictions and to influence those of others by the fire of his eloquence.

The pivot of his creative power and of his most assiduous

---

[49] H. H., i, 258-308.

[50] H. H., ii, 150-153; also Cook and Ewing, Louisa Fontenelle, Actress. B. Chr., 1935, pp. 88-91, with portrait.

[51] H. H., ii, 230-231.

[52] Ibid., 271-272.

[53] Ibid., 66-69. See Ewing, B. Chr., 1935, pp. 33-38.

[54] e.g., H. H., ii, 255.

[55] Ibid., 231.

[56] Ibid., 191-203.

[57] Ibid., 204-205.

mental efforts remained, however, during the whole of the Dumfries period, the two great song-collections of Johnson and Thomson,
especially that of the latter.   In our ninth chapter we have dealt
with these in as much detail as the compass of this work allows,
and we must refer the reader back to the pages in question.   It is
upon our assessment of Burns as critic and renovator of the songs
of Scotland that we must base our answer to the question as to
whether we are justified in speaking of a decline in his intellectual
faculties, that is, of real decadence.   There can only be one interpretation of the facts: it is not as one worn-out and incapable of
further development, for whom there could be no happier fate than
death, that we see Burns, but as a man whose active mind grappled
indefatigably with its problems; a man of high purpose and mighty
ideals; burning but not burned-out, when his body, falling a prey
to a grave malady, presumably aggravated by repeated and manifold excesses, left him in the lurch and collapsed.

The first signs of a threatened breakdown in his physical strength
seem to have been evident about the summer of 1794, while his
intellectual clarity and his creative power remained undimmed right
up to the last few days.   On 25th June he wrote to Mrs. Dunlop
that he feared he was about to suffer for the follies of his youth.
His medical friends threatened him with a "flying gout."   He
trusted, however, that they were mistaken.[58]   There is no doubt
that in this flying gout we must recognize the symptoms of a severe
heart disease the beginnings of which may be traced back to his
early years, and which, unheeded, neglected, or wrongly treated,
was now hastening on the catastrophe.   In a popular book (already
referred to) Sir James Crichton-Browne has described and commented upon the whole history of Burns's illness, and has proved
indisputably that the poet's early death was brought on not by the
abuse of alcohol, but by the plainly recognizable development
of that grave organic complaint.[59]   Currie states that about a year
before his death the decline in his powers was apparent also in his
outward appearance.[60]   The autumn of that year 1795, at any rate,
was bad.   In September he lost his only daughter, Elizabeth
Riddell, who died in Mauchline, too far away for her father to be

[58] Dunlop Corr., 405; Letters, 628.
[59] See also F. B. Snyder, "Burns's Last Years." *B. Chr.*, 1935, pp. 53-68.
[60] "Life of Burns," 218.

privileged to close her eyes or commit her to the grave. Soon afterwards he fell ill of a "rheumatic fever" which brought him, as he said in a letter to Cleghorn in January 1796, "to the borders of the grave."[61]   To his superior officer, Mitchell, from whom he had to ask an advance of a guinea on his salary after he got over the attack, he could, shortly before the close of the year 1795, address whimsical and optimistic lines, declaring that he still had a share of health and the promise of more life, and would take better care of both in future.[62]   But the improvement did not last.   His letters begin to sound depressed, and he and his friends long for the warmer season, expecting from the sun the health it could no longer bring.   During this hard time Burns's colleagues in the Excise stood loyally by him.   Adam Stobie, who took his place in the service, refused every penny of the remuneration due to him, so that Burns could draw his full salary till the end.   His superiors, Mitchell and Findlater, did all in their power to help him. Robert Graham offered his assistance, though too late.   And instead of Jean, who was again expecting to become a mother, Jessy Lewars, the young sister of another colleague, nursed him devotedly. In June, when the longed-for summer had actually come, Burns knew that his life was drawing to its close, and meditated in bitter agony of soul upon the fate of the family he must leave behind:

> "As to my individual Self, I am tranquil;—I would despise myself
> if I were not: but Burns's poor widow! & half a dozen of his dear
> little ones, helpless orphans, there I am weak as a woman's tear.—
> "Enough of this! 'tis half my disease!"

he wrote to James Clarke, his former protégé.[63]

This was one of the first of a number of heart-rending letters in which he took leave not of the great ones in the land, who for their own ends had lent their ephemeral support to the rising star, but of his collaborators, James Johnson[64] and George Thomson, of Alexander Cunningham and Frances Dunlop,[65] of his brother Gilbert at Mossgiel and his cousin James Burness in Montrose— friends whose loyalty he had proven through many a year.

At the end of June Burns went to Brow near Ruthwell on the

---

[61] Letters, 687.
[62] "To Collector Mitchell"; H. H., ii, 137-138.
[63] Letters, 698 (26th June 1796).
[64] Ibid., 696.
[65] Ibid., No. 702.   Facsimile in Dunlop Corr., p. 420.

Solway Firth, where it was hoped that sea-bathing and the mineral waters of the district would restore his strength;[66] and at first, indeed, he felt that the change of air was doing him good. He also had the pleasure of a last interview with Maria Riddell, and he enjoyed the sympathetic company of Henry Duncan, the active minister of Ruthwell, and his family. One last bitterness, however, was not spared him: he received a letter from a lawyer in Dumfries asking for payment of a few pounds which he owed his tailor for his Volunteer uniform. In morbid exaggeration of the importance of this letter his horror-stricken mind conjured up visions of arrest for debt and a dishonourable death in prison as the end of his earthly career. The thought was too much for him— he called aloud for help. In two letters, both written on 12th July, he, the proudest of men, asked James Burness and George Thomson for money. We quote the letter to Thomson:

> "After all my boasted independance, curst necessity compels me to implore you for five pounds.—A cruel scoundrel of a Haberdasher to whom I owe an account, taking it into his head that I am dying, has commenced a process, & will infallibly put me into jail.—Do, for God's sake, send me that sum, & that by return of post.—Forgive me this earnestness, but the horrors of a jail have made me half distracted.— I do not ask all this gratuitously; for upon returning health, I hereby promise & engage to furnish you with five pounds' worth of the neatest song-genius you have seen.—I tryed my hand on Rothiemurche this morning.—The measure is so difficult, that it is impossible to infuse much genius into the lines—they are on the other side. Forgive me!
>   Yours
>   R. Burns."[67]

Both Burness and Thomson at once complied with the dying poet's request, so that the imaginary danger could be banished.

On Monday, 18th July, Burns returned to Dumfries from Brow. He was so weak that he could scarcely walk from the carriage to the door of his house. A few lines which he addressed immediately after his arrival to his father-in-law in Mauchline, begging him to send Mrs. Armour to his wife's assistance without delay, contain the last words he ever penned.[68] After that he looked forward calmly and patiently—indeed, he was even capable of an occasional joke—to his approaching end.

---

[66] For their chemical composition, see Crichton-Brown, l.c., p. 11.

[67] Letters, 706. The poem mentioned, "Fairest Maid on Devon Banks," H. H., iii, 258, was Burns's last poem.

[68] Letters, 710.

On the morning of 21st July 1796 Robert Burns died in his thirty-eighth year.

During the last stages of his illness the sympathy of the people of Dumfries had been sincere and universal.[69] As he shed the vestments of his temporal life, blame and political enmity gradually fell silent, conscious that a genius was leaving the world, and that Scotland was about to lose the ardent patriot whose renown as a poet had brought greater fame to his country than any man before him. After his death he lay in a plain coffin, his face covered with a linen cloth, while the body and the bed, according to local custom, were richly strewn with flowers and herbs. Silent crowds streamed through the humble room and took farewell of the singer to whom they owed their finest songs. On Saturday, 23rd July, the poet's remains were removed to the town hall, and on the following Monday they were interred with high military and civil honours in the north-east corner of St. Michael's Cemetery. A picket of volunteers from his regiment fired a salute of three volleys over his grave, round which stood a vast company of mourners, silent with emotion. Then Life once more claimed its sacred rights.

Here ends our survey of the life and work of Robert Burns, whose earthly pilgrimage came to an untimely close, and whose artistic achievement stands before us as a titanic fragment.

In the first pages of this book we have quoted Goethe. In taking our leave we may be allowed to bring in an appreciation by the same inspired poet, in which he tries to account for the lasting fame of Burns by the living influence of his poetry on the mind of his people:

"Geprägte Form, die lebend sich entwickelt"

as he expresses it in another connection. In a conversation with Eckermann on 3rd May 1827, in which Goethe aims at comprehending the poet, the philosopher, and the historian as the product of their nation and their time, his reflections lead him to the

---

[69] We are here following the account of an eye witness, Allan Cunningham, in the *London Magazine*, for Aug. 1834, 117-122, entitled "Robert Burns and Lord Byron." See also letter from J. Syme to A. Cunningham, 23rd July 1796. *B. Chr.* 1935, pp. 43-44.

Scottish national poet and to the power and depth of his influence. He says:

> "Take Burns, for example. Wherein lies the cause of his greatness, except that the old songs of his forefathers were still living in the mouths of his people, that they were, so to speak, sung to him in his cradle, that as a boy he grew up amongst them, and the high excellence of these models so dwelt in him, that he had in them a living basis on which he could proceed. And, further, wherein is he great, except that his own songs at once found receptive ears amongst his people; they were re-echoed by the binders and reapers in the field, and he was greeted with them by his boon-companions in the alehouse. No wonder that something should come of it!"[70]

Thus it is. We add, that into little more than thirty-seven years of life there is compressed such a wealth of love and sorrow, of passion, success and disappointment, of errors and triumphs, as seldom falls to the lot of any individual. Burns's short career reflects the image of his age, with its limitations, its mistakes, its great thoughts and its attainments. His personality is as interesting from the human point of view as from the literary. The two elements cannot be considered apart: they are permeated with the same burning passion, the same pride, and the same manliness. His artistic mission is unmistakable: it consists in the revival, poetic purification and interpretation of the customs, songs, and legends of his native land, a task for which Nature had endowed him with brilliant and incomparable gifts. He was not always successful in achieving the full lucidity of his own peculiar style, and his poetry resembles his life in that it often strayed from the right path, and as a result bears the scars of many a voluntary and involuntary compromise, and lacks the ultimate purification and the final harmony of perfection. But at its best his poetry rises to the typical expression of the highest ideas that the eighteenth century was called upon to communicate to mankind. He took a literary tradition that was confined within the bounds of a too narrow realism and developed it to its furthest possible limits by infusing it with his own spirit, which was gripped and inspired by the great ideas of the time, and which reached out towards the universal. By thus combining the finite with the infinite, he left behind him a legacy of unequalled magnificence. This is not the place to speak of his influence on posterity. He has been granted the happiest lot

---

[70] Goethe-Carlyle Correspondence, ed. C. E. Norton, p. 137.

that can fall to any poet: he is enshrined for ever in the hearts of his fellow-countrymen, and has become such an essential part of their spiritual possessions that it is impossible to imagine Scotland without Robert Burns. He has remained a living force in the nation. The sun that rose over the grave by the churchyard wall in Dumfries was the sun of immortality.

NULLA CRUX, NULLA CORONA!

APPENDIX

———

HERON'S MEMOIR OF BURNS

INTRODUCTORY REMARKS

Heron's *Memoir* is more frequently quoted in Burns Literature than it has actually been seen or read. We reprint it here from the Edinburgh Edition, 1797, which had been preceded in the same year by a first publication in *The Monthly Magazine, and British Register,* vol. III, pp. 213-216 and 552-562, signed "H" and dated June 1797. On the whole, the two texts agree with each other. In our reprint minor alterations have been neglected, while the more important ones will be found in the footnotes, where M.M. refers to *The Monthly Magazine.* In so far as the variants affect the contents themselves, they, of course, merit our attention. To the Edinburgh Edition Heron prefixed a few sentences on biography in general, and he undoubtedly bestowed a certain amount of care upon this treatise. From *The Monthly Magazine* it was reprinted in *The Edinburgh Magazine, or Literary Miscellany* (1797), in the *Philadelphia Monthly Magazine* (1798), in *Chambers's Biographical Dictionary of Eminent Scotsmen* (1835 and 1855), in this case with a sort of running commentary, and as an introduction to two Irish editions of Burns's *Poems,* viz., Belfast, 1800, and Cork, 1804.

As to the tangled skein of Heron's ill-fated life, there is a well-informed account of it in the *Dictionary of National Biography,* vol. XXVI (by T. F. Henderson). Isaac Disraeli moralizes on it in his *Calamities of Authors,* 1812, vol. I, 218-55. Among more recent studies we may refer to a painstaking article by W. McIlwraith in *Burns Chronicle,* vol. XXII (1913), pp. 51-65, and to C. Carswell's essay, *R. Heron: A Study in Failure,* in *The Scots Magazine* for October 1932, pp. 37-48, the last-named based upon Heron's *Journal of my Conduct,* 1789-98 (MS. in the Laing Collection, Edinburgh University Library).

Commencing his career as a gifted and very ambitious young man with considerable receptive faculties and a fairly wide intellectual horizon, Heron developed into a miserable creature impaired both mentally and physically, who ended his days in the hospital of the London Newgate Prison. He was a weaver's son from New Galloway. But the fruits of the soil are not all good.

This was a poisonous growth: unreliable, lazy, cruel, unbridled and, what was worst of all, utterly false l th to himself and to others, a vice which inevitably brought shame even upon his considerable talents. The whole blend was utterly venomous. When we meet with the sanctimonious rubbish and smug moral admonition which infest his writings, and at the same time remember the malodorous life of this arch-Pharisee, we are tempted to consign him, if not to eternal damnation, yet at least to eternal oblivion. What stands in the way of this step is just this little treatise on Burns.

As far as we can trust his words, Heron, too, was gripped and overwhelmed by the power of the Kilmarnock Poems. As assistant to Drs. Blacklock and Blair he must at least have seen the poet during the latter's sojourn in Edinburgh. In any case he moved in the circle of Burns's patrons and met men who could tell him of his doings (cp., for instance, *Memoir*, p. 25, 27, 31, &c.). He had a personal encounter with the poet at Ellisland in 1789, when Burns gave him a letter to Dr. Blacklock, which he omitted to deliver. Two stanzas in Burns's Epistle to Dr. Blacklock, dated 21st October 1789, refer to Heron's frivolity and show that the poet had a pretty fair idea of his messenger's character:

> The Ill-Thief blaw the Heron south,
> And never drink be near his drouth!
> He tauld mysel by word o' mouth,
>   He'd tak my letter:
> I lippen'd to the chiel in trowth,
>   And bade nae better.
>
> But aiblins honest Master Heron
> Had at the time some dainty fair one
> To ware his theologic care on
>   And holy study,
> And, tired o' sauls to waste his lear on,
>   E'en tried the body.

Thereupon Heron disappears from Burns's life, whereas Heron himself obviously follows the poet's further career with undiminished interest. He senses his presence, he at the same time admires and envies him. In some tortuous psychic way or other he compares his own brittle volition with the inspired sureness of purpose of Burns and utilizes the poet's frailties, concerning which an exaggerated report may have reached him, in order to censure him in hypocritical austerity, thereby both scourging and justifying himself. An obnoxious picture: for compared with Heron, Burns was a saint! Thus in Heron's writings there is no lack of allusions to Burns. He quotes Burns's *Address to the Shade of Thomson* at the end of his *Life of Thomson* in his edition of *The Seasons* (Perth, 1793, pp. li-lii). In this passage he mentions the *Poems in the Scottish Dialect,* saying that "they are well known among us, and universally admired." In the same year Heron's *Observations made in a Journey through the Western Counties of Scotland* appeared, likewise in Perth. The descriptions of *Ayr and its Environs* (II, 333 ff.) contains a few pages on Burns which look like a first draft of the *Memoir.* Heron later took out sentences here and there and explained them. We quote the pages in question: [1]

> The Poems of *Robert Burns,* a native of the parish of *Mauchlin* in Kyle, are in every person's hands. Burns had received only that education in reading, writing, and arithmetic which the children of the peasantry throughout Scotland, commonly obtain at the parish-schools. [347] But the circumstances of his early youth had given a tone of lively sensibility to his feelings, had strengthened his judgement to solid thought, had sharpened his penetration, to discern the lights and shades of the human character, and had given a bold, excursive energy to his imagination. By one accident or another, he had contracted a taste for reading. Books of Scottish and of English Poetry had fallen into his hands. "He was smit with the love of Poesy and of Song." He began to write verses. And, at first, no doubt, would produce verses more remarkable for fancy and for sentiment, than for rich poetic phrase, or for melodious versification. Practice seems to have soon given him the powers and the skill of a master in the use of the language and measures of poetry. As he came to use these with greater facility, he would more boldly and more frequently express his fancies and sentiments in verse. He soon became distinguished in his neighbourhood, as a poet. His poetical talents drew upon him the notice of some gentlemen of taste. He was encouraged to publish a collection of his Poems. I have witnessed the passionate eagerness with which they were received and read by all, from the parson to the plowman,—from the gentleman and lady in the parlour, to the cinder-wench, kneeling to read them before the kitchen-fire.—By the kindness —chiefly of the late, amiable and ingenious [348] *Dr. Blacklock,* he was invited to Edinburgh, and encouraged to publish a second edition of his Poems,—for the first had been printed, I think, at *Kilmarnock.* He was eagerly caressed by all ranks; by the rich and the poor; by the learned and the gay; by young and old; by men and women. Every one was earnest to have the honour of subscribing for his book. At every table his company was courted. In every party of pleasure, he

---

[1] See also *B. Chr.,* 1st series, vol 20, pp. 137-138 (signed "Ballochmyle").

was earnestly solicited to make one. On this new scene, amidst these
flattering, trying circumstances, sufficient to turn the head of any
young man who was not endowed with more than ordinary portion of
sound sense and moderation of mind;—*Burns* conducted himself with
wonderful prudence and propriety. He was neither elated to folly by
the notice of his superiors; nor awed into silliness in their presence.
He conversed with decent and manly freedom of speech and sentiment;
without discovering any thing of that silly vanity of his poetry which
to one in his circumstances might have been easily pardoned. It was
said, in my hearing, by one of the greatest men in this, or perhaps any
age,[2] that he had never met with a man who discovered, in conversation, greater energy of mind than *Burns*. His manners, too, soon
shewed enough of the ease of a gentleman, to prove, that, "wherever
there is strength of cultivated [349] mind, the exterior polish may be
easily superinduced."

   The Poems which thus brought Mr. Burns into fashion,—for a
winter, have all considerable merit. Some of them I think the first
pieces of their kind in ours, or in any language with which I am
acquainted. *The Cotter's Saturday Night,* which is really a faithful
description from the life, proves, that the manners of our rustics can
afford subjects for pastoral poetry more elevated and more amiable
than those which are exhibited in *Gay's Shepherd's Week;*—that
Pastoral Poetry needs not to employ itself upon fictitious manners and
modes of life, but may, with higher poetical advantages, paint the
humble virtues, the simple pleasures, the inartificial manners of our
peasantry, such as they actually exist. The Poem on the rustic rites
and festivity of the *Hallowe'en* is finely fanciful, and most divertingly
comic; but, the subject was indeed rich in materials for the man of
fancy, and humour. A later composition of Mr. Burns's, a Tale,
intituled *Alloway Kirk,* in which the vulgar ideas concerning witch-
craft are happily introduced, has very high merit of the same cast as
that of *Hallowe'en.* As a Tale, it wants indeed, the inimitable, arch
simplicity of the Tales of Fontaine. But, it has beauties of a higher
kind. I have been more entertained [350] by it than by any of
Prior's. Burns seems to have thought, with Boccace and Prior, that
some share of indelicacy was a necessary ingredient in a Tale. Pity
that he should have debased so fine a piece, by any thing, having
even the remotest relation to obscenity! Many of his other poems are
perhaps superior to these in merit; although these be my favourites.
In all of them we find that originality of sentiment and of imagery
which none can display, but he who looks around, on nature and on
life, with the eye of a man of genius.—

Finally, there is the *Memoir*. Heron had no small opinion of

---

   [2] Who, alas! is no more. [William Robertson, the historian (1721-1793). s.
Memoir, p. 25.]

its merits, and refers specifically to it when enumerating his works
in his pitiful letter to the Literary Fund (1807):

> "[I wrote] a Memoir of the life of Burns the Poet, which suggested
> and promoted the subscription for his family; has been many times
> reprinted and formed the basis of Dr. Currie's life of him, as I learned
> by a letter from the Doctor to one of his friends . . ."
>
> (Disraeli, as above, p. 221.)

After this bombast, which resembles its author in that it contains more falsehood than truth, how is one to assess the *Memoir* as
a whole? Certainly not as a biography, as it has often been called.
It lacks the necessary foundations for that. Rather is it the reflection of a contemporary impression, seen in a dark and distorted
mirror. With this reservation, it retains its value. If one reads it
closely, one is rewarded with a striking opinion here and there, and
an occasional remark about people and events which will stick to
the memory. Any adverse criticism which Heron has passed on
Burns's life, especially concerning his last years, is as unlikely to
damage him to-day as we are to adopt the insipid advice and
unctuous effusions of the *Memoir*. We treat this text as a historical
curiosity, and content ourselves with linking up one of the earliest
sketches with this our latest, elaborate appreciation of the poet, be it
only to indicate the difficulties and the length of the road that had
to be traversed from there to here.

In the reproduction of the *Memoir* which follows, the original
page references appear in square brackets. The reader will note
that on several occasions words have been split in the original text
to carry them on to new pages.

A

MEMOIR

OF

THE LIFE

OF THE LATE

ROBERT BURNS

Written by R. Heron.

And thou, sweet poesy, thou loveliest maid,
Still first to fly, where sensual joys invade;
Unfit, in these degenerate times of shame,
To catch the heart, or strike for honest fame;
Dear charming nymph, neglected and decried,
My shame in crowds, my solitary pride;
Thou source of all my bliss, and all my woe,
Who found'st me poor at first, and keep'st me so;
Thou guide by which the nobler art, excel,
Thou nurse of every virtue, fare thee well!

GOLDSMITH's *Deserted Village.*

EDINBURGH:

PRINTED FOR T. BROWN, NORTH BRIDGE STREET.

1797.

A

MEMOIR

OF

THE LIFE

OF THE LATE

ROBERT BURNS

BIOGRAPHY is, in some instances, the most trifling and contemptible, in others, the most interesting and instructive of all the species of literary composition. It would be difficult to persuade one's self to agree with several late historians of the lives of poets, philosophers, and statesmen; that, the mere, industrious accumulation of dates, anecdotes, and witticisms, of transactions in which no peculiarities of genius and character were displayed, or of obscure events by which the habits of feeling, thought, or action, were in no way remarkably influenced; can deserve to be ambitiously studied, or [2] admired, as the perfection of biographical writing. The following memoir of the life of one who was a GREAT MAN, *solely of* GOD ALMIGHTY's *making such;* has been composed under the direction of a very different, although perhaps not a more correct, critical principle. If, however, this principle be just; it is the proper business of the biographer; TO TRACE THE GRADUAL DEVELOPMENT OF THE CHARACTER AND TALENTS OF HIS HERO, WITH ALL THE CHANGES WHICH THESE UNDERGO FROM THE INFLUENCE OF EXTERNAL CIRCUMSTANCES, BETWEEN THE CRADLE AND THE GRAVE; AND AT THE SAME TIME, TO RECORD ALL THE EMINENT EFFECTS WHICH THE DISPLAY OF THAT CHARACTER, AND THE EXERCISE OF THOSE TALENTS, HAVE PRODUCED UPON NATURE AND ON HUMAN SOCIETY, IN THE SPHERE WITHIN WHICH THEY WERE EXHIBITED AND EMPLOYED. The writer's wishes will be amply gratified; if this TRIFLE shall be found to afford any exposition of the nicer laws of the formation and progress of human character, such as shall not be scorned as *data* by the moral philosopher, or as facts to enlighten his imitations, by the dramatist; if it shall be received [3] by the world in general, as an honest though humble tribute to the merits of illustrious genius; and above all, if it shall be regarded by the candid and the good, as presenting some details and reflections, of which the direct tendency is, to recommend that steady VIRTUE, without which even genius in all its omnipotence is soon reduced to paralytic imbecility, or to maniac mischievousness.

[1] ROBERT BURNS was a native of *Ayrshire,* one of the western counties of *Scotland.* He was the son of humble parents. His[2] father passed through life in the condition of a hired labourer, or a[3] small farmer. Even in this situation,[4] it was not hard fcr him to send his children to the parish-school, to receive the ordinary instruction in reading, writing, arithmetic, and the principles of religion. By such a[5] course of education, young Robert profited to a degree that might have encouraged his friends to destine him to one of the liberal professions, had not his father's poverty made it necessary to remove him from the school, as soon as he had grown up, to earn for himself the means of support, as a[6] ploughboy or a shepherd.

[4] THE establishment of PARISH-SCHOOLS; but for which, perhaps, the infant energies of this young genius might never have received that first impulse by which alone they were to be excited into action; is one of the most beneficial that have been ever instituted in any country; and one that,[7] I believe, is no where so firmly fixed, or extended so completely throughout a whole kingdom, as in Scotland. Every[8] parish has, here,[9] a schoolmaster, almost as invariably as it has a clergyman. For a sum rarely exceeding twenty pounds, in salary and fees, this person instructs the children of the parish in reading, writing, arithmetic, book-keeping, Latin, and Greek. The schoolmasters are generally students in philosophy or theology. Hence,[10] the establishment of the parish-schools, beside its direct utilities, possesses also the accidental advantage of furnishing an excellent nursery[11] of future candidates for the office of parochial clergymen. So small are the fees for teaching, that no parents, however poor, can want the means to give their children at least such education[12] as young BURNS received.

---

[1] Heron's article in the *Monthly Magazine* begins here. It is in two parts: pp. 213-216 and 552-562.

[2] parents. His] parents: and his M.M.

[3] a] of a M.M.

[4] situation, it] sit., however, it M.M.

[5] such a] this M.M.

[6] a pl.] a hired pl. M.M.

[7] that] which M.M.

[8] Here, every M.M.

[9] *not in* M.M.

[10] theology; and hence M.M.

[11] nursery] school M.M.

[12] ed.] education at school, M.M.

From the *spring* labours of a ploughboy, from the *summer* employment of a shepherd, the peasant-youth often [5] returns, for a few months, eager to receive new instruction in[13] the parish-school.

IT was so with BURNS. He returned from labour to learning, and from learning went again to labour; till his mind began to open to the charms of taste and knowledge; till he began to feel a passion for books and for the subjects of books, which was to give a colour to the whole thread of his future life. On nature, he soon began to gaze with new discernment, and with new enthusiasm. His mind's eye opened to perceive affecting beauty and sublimity, where, by the mere gross peasant, there was nought to be seen, but water, earth, and sky, but animals, plants, and soil: even as the eyes of the servant of Elisha were suddenly enlightened to behold his master and himself guarded from the Syrian bands, by horses and chariots of fire, to all but themselves, invisible.

WHAT might perhaps first contribute to dispose his mind to poetical efforts, is, a particular practice[14] in the devotional piety of the Scottish peasantry. It is still common for them to make their children get by heart the psalms of David, [6] in that version of homely rhymes, which is used in their churches. In the morning, and in the evening of every day; or, at least on the evening of every Saturday and Sunday; these psalms are sung in solemn family-devotion, a chapter of the bible is read, an extemporary prayer is fervently uttered. The whole books of the sacred scriptures are continually in the hands of almost every peasant. And it is impossible, that there should not be occasionally some souls among them, awakened to the divine emotions of genius, by that rich assemblage which these[15] books present, of almost all that is interesting in incidents, or picturesque in imagery, or affectingly sublime or tender in sentiments and character. It is impossible that those rude rhymes, and the simple artless music with which they are accompanied, should not occasionally excite some ear[16] to a fond perception of the melody of verse. That BURNS had felt these impulses, will appear undeniably certain to whoever shall carefully peruse his *Cottar's Saturday's Night;* or shall remark, with nice observation, the various fragments of *scripture* sentiment, of *scripture* imagery, of *scripture* language, which are scattered throughout his works.

[7] STILL more interesting to the young peasantry, are those ancient ballads of love and war, of which a great number are yet popularly known and sung in Scotland. While the prevalence of the Gaelic language in the northern parts of this country, excluded from those

---

13 rec. n. instr. in] eagerly to pursue his education at M.M.
14 a part. pract.] one particular M.M.
15 those M.M.
16 *correcting* 'care' *in* M.M.

regions the old Anglo-Saxon songs and minstrels: These songs and
minstrels were, in the mean time, driven by the Norman conquests and
establishments, out of the southern counties of England; and were forced
to wander, in exile, *towards its northern confines, or even into*[17] the
southern districts of the Scottish kingdom. Hence, in the old English
songs, is every eminent bard[18] still related to have been of the *north
country;* but,[19] on the contrary, in the old Scottish songs, it is always
the *south country,* to which every favourite minstrel is said to belong.
Both these expressions are intended to signify one district;[20] a district
comprehending precisely the southern counties of Scotland, with the
most northern counties of England. In the south of Scotland, almost
all the best of those ballads are still[21] often sung by the rustic maid or
matron at her spinning-wheel. They are listened to, with ravished
ears, by old and young. Their rude me[8]lody; that mingled curiosity
and awe, which are naturally excited by the very idea of their antiquity;
the exquisitely tender and natural complaints sometimes poured forth
in them; the gallant deeds of knightly heroism, which they sometimes
celebrate; their wild tales of demons, ghosts and fairies, in whose
existence superstition alone has believed; the manners which they
represent; the obsolete, yet picturesque and expressive language in which
they are often clothed; give them wonderful power to transport every
imagination, and to agitate every heart. To the soul of BURNS, they
were like a happy breeze touching the strings[22] of an Æolian harp, and
calling forth the most ravishing melody.

BESIDE all this, the *Gentle Shepherd,* and the other poems of *Allan
Ramsay,* have long been highly popular in Scotland. They fell early
into the hands of BURNS. And while the fond applause which they
received, drew his emulation; they presented to him likewise treasures
of phraseology, and models of versification. *Ruddiman's Weekly
Magazine* was, during this time, published; was supported chiefly by
the original com[9]munications of correspondents; and found a very
extensive sale. In it, BURNS read, particularly, the poetry of *Robert
Ferguson,* written chiefly in the Scottish dialect, and exhibiting many
specimens of uncommon poetical excellence. The *Seasons* of *Thomson,*
too, the *Grave* of *Blair,* the far-famed *Elegy* of *Gray,* the *Paradise Lost*
of *Milton,* the wild strains of *Ossian,*[23] perhaps the *Minstrel* of *Beattie,*
were so commonly read, even among those with whom BURNS would
naturally associate, that poetical curiosity, although less ardent than

---

17 toward—into] beyond its northern confine, into M.M.
18 em. bard] famous minstrel M.M.
19 but] while M.M.
20 Both—district] It is the same district to which both allude, M.M.
21 still *not in* M.M.
22 strings] wires M.M.
23 the w. str. of O. *not in* M.M.

his, could, in such circumstances, have little difficulty in procuring them.

WITH such means to give his imagination a poetical bias, and to favour the culture of his taste and genius, BURNS gradually became a poet. He was not[24] one of those forward children, who, from a mistaken impulse, begin prematurely to write and to rhyme, and hence, never attain to excellence. Conversing familiarly for a long while, with the works of those poets who were known to him: Contemplating the aspect of nature; in a district which exhibits an uncommon assemblage of the beautiful and the ruggedly grand, of the cultivated [10] and the wild: Looking upon human life with an eye quick and keen, to remark as well the stronger and leading, as the nicer and subordinate features of character:[25] *It was thus that he slowly and unconsciously acquired a poetical temper of soul, and a poetic cast of thought.* He was distinguished among his fellows, for extraordinary intelligence, good sense, and penetration, long ere they suspected him to be capable of writing verses. His mind was mature, and well stored with such knowledge as lay within his reach;[26] he had made himself master of powers of language, superior to those of almost any former writer in the Scottish dialect; before he conceived the idea of surpassing *Ramsay* and *Ferguson*.

IN the mean time, beside the studious bent of his genius, there were other features[27] in his opening character, which might seem to mark him for a poet. He began early in life to regard with sullen disdain and aversion, all that was sordid in the pursuits and interests of the peasants among whom he was placed. He became discontented with the humble labours to which he saw himself confined, [11] and with the poor subsistence that was all he could earn by them. He was excited to look[28] upon the rich and great, whom he saw around him, with an emotion between envy and contempt; as if something had still whispered to his heart, that there was injustice in the exterior inequality between his fate and theirs. While such emotions arose in his mind, he conceived an inclination,—very common among the young men of the more uncultivated parts of Scotland,—to go abroad to *America* or the *West Indies,* in quest of a better fortune.—His heart was, at the same time,[29] expanded with passionate ardour, to meet the impressions of love and *friendship.* With several of the young peasantry, who were his fellows

---

24 not] not, however, M.M.

25 character] *instead of the next sentence* M.M. *has*:—to discriminate the generous, the honourable, the manly, in conduct, from the ridiculous, the base, and the mean: he was distinguished, &c.

26 reach] search M.M.

27 o.f.] some other particulars M.M.

28 He could not help looking M.M.

29 At the same time, his heart was expanded M.M.

in labour, he contracted an affectionate intimacy.[30] He eagerly sought admission into the brotherhood of *Free Masons;* which is recommended to the young men of this country, by nothing so much as by its seeming to extend the sphere of agreeable acquaintance, and to knit closer the bonds of friendly endearment. In some *Mason Lodges* in his neighbourhood, BURNS had soon the fortune, whether good or bad, to gain the notice of several gentlemen who were better able than his [12] fellow-peasants, to estimate the true value of such a mind as his.[31] One or two of them might be men of convivial dispositions, and of religious notions rather licentious than narrow; who encouraged his talents, by occasionally inviting him to be the companion of their looser hours; and who were at times not ill pleased to direct the force of his wit and humour against those sacred things which they affected outwardly to despise as mere *bugbears,* while perhaps[32] they could not help inwardly trembling before them as realities. For a while, the native rectitude of his understanding, and the excellent principles in which his infancy had been educated, withstood every temptation to intemperance or impiety. Alas! it was not always so.—*He was even in the first years of his rising youth, an ardent lover: feeling the passion, not affected, light, and sportive; but solemn, anxious, fervent, absorbing the whole soul; such as it is described by Thomson in his enrapturing poem on *Spring.*[*33] When his heart was first struck by the charms of village beauty; the *love* he felt was pure, tender,[34] and sincere, as that of the youth and maiden in his own *Cottar's Saturday's Night.* If the ardour of his passion hurried him afterwards to triumph over [13] the chastity of the maid he loved; the tenderness of his heart, the manly honesty of his soul, soon made him offer, with eager solicitude, to repair by marriage the injury of love.

ABOUT this time in the progress of his life and character, did he first begin to be publicly distinguished as a POET. A *masonic* song, a satirical epigram, a rhyming epistle to a friend, attempted with success; taught him to know his own powers, and gave him confidence to try tasks more arduous, and which should command still higher applause. The annual celebration of the *Sacrament of the Lord's Supper,* in the rural parishes of Scotland, has much in it of those old *Popish* festivals, in which superstition, traffic, and amusement, used to be strangely intermingled. BURNS saw, and seized, in it, one of the happiest of all subjects, to afford scope for the display—of that strong and piercing sagacity by which he could almost intuitively distinguish the reasonable

[30] intimacy of acquaintance M.M.

[31] as his.] as his, than were his fellow-peasants, with whom alone he had hitherto associated M.M.

[32] perhaps *not in* M.M.

[33] *The sentence* He was . . . Spring, *not in* M.M.

[34] tender, simple M.M.

from the absurd, and the becoming from the ridiculous;—of that picturesque power of fancy, which enabled him to represent scenes, and persons, and groupes, and looks, attitudes,[35] and gestures,[36] in a manner [14] almost as lively and impressive, even in words, as if all the artifices and energies of the pencil had been employed;—of that knowledge which he had necessarily acquired of the manners, passions, and prejudices of the rustics around him, of whatever was ridiculous, no less than of whatever was affectingly beautiful, in rural life. A thousand prejudices of *Popish,* and perhaps too of ruder *Pagan* superstition, have from time immemorial; been connected in the minds of the *Scottish* peasantry, with the annual recurrence of the *Eve of the Festival of all the Saints,* or *Hallowe'en.* These were all intimately known to BURNS, and had made a powerful impression upon his imagination and feelings. Choosing them[37] for the subject of a poem, he[38] produced a piece, which is, almost to frenzy, the delight of those who are best acquainted with its subject; and which will not fail to preserve the memory of the prejudices and usages which it describes, when they shall, perhaps, have ceased to give one merry evening in the year to the cottage fire-side. The simple joys, the honest love, the sincere friendship, the ardent devotion of the cottage; whatever in the more solemn part of the rustic's life is humble and artless, [15] without being mean or unseemly; or tender and dignified, without aspiring to stilted grandeur, or to unnatural, buskined pathos; had deeply impressed the imagination of the rising poet; had in some sort wrought itself into the very texture of the fibres of his soul. He tried to express in verse what he most tenderly felt, what he most enthusiastically imagined; and composed the *Cottar's Saturday's Night.*

THESE pieces, the true effusions of genius, informed by reading and observation, and prompted by its own native ardour, as well as by friendly applause; were soon communicated from one to another[39] among the most discerning of BURNS's acquaintance; and were, by every new reader, perused and re-perused with an eagerness of delight and approbation, which would not suffer him long to withhold them from the press. A *subscription* was proposed; was earnestly promoted by some gentlemen, who were glad to interest themselves in behalf of such signal poetical merit; was soon crowded with the names of a considerable number of the inhabitants of Ayrshire; who, in the proffered purchase, sought not less to gratify their own passion for *Scottish* poesy, than to encourage [16] the wonderful ploughman.

---

35 attitude M.M.

36 gesture M.M.

87 He chose them M.M.

38 he] and M.M.

39 comm. from one to another] handed about M.M.

At the manufacturing village of KILMARNOCK[40] were the poems of BURNS, for the first time, printed. The whole edition was quickly distributed over the country.

THEY were every where received with eager admiration and delight.[41] They eminently possessed all those qualities which never fail[42] to render any literary work quickly and permanently popular. They were written in a phraseology, of which all the powers were universally felt; and which, being at once, *antique, familiar,* and now *rarely written,* was hence fitted for all the dignified and picturesque uses of poetry, without being disagreeably obscure.[43] The imagery, and[44] the sentiments, were, at once, faithfully natural, and irresistibly impressive and interesting. Those topics of satire and scandal in which the rustic delights; that *humorous* imitation of character, and that *witty* association of ideas familiar and striking but[45] not naturally allied to one another, which have[46] force to shake his sides with laughter; those fancies of superstition at which he still wonders and trembles; those affecting sentiments and images of true religion, which are at once dear and awful to his heart; were all represented by BURNS with [17] all a poet's magic power. Old and young, high and low, grave and gay, learned or ignorant, all were alike delighted, agitated, transported. I was at that time resident in *Galloway,* contiguous to *Ayrshire*: and I can well remember, how that even plough-boys and maid-servants would have gladly bestowed[47] the wages which they earned the most hardly, and which they wanted to purchase necessary clothing, if they might but procure the works of BURNS. A copy happened to be presented from a gentleman in Ayrshire to a friend in my neighbourhood. He put it into my hands, as a work containing some effusions of the most extraordinary genius. I took it, rather that I might not disoblige the lender, than from any ardour of curiosity or expectation. "An unlettered ploughman, a poet!" said I, with contemptuous incredulity. It was on a Saturday evening. I opened the volume, by accident, while I was undressing, to go to bed. I closed it not, till a late hour on the rising Sunday morn, after I had read over every syllable it contained. And,

Ex illo Corydon, Corydon est tempore nobis! Virg, Ec. 7.[48]

---

40 at Kilmarnock M.M.

41 It is hardly possible to express, with what eager ad. and delight they were every where rec. M.M.

42 wh. n. f.] which the most invariably contribute M.M.

43 without being d. obsc.] without making it unintelligible M.M.

44 and *not in* M.M.

45 yet M.M.

46 has M.M.

47 bestowed] parted with M.M.

48 End of the first part of the article in *Monthly Magazine*. It is continued on p. 552.

[18] In the mean time, some few copies of these fascinating poems found their way to Edinburgh: and one was communicated to the late amiable and ingenious Dr. Thomas Blacklock. There was, perhaps, never one among all mankind whom you might more truly have called *an angel upon earth* than Dr. Blacklock! He was guileless and innocent as a child, yet endowed with manly sagacity and penetration. His heart was a perpetual spring of overflowing benignity. His feelings were all tremblingly alive to the sense of the sublime, the beautiful, the tender, the pious, the virtuous. Poetry was to him the dear solace of perpetual blindness. Cheerfulness, even to gaiety, was, notwithstanding that irremedial misfortune under which he laboured, long the predominant colour of his mind. In his latter years, when the gloom might otherwise have thickened around him, hope, faith, devotion the most fervent and sublime, exalted his mind to heaven, and made him still maintain much of his wonted cheerfulness in the expectation of a speedy dissolution.

This amiable man of genius read the poems of Burns with a nice perception, with a keen[19]ly[49] impassioned feeling of all their beauties. Amid that tumult of emotions of benevolence, curiosity, and[50] admiration, which were thus excited in his bosom; he eagerly addressed some encouraging verses to the rustic bard; which, conveying the praises of a poet, and a judge of poetical composition; were much more grateful to Burns, than any applauses he had before received from others. It was Blacklock's invitation that finally determined him to abandon his first intentions of going abroad to the West Indies; and rather to repair to Edinburgh, with his book, in hopes, there to find some powerful patron, and, perhaps, to make his fortune by his poetry.

In the beginning of the winter 1786-87, Burns came to Edinburgh. By Dr. Blacklock he was received with the most flattering kindness; and was earnestly introduced to every person of taste and generosity among the good old man's friends. It was little Blacklock had in his power to do, for a brother poet. But that little he did with a fond alacrity, and with a modest grace, which made it ten times more pleasing, and more effectually useful to [20] him, in whose favour it was exercised, than even the very same services would have been from almost any other benefactor. Others soon[51] interposed, to share with Blacklock in the honour of patronizing Burns. He had brought, from his Ayrshire friends, some letters of recommendation. Some of his rural acquaintances[52] coming, as well as himself, to Edinburgh for the winter, did him what offices of kindness they conveniently could. Those very few, who possessed at once true taste and ardent philan-

---

[49] keenly] tremblingly M.M.
[50] and *not in* M.M.
[51] soon] s. officiously M.M.
[52] acquaintance M.M.

thropy, were soon earnestly united in his praise. They who were disposed to favour any good thing belonging to Scotland, purely because
it was Scottish, gladly joined the cry. Those who had hearts and
understandings to be charmed, without knowing why, when they saw
their native customs, manners, and language made the subjects and
the materials of poesy, could not suppress that voice of feeling which
struggled to declare itself for BURNS. For the dissipated, the licentious,
the malignant wits, and the free-thinkers, he was so unfortunate as to
have satire, and obscenity, and ridicule of things sacred, sufficient to
captivate their fancies. Even for the pious, he had passages in which
the inspired language of devotion might seem to come [21] mended
from his tongue. And then, to charm those whom nought can charm[53]
—but wonders; whose taste leads them to admire only such things as
a juggler eating fire; a person who can converse as if his organs of
speech were in his belly; a lame sailor writing with his toes, for want
of fingers; a peer or a ploughman making verses; a small coal-man
directing a concert;—why, to those people, the Ayrshire poet might
seem precisely one of the most wonderful of the wonders after which
they were wont to gape.—Thus did BURNS, ere he had been many
weeks in Edinburgh, find himself the object of universal curiosity,
favour, admiration, and fondness. He was sought after, courted with
attentions the most respectful and assiduous, feasted, flattered, caressed
by all ranks, as the first boast of our country; whom it was scarcely
possible to honour and reward to a degree equal to his merits. In comparison with the general favour which now promised to more than
crown his most sanguine hopes, it could hardly be called *praise* at all,
which he had obtained in Ayrshire.

IN this posture of our poet's affairs, a new edition of his poems
was earnestly called for. He [22] sold the copy-right to Mr. CREECH,
for one hundred pounds. But, his friends, at the same time, suggested,
and actively promoted *a subscription* for an edition to be published for
the benefit of the author, ere the bookseller's right should commence.
Those gentlemen who had formerly entertained the public of Edinburgh
with the periodical publication of the papers of the MIRROR; having
again combined their talents in producing the LOUNGER; were, at this
time, about to conclude this last series of papers. Yet, before the
LOUNGER relinquished his pen, he dedicated *a number* to a commenda-
tory criticism of the poems of the Ayrshire bard. That criticism is now
known to have been composed *by HENRY MACKENZIE, Esq.; whose
writings are universally admired for an *Addisonian* delicacy and felicity
of wit and humour, by which the CLIO of the *Spectator* is more than
rivalled; for a wildly tender pathos that excites the most exquisite vibra-
tions of the finest chords of sympathy in the human heart; for a lofty,

---

53 can charm] delights M.M.

vehement, persuasive eloquence, by which the immortal *Junius* has been sometimes perhaps excelled, and often almost equalled!*[54] The subscription-papers were rapidly filled. The ladies, especially, vied with one another—who should be the [23] first to subscribe, who should procure the greatest number of other subscribers, for the poems of a bard who was now, for some moments, the idol of fashion. The *Caledonian Hunt,* a gay *club,* composed of the most opulent and fashionable young men in Scotland, professed themselves the patrons of the Scottish poet, and eagerly encouraged the proposed republication of his poems. Six shillings were all the subscription-money demanded for each copy. But many voluntarily paid half-a-guinea, a guinea, or two guineas. And it was supposed that the poet might derive from the subscription, and the sale of his copy-right, a clear profit of, at least, seven hundred pounds; a sum that, to a man who had hitherto lived in his indigent circumstances, would be absolutely more than the vainly expected wealth of Sir Epicure Mammon!

BURNS, in the mean time, led a life differing from that of his original condition in Ayrshire, almost as widely as differed the scenes and amusements of London, to which OMIAH was introduced, under the patronage of the Earl of SANDWICH, from those to which he had been familiar in the Friendly Isles. The conversation of even the most eminent authors, is often found [24] to be so unequal to the fame of their writings, that he who *read* with admiration, can *listen* with none but sentiments of the most profound contempt. But, the conversation of BURNS was, in comparison with the *formal* and *exterior* circumstances of his education, perhaps even more wonderful than his poetry. He affected no soft airs, no[55] graceful motions of politeness, which might have ill accorded with the rustic plainness of his native manners. Conscious superiority of mind taught him to associate with the great, the learned, and the gay, without being over-awed into any such bashfulness as might have made him confused in thought, or hesitating in elocution. He possessed, withal, an extraordinary share of plain common sense, or *mother-wit,* which prevented him from obtruding upon persons, of whatever rank, with whom he was admitted to converse, any of those effusions of vanity, envy, or self-conceit, in which authors are exceedingly apt to indulge, who have lived remote from the general practice of life, and whose minds have been almost exclusively confined to contemplate their own studies and their own works. In conversation he displayed a kind of intuitive quickness and rectitude of judgment upon every subject that arose. The [25] sensibility of his heart, and the vivacity of his fancy, gave a rich colouring to whatever

---

54 by H. M., Esq. . . . equalled] by the right hon. Lord CRAIG, one of the senators of the college of justice, who had adorned the MIRROR with a finely written essay, in recommendation of the poetry of MICHAEL BRUCE. M.M.

55 no] or M.M.

reasoning he was disposed to advance: and his language in common discourse,[56] was not at all less happy than in his writings. For these reasons, he did not cease to please immediately after he had been once seen. Those who had met and conversed with him once, were pleased to meet and converse with him again and again. I remember, that the late Dr. ROBERTSON once observed to me, that he had scarcely ever met ,with any man whose conversation discovered greater vigour and activity of mind than did that of BURNS. Every one wondered that the rustic bard was not *spoiled* by so much caressing, favour, and flattery as he found: and every one went on to *spoil* him, by continually repeating all these, as if with an obstinate resolution that they should, in the end, produce their effect. Nothing, however, of change in his manners, appeared, at least for a while—to show that this was at all likely to happen. He, indeed, maintained himself with considerable spirit, upon a footing of equality with all with whom he had occasion to associate or converse. Yet he never arrogated any superiority, save what the fair and manly exertion of his powers, at the time, could unde[26]niably command. Had he but been able to give a steady preference to the society of the virtuous, the learned, and the wise, rather than to that of the gay and the dissolute, it is probable that he could not have failed to rise to an exaltation of character and of talents fitted to do high honour to human nature.

UNFORTUNATELY, however, that happened which was natural in those unaccustomed circumstances in which BURNS found himself placed. He could not assume enough of superciliousness, to reject the familiarity of all those who, without any sincere kindness for him, importunately pressed to obtain his acquaintance and intimacy. He was insensibly led to associate less with the learned, the austere, and the rigorously temperate, than with the young, with the votaries of intemperate joys, with persons to whom he was recommended chiefly by licentious wit, and with whom he could not long associate without sharing in the excesses of their debauchery. Even in the country, men of this sort had begun to fasten on him, and to seduce him to embellish the gross pleasures of their looser hours with the charms of his wit and fancy. [27] And yet, I have been informed by Mr. ARTHUR BRUCE, a gentleman of great worth and discernment, to whom BURNS was, in his earlier days, well known; that he had, in those times, seen the poet steadily resist such solicitations and allurements to excess in convivial enjoyment, as scarcely any other person could have withstood. But, the enticements of pleasure too often unman our virtuous resolution, even while we wear the air of rejecting them with a stern brow. We resist, and resist, and resist; but, at last, suddenly turn and passionately embrace the enchantress. The *bucks* of Edinburgh accomplished, in regard to BURNS,

---

[56] in c. disc.] in conversation M.M.

that in which the *boors* of Ayrshire had failed. After residing some months in Edinburgh, he began to estrange himself, not altogether, but in some measure, from the society of his graver friends. Too many of his hours were now spent at the tables of persons who delighted to urge conviviality to drunkenness, in the tavern, in the brothel, on the lap of the woman of pleasure. He *suffered* himself to be surrounded by a race of miserable beings who were proud to tell; that they had been in company with BURNS; and had seen BURNS as loose and as foolish as themselves. [28] He was not yet irrecoverably lost to temperance and moderation: but he was already almost too much captivated with their wanton rivals, to be ever more won back to a faithful attachment to *their* more sober charms. He now also began to contract something of new arrogance in conversation. Accustomed to be, among his favourite associates, what is vulgarly but expressively called, *the cock of the company;* he could scarcely refrain from indulging in similar freedom and dictatorial decision of talk, even in the presence of persons who could less patiently endure his presumption.

THUS passed two winters, and an intervening summer, of the life of BURNS. The subscription-edition of his poems, in the mean time, appeared; and, although not enlarged beyond that which came from the *Kilmarnock* press, by many[57] new pieces of eminent merit, did not fail to give entire satisfaction to the subscribers. He at one time, during this period, accompanied, for a few weeks, into *Berwickshire, Robert Ainslie, Esq.,*—a gentleman of the purest and most[58] correct manners, who was accustomed sometimes to soothe the toils of a laborious profession, by an [29] occasional converse with polite literature, and with general science. At another time, he wandered on a jaunt of four or five weeks, through the *Highlands,* in company with the late Mr. WILLIAM NICOL; a man who had been before the companion and friend of Dr. GILBERT STUART; who in vigour of intellect, and in wild, yet generous, impetuosity of passion, remarkably resembled both STUART and BURNS; who, for his skill and facility of Latin composition, was perhaps without a rival in Europe; whose virtues and genius were clouded by habits of Bacchanalian excess; whose latter years were vexatiously embittered by a contest with a *person of far meaner talents, and narrower intelligence;*[59] who by the most unwearied and extraordinary professional toil, in the midst of as persevering dissipation, by which alone it was at any time interrupted, won and accumulated an honourable and sufficient competence for his family; and, alas! who died, within these few weeks, of a jaundice, with a complication of other

---

57 many] any M.M.

58 most *in* M.M.; more *in the memoir is a misprint.*

59 person . . . intelligence] creature, that, although accidentally exalted into competition with him, was unworthy even to *unloose his shoe-latchet* M.M. [This refers to Nicol's quarrel with Dr. A. Adam, rector of the High School, Edinburgh.]

complaints, the effects of long-continued intemperance! So much did the zeal of friendship, and the ambition of honest [30] fame, predominate in Nicol's mind, that he was, in his last hours, exceedingly pained by the thought that since he had survived Burns, there remained none who might rescue his mixed character from misrepresentation, and might embalm his memory in never-dying verse!

In their excursion, Burns and his friend Nicol were naturally led to visit the interesting scenery adjacent to the duke of Athol's seat at *Dunkeld,* on the banks of the Tay. While they were in a contiguous inn, the duke, accidentally informed of Mr. Burns's arrival so near, invited him, by a polite message, to *Dunkeld-house.* Burns did not fail to attend his obliging inviter; was received with flattering condescension; made himself sufficiently agreeable by his conversation and manners; was detained for a day or two by his Grace's kind hospitality; and, ere he departed, in a poetical petition, in the name of the river *Bruar,* which falls into the Tay, within the duke's pleasure-grounds at *Blair-Athol;* suggested some new improvements of taste, which I believe to have been since happily made, in compliance with his advice. I relate this little incident, to do honour rather [31] to the duke of Athol, than to Burns: for, if I be not exceedingly mistaken, nothing that history can record of George the Third, will in future times, be accounted more honourable to his memory, than the circumstances and the conversation of his well known interview with Dr. Johnson. The two congenial companions, Burns and Nicol; after visiting many other of those romantic, picturesque, and sublime scenes, of which the fame attracts travellers of taste to the Highlands of Scotland; after fondly lingering here and there for a day or two at a favourite inn; returned at last to Edinburgh: and Burns was now to close accompts with his bookseller, and to retire with his profits in his pocket to the country.

Mr. Creech has obligingly informed me, that the whole sum paid to the poet for the copy-right, and for the subscription copies of his book, amounted to nearly eleven hundred pounds. Out of this sum, indeed, the expences of printing the edition for the subscribers, were to be deducted. I have likewise reason to believe, that he had consumed a much larger proportion of these gains, than prudence could approve; [32] while he superintended the impression, paid his court to his patrons, and waited the full payment of the subscription-money.

He was now at last to fix upon a plan for his future life. He talked loudly of independence of spirit, and simplicity of manners; and boasted his resolution to return to the plough. Yet, still he lingered in Edinburgh, week after week, and month after month; perhaps expecting that one or another of his noble patrons might procure him some permanent and competent annual income, which should set him above all necessity of future exertions to earn for himself the means of subsistence; perhaps unconsciously reluctant to quit the pleasures of that voluptuous town-life to which he had for some time too willingly accustomed himself. An accidental dislocation or fracture of an arm or a leg, confining him for some weeks to his apartment, left him, during this time, leisure for serious reflection: and he determined to retire from the town, without longer delay. None of all his patrons interposed to divert him from his purpose of returning to the plough, by the offer of any small pension, or any sinecure place of moderate emolument, [33] such as might have given him competence without withdrawing him from his poetical studies. It seemed to be forgotten, that a ploughman thus exalted into a man of letters, was unfitted for his former toils, without being regularly qualified to enter the career of any new profession; and that it became incumbent upon those patrons who had called him from the plough, not merely to make him their companion in the hour of riot, not simply to fill his purse with gold for a few transient expences; but to secure him, as far as was possible, from being ever over-whelmed in distress, in consequence of the favour which they had shown him, and of the habits of life into which they had seduced him. Perhaps, indeed, the same delusion of fancy betrayed both Burns and his patrons into the mistaken idea that, after all which had passed, it was still possible for him to return, in cheerful content, to the homely joys and simple toils of undissipated rural life.

In this temper of Burns's mind, in this state of his fortune, a *farm* and the *excise* were the objects upon which his choice ultimately fixed for future employment and support. Mr. Alexan[34]der Wood, the surgeon who attended him during the illness occasioned by his hurt; no sooner understood his patient's wish, to seek a resource in the service of the *excise;* than he, with the usual activity of his benevolence, effectually recommended the poet to the commissioners of excise: and the name of Burns was enrolled in the list of their *expectant-officers.* Peter Millar, Esq. of *Dalswinton,* deceived, like Burns himself, and Burns's other friends, into an idea, that the poet and exciseman might yet be respectable and happy as a farmer; generously proposed to establish him in a farm, upon conditions of lease, which prudence and industry might easily render exceedingly advantageous. Burns eagerly accepted the offers of this benevolent patron. Two of the poet's friends from *Ayrshire* were invited to survey that farm in *Dumfriesshire,* which Mr. Millar offered. A lease was granted to the poetical farmer, at the[60] annual rent which his own friends declared, that the due cultivation of his farm might easily enable him to pay. What yet remained of the profits of his publication, was laid out in the purchase of farm-stock. And Mr. Millar might, for some short time, please himself with the persuasion, [35] that he had approved himself the liberal patron of genius; had acquired a good tenant upon his estate; and had placed

---

[60] the] that M.M.

a deserving man in the very situation in which alone he himself desired to be placed, in order to be happy to his wishes.

BURNS, with his JANE, whom he now married, took up their residence upon his farm. The neighbouring farmers and gentlemen, pleased to obtain for an inmate among them, the poet by whose works they had been delighted; kindly sought his company, and invited him to their houses. He found an inexpressible charm in sitting down, beside his wife, at his own fire-side; in wandering over his own grounds; in once more putting his hand to the spade and the plough; in forming his inclosures, and managing his cattle. For some moments, he felt almost all that felicity which fancy had taught him to expect in his new situation. He had been, for a time, idle: but his muscles were not yet unbraced for rural toil. He had been admitted to flatter ladies of fashion; he had been occasionally seduced by the allurements of venal beauty: But, he now seemed to find a joy in being the husband of the mistress of his affections, in seeing himself the [36] father of her children, such as might promise to attach him for ever to that modest, humble, domestic life in which alone he could hope to be permanently happy. Even his engagements in the service of the excise, did not at the very first, threaten necessarily to debase him by association with the mean, the gross, and the profligate, to contaminate the poet, or to ruin the farmer.

BUT, it could not be. It was not possible for BURNS now to assume that soberness of fancy and passions, that sedateness of feeling, those habits of earnest attention to gross and vulgar cares, without which, success in his new situation was not to be expected. A thousand difficulties were to be encountered and overcome, much money was to be expended, much weary toil was to be exercised, before his farm could be brought into a state of cultivation, in which its produce might enrich the occupier. The prospect before him, was, in this respect, such as might well have discouraged the most stubbornly laborious peasant, the most sanguine projector in agriculture. Much[61] more, therefore, was it likely, that this prospect should quickly dishearten BURNS; [37] who had never loved labour; and who was, at this time, certainly not at all disposed to enter into agriculture with the enthusiasm of a projector. Beside all this, I have reason to believe, that the poet had made his bargain rashly, and had not duely availed himself of his patron's generosity. His friends from Ayrshire, were little acquainted with the soil, with the manures, with the markets, with the dairies, with the modes of improvement in Dumfriesshire. They had set upon his farm, rather such a value of rental, as it might have borne in Ayrshire, than that which it could easily afford in the local circumstances in which it was actually placed. He himself had inconsiderately submitted to their judgment, without once doubting whether they might

61 Much] : and much M.M.

not have erred against his interests, without the slightest wish to make a bargain artfully advantageous for himself. And the necessary consequence was, that he held his farm at too high a rent, contrary to his landlord's intention.—The business of the excise too, as he began to be more and more employed in it, distracted his mind from the care of his farm, led him into gross and vulgar society, and exposed him to many unavoidable temptations to drunken excess, such as [38] he had no longer sufficient fortitude to resist. Amidst the anxieties, distractions, and seducements, which thus arose to him; home became insensibly less and less pleasing; even the endearments of his JANE's affection began to lose their hold on his heart; he became every day less and less unwilling to forget in riot those gathering sorrows which he knew not to subdue.

MR. MILLAR, and some others of his friends, would gladly have exerted an influence over his mind, which might have preserved him, in this situation of his affairs, equally from despondency, and from dissipation. But BURNS's temper spurned all controul from his superiors in fortune. He resented, as an arrogant encroachment upon his independence, that tenor of conduct by which Mr. MILLAR wished to turn him from dissolute conviviality, to that steady attention to the business of his farm, without which it was impossible to thrive in it. In the neighbourhood were other gentlemen occasionally addicted, like BURNS, to convivial excess; who, while they admired the poet's talents, and were charmed with his licentious wit; forgot the care of his real interests in the pleasure which they found [39] in his company, and in the gratification which the plenty and festivity of their tables appeared evidently to afford him. With these gentlemen, while disappointments and disgusts continued to multiply upon him in his present situation, he persisted to associate every day more and more eagerly. His crosses and disappointments drove him every day more and more into dissipation; and his dissipation tended to enhance whatever was disagreeable and perplexing in the state of his affairs. He sank, by degrees, into the boon companion of mere excisemen: and almost every drunken fellow, who was willing to spend his money lavishly in the ale-house, could easily command the company of BURNS. The care of his farm was thus neglected: Waste and losses wholly consumed his little capital: He resigned his lease into the hands of his landlord; and retired, with his family, to the town of Dumfries: Determining to depend entirely for the means of future support upon his income as an excise-officer.

YET, during this unfortunate period of his life, which passed between his departure from Edinburgh to settle in Dumfriesshire, and his leaving the country in order to take up his residence in [40] the town of Dumfries, the energy and activity of his intellectual powers appears to have been not at all impaired. He made a collection of Scottish

songs, which were published, the words with the music, by a Mr.
JOHNSTONE, an engraver, in Edinburgh, in three small volumes, in
octavo. In making this collection, he, in many instances, accom-
modated new verses to the old tunes, with admirable felicity and skill.
He composed several other poems, such as the tale of *Tam o' Shanter,*
the *Whistle, Verses on a wounded Hare,* the *Pathetic Address to R****
G*** of F***, and some others which he afterwards permitted Mr.
CREECH to insert in the *fourth* and *fifth* editions of his poems. He
assisted in the temporary institution of a small, subscription-library,
for the use of a number of the well-disposed peasants in his neighbourhood. He readily aided, and by his knowledge of genuine Scottish
phraseology and manners, greatly enlightened, the antiquarian researches
of the late ingenious Captain GROSE. He still carried on an epistolary
correspondence, sometimes gay, sportive, humorous, but always
enlivened by bright flashes of genius, with a number of his old friends,
and on a very wide [41] diversity of topics. At times, as it should
seem from his writings of this period he reflected, with inexpressible
heart-bitterness, on the high hopes from which he had fallen; on the
errors of moral conduct, into which he had been hurried, by the ardour
of his soul, and, in some measure, by the very generosity of his nature;
on the disgrace and wretchedness into which he saw himself rapidly
sinking; on the sorrow with which his misconduct oppressed the heart
of his JANE; on the want and destitute misery in which it seemed probable that he must leave her and their infants. Nor, amidst these
agonizing reflections, did he fail· to look, with an indignation half
invidious, half contemptuous, on those, who, with moral habits not
more excellent than his, with powers of intellect far inferior, yet
basked in the sun-shine of fortune, and were loaded with the wealth
and honours of the world, while *his* follies could not obtain pardon,
nor his wants an honourable supply. His wit became, from this time,
more gloomily sarcastic; and his conversation and writings began to
assume something of a tone of misanthropical malignity, by which
they had not been before, in any eminent de[42]gree, distinguished.
But, with all these failings; he was still that exalted mind which had
raised itself above the depression of its original condition, with all the
energy of *the lion, pawing to set free his hinder limbs from the yet
incumbering earth:* He still appeared *not less than*[62] *archangel ruined!*
    WHAT more remains there for me to relate? In Dumfries his dis-
sipation became still more deeply habitual. He was here exposed more
than in the country, to be solicited to share the riot of the dissolute and
the idle. Foolish young men, such as writers' apprentices, young
surgeons, merchants' clerks, and his brother excisemen, flocked eagerly
about him, and from time to time pressed him to drink· with them,
that they might enjoy his wicked wit. His friend NICOL made one or

---

[62] than *missing* in M.M.

two autumnal excursions to Dumfries, and when they met in Dumfries, friendship, and genius, and wanton wit, and good liquor could never fail to keep BURNS and NICOL together, till both the one and the other were as dead drunk as ever SILENUS was. The *Caledonian Club,* too, and the *Dumfriesshire and Galloway Hunt,* had occasional meetings in Dumfries, af[43]ter BURNS came to reside here: and the poet was, of course, invited to share their conviviality, and hesitated not to accept the invitation. The morals of the town were, in consequence of its becoming so much the scene of public amusement, not a little[63] corrupted: and, though a husband and a father, poor BURNS did not escape suffering by the general contamination, in a manner which I forbear to describe. In the intervals between his different fits of intemperance, he suffered still the keenest anguish of remorse and horribly afflictive foresight. His JANE still behaved with a degree of maternal and conjugal tenderness and prudence, which made him feel more bitterly the evil of his misconduct, although they could not reclaim him. At last, crippled, emaciated, having the very power of animation wasted by disease, quite broken-hearted by the sense of his errors, and of the hopeless miseries in which he saw himself and his family depressed; with his soul still tremblingly alive to the sense of shame, and to the love of virtue; yet even in the last feebleness, and amid the last agonies of expiring life, yielding readily to any temptation that offered the semblance of intemperate enjoyment; he died at Dumfries, in the summer of the year [44] 1796, while he was yet three or four years under the age of forty.

AFTER his death, it quickly appeared that his failings had not effaced from the minds of his more respectable acquaintance, either the regard which had once been won by his social qualities, or the reverence due to his intellectual talents. The circumstances of want in which he left his family, were noticed by the gentlemen of Dumfries, with earnest commiseration. His funeral was celebrated, by the care of his friends, with a decent solemnity, and with a numerous attendance of mourners, sufficiently honourable to his memory. Several copies of verses, having, if *no other merit, at least that of a good subject;* were inserted in different newspapers, upon the occasion of his death. A contribution by subscription, was proposed, in order to raise a small fund, for the decent support of his widow, and the education of his infant children. This subscription has been very warmly promoted, and not without considerable success, by *John Syme* Esq. of Dumfries; by *Alexander Cunningham,* Esq.[64] in Edinburgh; and by Dr. *James Currie* and Mr. *Roscoe* [45] of Liverpool. Mr. *Stephen Kemble,* manager of the theatre-royal at Edinburgh, with ready liberality, gave a benefit-night for this generous purpose. A publication of the poet's

---

[63] not a little] deplorably M.M.
[64] esq. writer to the signet M.M.

posthumous works is now in preparation, the profits of which are to be appropriated to the same pious use. It is hoped, that such a sum may be made up, in all, as shall secure his widow from destitute want, and shall bestow upon his children the advantages of a liberal education. It will be rather a tribute to BURNS, than the mere dole of charity.

I shall conclude this paper with a short estimate of what appear to me to have been BURNS's real merits, as a poet and as a man.

THE most remarkable quality he displayed, both in his writings and his conversation, was, certainly, an enlarged, vigorous, keenly discerning, COMPREHENSION[65] OF MIND. Whatever be the subject of his verse; he seems still to grasp it with giant force; to wield and turn it with easy dexterity; to view it on all sides, with an eye which no turn of outline and no hue of colouring can elude; to mark all its relations to the group of surrounding objects; [46] and then to select what he chooses to represent to our imaginations, with a skilful and happy propriety, which shows him to have been, at the same time, master of all the rest. It will not be very easy for any other mind, however richly stored with various knowledge; for any other imagination, however elastic and inventive; to find any new and suitable topic that has been omitted by BURNS, in celebrating the subjects of all his greater and more elaborate poems. It is impossible to consider, without astonishment, that amazing fertility of invention which is displayed, under the regulation of a sound judgment, and a correct taste, in the pieces intituled *the Twa Dogs; the Address to the De'il; Scotch Drink; the Holy Fair; Hallowe'en; the Cottar's Saturday Night; To a Haggis; To a Louse; To a Mountain Daisy; Tam O'Shanter; on Captain Grose's Peregrinations; The humble Petition of Bruar water; The Bard's Epitaph.* Shoemakers, footmen, threshers, milk-maids, peers, stay-makers, have all written verses, such as deservedly attracted the notice of the world. But in the poetry of these people, while there was commonly some genuine effusion of the sentiments of agitated nature, some exhibition of such imagery [47] as at once impressed itself upon the heart; there was also ever much to be excused in consideration of their ignorance, their want of taste, their extravagance of fancy, their want or abuse of the advantages of a liberal education. BURNS has no pardon to demand for defects of this sort. He might scorn every concession which we are ready to grant to his peculiar circumstances, without being, on this account, reduced to relinquish any part of his claims to the praise of poetical excellence. He touches his lyre, at all times, with the hand of a master. He demands to be ranked, not with the WOODHOUSES, the DUCKS, the RAMSAYS, but with the MILTONS, the POPES, the GRAYS. No poet was ever more[66] largely endowed with that strong

65 comprehension] conscious compr. M.M.
66 No poet w. e. more] He cannot be denied to have been M.M.

common sense which is necessarily the very source and principle of all fine writing.

THE next remarkable quality in this man's character, seems to have consisted in native strength, ARDOUR, and delicacy of FEELINGS, passions, and affections. *Si vis me flere; dolendum primum est ipsi tibi.* All that is valuable in poetry, and, at the same time, peculiar to it, consists in the effusion of particular, not gene[48]ral, *sentiment,* and in the picturing out of particular *imagery.* But education, reading, a wide converse with men in society, the most extensive observation of external nature, however useful to improve, cannot, even all combined, confer, the power of comprehending[67] either *imagery* or *sentiment* with such force and vivacity of conception, as may enable one to impress whatever he may choose upon the souls of others, with full, irresistible, electric energy. This is a power which nought can bestow, save native soundness, delicacy, quickness, ardour, force of those parts of our bodily organization, of those energies in the structure of our minds, on which depend all our sensations, emotions, appetites, passions, and affections. Who ever knew a man of high original genius, whose senses were imperfect, his feelings dull and callous, his passions all languid and stagnant, his affections without ardour, and without constancy? Others may be artisans, speculatists, imitators in the fine arts. None but the man who is thus richly endowed by nature, can be a poet, an artist, an illustrious inventor in philosophy. Let any person *first* possess this original soundness, vigour, and delicacy of the primary energies of mind; and *then* let him re[49]ceive some impression upon his imagination which shall excite a passion for this or that particular pursuit: he will scarcely fail to distinguish himself by illustrious efforts of exalted and original genius. Without having, *first,* those simple ideas which belong, respectively, to the different senses; no man can ever form for himself the complex notions, into the composition of which such simple ideas necessarily enter. Never could BURNS, without this delicacy, this strength, this vivacity of the powers of bodily sensation, and of mental feeling, which I would here claim as the indispensible native endowments of true genius; without these, never could he have poured forth those sentiments, or pourtrayed those images, which have so powerfully impressed every imagination, and penetrated every heart. Almost all the sentiments and images diffused throughout the poems of BURNS, are fresh from the mint of nature. He sings what he had himself beheld with interested attention,—what he had himself felt with keen emotions of pain or pleasure. You actually see what he describes: you more than sympathize with his joys: your bosom is inflamed with all his fire: your heart dies away within you, in[50]fected by the contagion of his despondency. He exalts, for a time, the genius of his reader to the elevation of his own; and, for the moment, confers upon

---

[67] compr.] apprehending M.M.

him all the powers of a poet. Quotations were endless. But any person of discernment, taste, and feeling, who shall carefully read over BURNS's book, will not fail to discover, in its every page, abundance of those sentiments and images to which this observation relates.—It is originality of genius, it is soundness of perception, it is delicacy of passion, it is general vigour and impetuosity of the whole mind, by which such effects are produced. Others have sung, in the same Scottish dialect, and in similar rhymes, many of the same topics which are celebrated by BURNS. But, what with BURNS awes or fascinates; in the hands of others only disgusts by its deformity, or excites contempt by its meanness and uninteresting simplicity.

A *THIRD* quality which the life and the writings of BURNS show to have belonged to his character, was, a quick and correct DISCERNMENT of the distinctions between RIGHT and WRONG, between TRUTH and FALSEHOOD; and this, ac[51]companied with a passionate preference of whatever was *right* and *true,* with an indignant abhorrence of whatever was *false* and morally *wrong.* It is true that he did not always steadily distinguish and eschew the evils of drunkenness and licentious love; it is true that these, at times, seem to obtain even the approbation of his muse. But there remains in his works enough to show, that his cooler reason, and all his better feelings, earnestly rejected those gay vices, which he could sometimes, unhappily, allow himself to practise, and would sometimes recommend to others, by the charms which his imagination lent them. What was it but the clear and ardent discrimination of justice from injustice, which inspired that indignation with which his heart often burned, when he saw those exalted by fortune, who were not exalted by their merits? His *Cottar's Saturday Night,* and all his graver[68] poems, breathe a rich vein of the most amiable, yet manly, and even delicately correct, morality. In his pieces of satire, and of lighter humour, it is still upon the accurate and passionate discernment of falsehood, and of moral turpitude, that his ridicule turns. Other poets are often as remarkable for the incorrectness, or even the absurdity of their [52] general truths; as for interesting sublimity or tenderness of sentiment, or for picturesque splendour of imagery. BURNS is not less happy in teaching general truths, than in that display of sentiment and imagery, which more peculiarly belongs to the province of the poet. BURNS's morality deserves this high praise; that it is not a system merely of *discretion;* it is not founded upon any scheme of superstition; but seems to have always its source, and the test by which it is to be tried, in the most diffusive benevolence, and in a regard for the universal good.

THE only other leading feature of character that appears to be strikingly displayed in the life and writings of BURNS, is a *lofty-minded* CONSCIOUSNESS *of his own* TALENTS *and* MERITS. Hence, the fierce and

---

68 graver] grave M.M.

contemptuous asperity of his satire; the sullen and gloomy dignity of his complaints, addressed, not so much to alarm the soul of pity, as to reproach injustice, and to make fortunate baseness shrink abashed; that general gravity and elevation of his sentiments, which admits no humbly insinuating sportiveness of wit, which scorns all compromise between the *right* and the *expedient,* which decides with the autho[53]ritative voice of a judge from whom there is no appeal, upon characters, principles, and events, whenever they present themselves to notice. From his works, as from his conversation and manners, *pride* seems to have excluded the effusion of *vanity.* In the composition, or correctness of his poetry, he never suffered the judgment, even of his most respectable friends, to dictate to him. This line in one of his poems, ("When I *look back* on *prospects drear"*) was criticised; but he would not condescend either to reply to the criticism, or to alter the expression. Not a few of his smaller pieces are sufficiently trivial, vulgar, and hackneyed in the thought, are such as the pride of genius should have disdained to write, or, at least, to publish. But there is reason to believe that he despised such pieces, even while he wrote and published them; that it was rather in regard to the effects they had already produced upon hearers and readers, than from any overweening opinion of their intrinsic worth, he suffered them to be printed. His wit is always dignified. He is not a merry-andrew in a motley coat, sporting before you for your diversion: but a hero, or a philosopher, deigning to admit you to witness his re[54]laxations; still exercising the great energies of his soul; and little caring, at the moment, whether you do, or do not, cordially sympathize with his feelings.

His poems may be all distributed into the two classes of *pastorals* and *pieces upon common life and manners.* In the former class, I include all those in which rural imagery, and the manners and sentiments of rustics, are chiefly described. In the latter I would comprehend his epigrams, epistles, and, in short, all those pieces in which the imagery and sentiments are drawn from the condition and appearances of common life, without any particular reference to the country. It is in the first class, that the most excellent of his poems are certainly to be found. Those few pieces which he seems to have attempted in that miserable strain, called *the Della Crusca* style, appear to me to be the least commendable of all his writings. He usually employs those forms of *versification,* which have been used chiefly by the former writers of poetry in the Scottish dialect, and by some of the elder English poets. His *phraseology* is evidently drawn from those books of English poetry which were in his hands, from the writings of former [55] Scottish poets, and from those unwritten stores of the Scottish dialect, which became known to him, in the conversation of his fellow-peasants. Some other late writers in the Scottish dialect seem to think, that not to write English; is certainly, to write Scottish. BURNS, avoiding this error, hardly ever transgressed the propriety of English grammar, except in compliance with the long-accustomed variations of the genuine Scottish dialect.

From the preceding detail of the particulars of this poet's life, the reader will naturally and justly infer him to have been an honest, proud, warm-hearted man; of high passions, a sound understanding, a vigorous and excursive imagination. He was never known to descend to any act of deliberate meanness. In Dumfries, he retained many respectable friends, even to the last. It may be doubted whether he have[69] not, by his writings, exercised a greater power over the minds of men, and by consequence, on their conduct, upon their happiness and misery, upon the general system of life, than has been exercised by any half dozen of the most eminent statesmen of the present age. The power of the [56] statesman, is but shadowy, so far as it acts upon externals alone. The power of the writer of genius, subdues the heart and the understanding, and having thus made the very springs[70] of action its own, through them moulds almost all life and nature at its pleasure. Burns has not failed to command one remarkable sort of homage, such as is never paid but to great original genius. A crowd of poetasters started up to imitate him, by writing verses as he had done, in the Scottish dialect. But, *O imitatores! servum pecus!* To persons to whom the Scottish dialect, and the customs and manners of rural life in Scotland, have no charm; I shall possibly appear to have said too much about Burns. By those who passionately admire him, I shall, perhaps, be blamed, as having said too little.

FINIS.[71]

---

[69] have] has M.M.
[70] springs] spring M.M.
[71] Finis. *not in* M.M. There the article is signed H. and dated June, 1797.

BIBLIOGRAPHY

I. GENERAL BIBLIOGRAPHY.

1. British Museum Catalogue of Printed Books *s.n.* Burns. (New edition in course of publication.)
2. Catalogue of the Robert Burns Collection, Mitchell Library, Glasgow. Part II. 1933. As yet typewritten. (For details, cp. J. C. Ewing, A Guide to Burns Literature. *B. Chr.,* 1934, pp. 23-26.)
3. Memorial Catalogue of the Burns Exhibition 1896. Glasgow 1898.
4. The Bibliography of R. B., with Biographical and Bibliographical Notes, and Sketches of Burns Clubs, Monuments and Statues. Kilmarnock 1881. (Compiler: J. Gibson.)
5. Ewing, J. C., A Selected List of Editions of the Works of R. B., and of Books upon his Life and Writings. London 1899. (Reprinted from *The Library World.*)
6. *id.,* Bibliography of R. B. 1759-1796. (Reprinted from Publications of the Edinburgh Bibliographical Society, IX, 57-72.) Edinburgh 1909.
7. Craibe Angus, W., The Printed Works of R. B. A Bibliography in Outline. Glasgow 1909.

There are important biographical notes in Henley's and Henderson's Cent. Ed., e.g.: I, 311-318; II, 279-291; III, 291-299; IV, 73-81. The volumes of the *Burns Chronicle* form a sort of current bibliography and should, of course, be always consulted. An *Index* to the thirty-four volumes of the First Series (1892-1925), compiled by J. C. Ewing, has been published for the Burns Federation, Kilmarnock 1935.

II. EDITIONS.

(a) *Complete Works (Poetry and Prose).*

1. The Works, &c. 4 vols. ed. J. Currie. Liverpool (London, Edinburgh) 1800. Frequently reprinted: 1801, 1802, 1803, 1806, &c. In some editions R. H. Cromek's Reliques of R. B., first published in 1808, have been added as vol. 5.
2. The Globe Edition. Poems, Songs, Letters, ed. A. Smith, London 1868. Numerous reprints; contains only a selection of the letters. Text unsatisfactory.

3. The Works of R. B. ed. W. Scott Douglas. 6 vols. Edinburgh 1877-1879; repr. London 1891. vols. 1-3: Poetry; vols. 4-6: Prose.—A Summary of B.'s Career and Genius, by John Nichol, was published for the subscribers of this edition in 1882.

4. The Complete Works of R. B. (Gebbie Self-Interpreting Edition.) 6 vols. Philadelphia 1886.

5. The Life and Works of R. B. ed. R. Chalmers, revised by William Wallace. 4 vols. Edinburgh and London 1896.—Chambers's original ed. appeared in 1851-52; reissued 1856-57 and 1891.

6. The Complete Writings of R. B. 10 vols. Boston and London 1927. vols. 1-6 Poetry; vols. 7-10 Prose.—Introduction by John Buchan; Letters ed. by Francis H. Allen.

(b) *Poetical Works.*

1. The Poetical Works of R. B. (The Aldine Edition). 2 vols. London 1830; 3 vols. 1839, with Memoir by Sir Harris Nicolas; 3 vols. 1893, with Memoir by G. A. Aitken.

2. The Complete Poetical Works of R. B. ed. W. Scott Douglas. 2 vols. Kilmarnock 1871. Contains a Bibliotheca Burnsiana in vol. II, pp. 419-444.—13th ed., 2 vols. in one, Edinburgh and Glasgow 1923.

3. The Poetry of R. B. (The Centenary Burns.) edd. W. E. Henley and T. F. Henderson. 4 vols. Edinburgh 1896-97; cheap and handy reprint 1901. vol. IV contains Henley's much-discussed Essay on Burns, published separately in 1898.

4. Poems and Songs. ed. A. Lang, assisted by W. A. Craigie. London 1896. 4th ed. 1926.

5. Poetical Works. ed. J. Logie Robertson. Oxford University Press 1896.

(c) *The Kilmarnock Volume.*

For detailed descriptions of the editions of Burns's *Poems* published during his life-time see Ewing as above I, 6. There are several facsimiles of the 1786 edition, viz.:

1. Kilmarnock 1867 (James McKie).

2. Kilmarnock 1909 (D. McNaught).

3. Glasgow 1927 (John Smith & Son Ltd.).
   See also the page-for-page reproduction:

4. London (Frowde) 1911, anonymous, and:

5. Burns. Poems Published in 1786, with an Introduction and Notes by Margaret S. Cleghorn. Oxford 1913.

(d) *Songs.*

1. James C. Dick, The Songs of R. B. Now First Printed with the Melodies for which they were written. A Study in Tone-Poetry. With Bibliography, Historical Notes, and Glossary. London, &c. 1903.
2. *id.*, Notes on Scottish Song by Robert Burns written in an Interleaved Copy of *The Scots Musical Museum* with Additions by Robert Riddell and Others. London, &c. 1908.—This is supplemented and in part rectified in an important article by
3. Davidson Cook, Annotations of Scottish Songs by Burns. *B. Chr.,* XXXI (1922), pp. 1-21.
4. W. Dauney, Ancient Scotish Melodies. Edinburgh 1838. Appendix I: F. Dun, Analysis of the Structure of the Music of Scotland.
5. William Stenhouse, Illustrations of the Lyric Poetry and Music of Scotland. Edinburgh and London 1853. Additional Notes by David Laing.—Originally the commentary to a new edition of *The Scots Musical Museum* it had appeared in that form in 1839 and 1853.
6. John Glen, Early Scottish Melodies. Edinburgh 1900. Another commentary to the *Mus.*, essentially from the musical side and rather censorious with regard to Stenhouse.
7. Schwebsch, Erich, Schottische Volkslyrik in J. Johnson's The Scot's [sic!] Musical Museum. Palaestra 95. Berlin 1920.
8. Keith, Alexander, Burns and Folk-song. Aberdeen 1922.

(e) *Letters.*

1. De Lancey Ferguson, J., The Letters of R. B. Edited from the original manuscripts. 2 vols. Oxford 1931.
2. The Correspondence between Burns and Clarinda. With a Memoir of Mrs. McLehose. Arranged and Edited by her Grandson, W. C. McLehose. Edinburgh, &c. 1843.
3. Ewing, J. C., R. B.'s Letters Addressed to Clarinda. A History of its Publication and Interdiction with a Bibliography. Edinburgh 1921. Reprinted from Papers of the Edinburgh Bibliographical Society, vol. XI.
4. Robert Burns and Mrs. Dunlop. Correspondence now published in full for the first time. With elucidations by William Wallace. London 1898. cp. J. C. Ewing, Letter to the Editor of "The Bookman." Glasgow 1898.

III. LITERARY TRADITION. SOURCES.

1. Henderson, T. F., Scottish Vernacular Literature. A Succinct History. 3rd ed. Edinburgh 1910.

2. *id.*, Scottish Popular Poetry before Burns *in* Cambridge History of Engl. Literature, vol. IX, chap. 14, with bibliography by H. G. Aldis, pp. 542-568.

3. Haliburton, Hugh, Furth in Field. London 1894.—Part V: Of Burns in a new Aspect.

4. Molenaar, H., R. B.'s Beziehungen zur Literature *in* Münchener Beiträge zur Romanischen und Englischen Philologie, XVII. Erlangen u. Leipzig 1899. Reviewed by Ritter *in Archiv* vol. 105, pp. 403-427.

5. Meyerfeld, M., Robert Burns.   Studien zu seiner dichterischen Entwicklung. Berlin 1899.

6. Ritter, O., Quellenstudien zu R. B. 1773-1791. Berlin 1901. Supplemented by *id.*, Neue Quellenfunde zu R. B. Halle 1913, and: Burnsiana, *Anglia* XXXII, pp. 197-234. Articles by the same author: *Archiv* 108, pp. 141-142 (Quotations in B.); 117, 47-57; 118, 391-392; *Anglia* XXVII, 450-452 (on John Barleycorn); XXIX, 383-384 (on Charlie He's My Darling).

7. Anders, H., Neue Quellenstudien zu R. B. *Archiv* 119 (1907), pp. 55-85.
    On Song-books prior to and after Burns cp. Dick, as above II. d. 1 and 2; Glen *ibid.* 6, and

8. Stainer, Sir John, Catalogue of English Song Books. London 1891.
    The magnificent collection of Song-books brought together by John Glen is now in the National Library of Scotland. It has a separate catalogue.

9. Hecht, Hans, Songs from David Herd's Manuscripts. With Introduction and Notes. Edinburgh 1904.

10. Miller, Frank, The Mansfield Manuscript. Dumfries 1935. (From: Transactions of the Dumfriesshire and Galloway Natural History and Antiquarian Society.)

IV. BIOGRAPHY AND CRITICISM.

(a) *Early Appreciations*.

1. Ross, John D., Early Critical Reviews on R. B. Glasgow and Edinburgh 1900.

2. Heron, R., Memoir of the Life of R. B. ˙Edinburgh 1797. Reprinted in our Appendix.

3. Lockhart, J. G., The Life of R. B. Edinburgh 1828. Frequently reprinted and re-edited, e.g., by John H. Ingram, London 1890. A particularly beautiful edition is that by W. Scott Douglas, 2 vols. Liverpool 1914, with an Essay on Burns by Sir Walter Raleigh.—Lockhart's book called forth: —

4. Carlyle, Thomas, Burns. *Edinburgh Review,* December 1828, with slight textual variations in Critical and Miscellaneous Essays. See also Carlyle's fifth lecture On Heroes, Hero-Worship, and the Heroic in History.

5. Shairp, J. C., R. B. (English Men of Letters) London 1879. Opposing its general tendency there appeared: —

6. Stevenson, R. L., Some Aspects of R. B.; first in *The Cornhill Magazine,* vol. XL (1879), then in Familiar Studies of Men and Books (Swanston Edition vol. III, pp. 43-76): worth reading, although in part based upon unreliable material.

7. Blackie, J. St., Life of R. B. (Great Writers) London 1888.

(b) *Recent Lives.*

1. Angellier, Auguste, Etude sur la Vie et les Oeuvres de R. B. 2 vols. Paris 1893.

2. Setoun, G., R. B. (Famous Scots Series) Edinburgh and London 1896.
   Henley, W. E., see above II, b, 3.

3. Henderson, T. F., R. B. (Little Biographies) London 1904.

4. McNaught, Duncan, The Truth about Burns. Glasgow 1921.

5. Hughes, J. L., The Real R. B. London and Edinburgh 1922.

6. Dakers, A., R. B. His Life and Genius. London 1923.

7. Mackenzie, J., A New Life and Vindication of R. B. Edinburgh 1924.

8. Carswell, Catherine, The Life of R. B. London 1930.

9. *eadem,* R. B. (Great Lives) London 1933.

10. Snyder, F. B., The Life of R. B. New York 1932.

(c) *Episodes and Single Periods.*

1. Muir, J., R. B. till his Seventeenth (Kirkoswald) Year. Kilmarnock 1929.

2. Lowe, D., Burns's Passionate Pilgrimage or Tait's Indictment of the Poet. With Other Rare Records. Glasgow 1904.

3. McVie, John, Burns and Stair. Kilmarnock 1927.

4. Joly, W., R. B. at Mossgiel: with Reminiscences of the Poet by his Herd-Boy. Paisley 1881.

5. McDowall, W., B. in Dumfriesshire: A Sketch of the Last Eight Years of the Poet's Life. Edinburgh 1870, 3rd ed. 1881.

6. Gunning, J. P., Burns, Poet and Excise Officer. Dublin 1899.

7. Sinton, J., Burns, Excise Officer and Poet. 4th ed. Glasgow, &c. 1897.

8. Will, W., R. B. as a Volunteer. Aberdeen 1928.

9. Crichton-Browne, Sir James, Burns from a New Point of View. London 1937. Originally published in *The Glasgow Herald*.

(d) *Freemasonry and Religion.*

1. [Marshall, John,] A Winter with R. B. Edinburgh 1846.

2. Peacock, H. C., and Mackenzie, A., R. B. Poet-Laureate of Lodge Canongate Kilwinning. Edinburgh 1894.

3. Harvey, W., R. B. as a Freemason. Dundee 1921.

4. Wright, Dudley, R. B. and Freemasonry. Paisley 1921.

5. *id.*, R. B. and his Masonic Circle. London 1929.

6. Burns and the Ayrshire Moderates. A Correspondence [between Aliquanto Latior = Dr. John Gairdner and A. Taylor Innes.] Reprinted from *The Scotsman, 1883.*

7. Wotherspoon, James, Kirk Life and Kirk Folk. An Interpretation of the Clerical Satires of B. Edinburgh and London 1909.

8. Jamieson, A. B., Burns & Religion. Cambridge 1931. Bibliography on pp. 116-118.

(e) *Contemporaries, Friends.*

1. The Book of Robert Burns. 3 vols. Edinburgh 1889-1891. vols. 1 and 2 by Charles Rogers, vol. 3 by J. C. Higgins. A sort of Burns-cyclopedia, useful but not always accurate.

2. [Paterson, James,] The Contemporaries of Burns, and the more recent Poets of Ayrshire. Edinburgh 1840.

3. Kerr, Robert, Memoirs of the Life, Writings, and Correspondence of William Smellie. 2 vols. Edinburgh 1811.

4. Hadden, J. C., George Thomson, The Friend of B. His Life and Correspondence. London 1898.

5. Wood, J. Maxwell, R. B. and the Riddell Family. Dumfries 1922.

(f) *Introductory. Language.*

1. Craigie, Sir William A., A Primer of Burns, London 1896.

2. Neilson, W. A., R. B. How to Know Him. Indianapolis 1917.

3. Wilson, Sir James, The Dialect of R. B. as spoken in Central Ayrshire. Oxford Univ. Press 1923.

4. *id.*, Scottish Poems of R. B. in his Native Dialect. Oxford Univ. Press 1925.

5. Hahn, O., Zur Verbal- und Nominalflexion bei R. B. 3 Teile, Berlin 1887-89. (Beilage zum Programm der Victoriaschule, Berlin.)

6. Cuthbertson, John, Complete Glossary to the Poetry and Prose of R. B. Paisley 1886.

7. Reid, J. B., A Complete Word and Phrase Concordance to the Poems and Songs of R. B. Glasgow 1889.

(g) *Translations.*

1. Jacks, William, R. B. in other Tongues. Glasgow 1896.

V. Topography. The Social and Historical Blackground.

1. Dougall, C. S., The Burns Country. 3rd ed. London 1925.

2. Henderson, T. F., The Auld Ayrshire of R. B. London and Edinburgh 1906.

3. Gibb, J. Taylor, Mauchline, Town and District. Glasgow 1911.

4. Dickie, W., Dumfries and Round About. (Swan's Popular Guide.) Dumfries 1898.

5. Kay, John, A Series of Original Portraits and Caricature Etchings. 2 vols. 4to, Edinburgh 1837, 1838, 1877. Popular Letterpress Edition. 2 vols. London and Glasgow 1885.

6. Stevenson, R. L., Edinburgh. Picturesque Notes. (Swanston Edition, I, 271-335.)

7. Chambers, R., Traditions of Edinburgh. Edinburgh and London 1868.

8. Wilson, Sir Daniel, Memorials of Edinburgh in the Olden Time. 2 vols. Second Ed., Edinburgh and London 1891.

9. Harris, D. F., Saint Cecilia's Hall. Edinburgh and London 1899.

10. Edgar, Andrew, Old Church Life in Scotland. 2 vols. Paisley and London 1885-86.

11. Kerr, John, Scottish Education, School and University. Cambridge 1908 and 1913.

12. Graham, H. G., The Social Life of Scotland in the Eighteenth Century. London 1906. (Reprinted 1928.)

13. *id.,* Scottish Men of Letters in the Eighteenth Century. London 1908.

14. Robinson, C. Grant, England under the Hanoverians. London 1910.

15. Mathieson, W. L., The Awakening of Scotland. A History from 1747 to 1797. Glasgow 1910. For Burns and the French Revolution see Angellier (above IV, b, I). I, 486 ff., II, 206 ff.

16. Dowden, E., The French Revolution and English Literature. London 1897, pp. 141-152.

17. Cestre, Charles, La Révolution Française et les Poètes Anglais. Paris 1906, pp. 216-230.

INDEX.